PASTORAL THEOLOGY.

PRINTED BY MURRAY AND GIBB,

FOR

T. & T. CLARK, EDINBURGH.

LONDON, ... HAMILTON, ADAMS, AND CO.
DUBLIN, ... JOHN ROBERTSON AND CO.
NEW YORK, ... SCRIBNER, WELFORD, AND ARMSTRONG.

First Published 1875
This Old Paths edition 1992

ISBN   O-9632557-0-3

PASTORAL THEOLOGY:

A TREATISE

ON THE OFFICE AND DUTIES OF THE CHRISTIAN PASTOR.

BY THE LATE

PATRICK FAIRBAIRN, D.D.,

PRINCIPAL OF THE FREE CHURCH COLLEGE, GLASGOW; AUTHOR OF 'TYPOLOGY OF
SCRIPTURE,' 'COMMENTARY ON THE PASTORAL EPISTLES,' ETC. ETC.

With a Biographical Sketch of the Author by

REV. JAMES DODDS,

DUNBAR.

Old Paths
Publications

Old Paths Publications

Ernie Springer
223 Princeton Road
Audubon, NJ 08106
...ask for the old paths... *Jer. 6:16*

PREFACE.

THE lamented Author of this treatise lived to prepare it for the press. It seems to have been originally written in its present form, though it was repeatedly delivered to his class as a course of lectures. There can also be little doubt that it was intended to be a sequel or companion volume to his recently published work on the *Pastoral Epistles*. As such it may safely be accepted by the public; for the sound judgment, lofty aim, and evangelical spirit that characterize the work on the Epistles will not be found wanting in the present performance. Though probably not free from the defects almost inseparable from posthumous publications, the following pages will, it is hoped, amply sustain the high character of Principal Fairbairn as a theological professor. They relate to a subject which in these days is of growing importance, and which has by no means been exhausted, though several good practical works connected with it have of late made their appearance.

Principal Fairbairn left instructions that no extended memoir of him should be published by any of his friends. Accordingly, nothing of the kind has been attempted; but as he also indicated that he had no objection to a brief record of the leading events of his life being given to the public, it has been thought advisable by his trustees that such a summary should be prefixed to this work. A succinct Biographical Sketch has therefore been prepared by one who knew him long and well, who was among the first to become acquainted with his high merits as an author, and who always regarded with admiration his noble Christian character.

CONTENTS.

———◆———

CHAPTER V.

CHAPTER VI.

CHAPTER VII.

CHAPTER VIII.

CHAPTER IX.

BIOGRAPHICAL SKETCH.

———◆———

PATRICK FAIRBAIRN was born at Hallyburton, in the parish
of Greenlaw, Berwickshire, on the 28th January 1805. He
was the second son of a family of five children. The eldest
of the family, a brother, predeceased him ; the three younger
members, two brothers and a sister, still survive. His
father, a respectable farmer, was able to give all his children
a good education, and to educate two of them for the
Christian ministry, namely, the subject of this sketch, and
John, the third of the family, now minister of the Free
Church at Greenlaw.

Patrick, considered from his earliest years a highly promising boy, was sent to various schools in the district with
a view to his being prepared for the University. None of
these schools were of a superior kind ; yet he profited to such
an extent by the tuition they furnished, that he proceeded
to the University of Edinburgh in November 1818, before
he had completed his fourteenth year. Like many Scottish
youths of that period, he commenced his college studies
much too early, and had in subsequent years to work doubly
hard in order to make up for the deficiencies of his preliminary education. He attended the classes of Professors

Pillans, Dunbar, Wilson, Wallace, Dr. Ritchie, and Sir John Leslie.   He was noted as a diligent and well-conducted student ; but he seems to have made no very brilliant or distinguished figure in any leading branch of academic study.   His mind was of that order which comes to maturity rather slowly ; and he aimed at solid progress rather than showy distinction.

Early in his college career he resolved to study for the Christian ministry.   In this matter he was greatly influenced by his mother, who was a woman of fervent piety and great Christian worth.   All her children owed much to her prudent and prayerful training ; but Patrick seems to have been specially benefited by her influence and example.   On the occasion of her death in 1861, her distinguished son thus wrote of her : 'I doubt if I should ever have thought of giving myself to the ministry, had it not been for the early bent my mind received from her spirit and instructions. While I live I cannot but cherish her memory with affection and regard ; and I shall rest in the hope of meeting her in another and better state of existence.'

The young student never prized highly the advantages presented by the classes at the University as they were conducted in his time.   With one or two exceptions, the professors in the Arts Course were not successful teachers ; and few students ever thought of taking a degree.   Wilson was a brilliant lecturer, but he never attempted any systematic instruction in Moral Philosophy.   Wallace and Leslie were profound mathematicians, but failed in carrying their students along with them in the demonstrations of the class-room.   Patrick Fairbairn never ceased to lament the imperfect training he received at college.   The great improvements that have of late been effected in the Edinburgh University system were not even projected in his early academic days.

When he entered the Divinity Hall, he found matters worse than they were in the Faculty of Arts. Dr. William Ritchie, an old and infirm man, who had never been very efficient, was Professor of Systematic Divinity; Dr. Brunton was Professor of Hebrew; and Dr. Meiklejohn of Church History. There was nothing in the Hall to stimulate or reward the exertions of the students. Dulness and routine prevailed in all the classes; there was in none of them much evangelical life or theological enthusiasm. Several able young men were fellow-students with Patrick Fairbairn, and like him afterwards made a distinguished figure in the Church; but they owed little of their learning to the instructions of the theological professors. It was not till Dr. Chalmers had been appointed to the Chair of Systematic Theology, and Dr. Welsh to the Chair of Church History, that the Edinburgh Divinity Hall acquired a character worthy of the famous University to which it belongs.

It must here be mentioned that the young Berwickshire student received much assistance in the course of his philosophical studies from a Mr. Hay, a small merchant in the quiet little town of Gordon, near Greenlaw. This Mr. Hay belonged to a class of men who were, perhaps, once more numerous in Scotland than they are now,—men who, though moving in a humble station, and possessed of limited means, yet contrived to cultivate literature and philosophy in a remarkable manner, and to gather all sorts of information from such miscellaneous collections of books as they were able to purchase or borrow. This Gordon philosopher delighted to impart to superior young men the various knowledge he had accumulated, and to kindle in their minds that genuine love of moral and metaphysical speculation with which he was himself inspired.

During a considerable period of his University career, Mr. Fairbairn attended the ministry of Dr. Robert Gordon, then held in the highest repute as a powerful evangelical preacher. The high intellect of Dr. Gordon, joined to his solemn and impressive pulpit oratory, peculiarly attracted the better class of theological students, and indeed many leading professional men in Edinburgh. His influence in recommending the gospel to the more cultivated classes of society was very great ; and down to the close of his life he was, as a highly intellectual yet truly spiritual preacher, almost unrivalled. It is well known that the late Principal Cunningham was profoundly influenced in early life by one of Dr. Gordon's printed sermons, and that ever afterwards he regarded him with special affection. Patrick Fairbairn must also be set down as one of those young men of high promise who received great benefit, at a critical period of life, from Dr. Gordon's powerful ministrations. There was another excellent Edinburgh minister to whom the youthful student was introduced in his college days, and to whom he became united by the ties of the closest friendship. This was the late Dr. James Henderson of Free St. Enoch's Church, Glasgow, who in the early part of his life was minister of Stockbridge Chapel of Ease, Edinburgh. After living on terms of cordial intimacy for half a century, the two friends were but a short while separated by death, Dr. Henderson surviving Principal Fairbairn little more than a month.

Always an exemplary and laborious student, Mr. Fairbairn before leaving the Hall attracted the special attention of Dr. Brunton, who procured for him the situation of tutor in the family of his brother-in-law, Captain Balfour, a large Orkney proprietor. He went to Orkney in 1827; and by the way in which he performed his duties, he so commended himself to Captain Balfour, that through the interest of that gentleman he was appointed by the Crown in 1830 to the Parliamentary Parish of North Ronaldshay. He had been licensed to preach the gospel by the Presbytery of Dunse, on the 3d October 1826.

North Ronaldshay is the most northerly of the Orkney Islands, and is of no great size or importance. The inhabitants were addicted to some strange and semi-barbarous customs when Mr. Fairbairn entered upon his charge. Many of them had the repute of being 'wreckers;' and the morality of the island was by no means high. They had not been accustomed to an evangelical ministry, or any of the best influences of the gospel. Indeed, during the last and the earlier part of the present century, the ministers of the Established Church in Orkney were, as a class, by no means distinguished for sound doctrine or Christian practice. Not a few of them had actually done much to bring the ministry into contempt by unbecoming conduct. But when Mr. Fairbairn commenced his pastoral duties he immediately took high ground, and both as a preacher and as a pastor he strenuously endeavoured to instruct and reform his parishioners. The good fruits of his faithful ministry were soon manifested in the improved character and habits of the islanders. The improvement effected by the young minister was so marked, that it attracted the attention of all who visited, or were specially interested in, North Ronaldshay.

It may be truly said, that the studies which laid the foundation of Mr. Fairbairn's theological eminence began only after he had left the Divinity Hall. About the time when he was licensed as a preacher, or looked forward to ordination as a minister in Orkney, he formed a regular plan of professional study of no slight or superficial character, but solid, laborious, and systematic ; and that plan he carried out with unflinching perseverance. He determined to make himself thoroughly master of the Hebrew and German languages, in order more effectually to equip himself as a scientific theologian ; and having become in good time an excellent Hebrew and German scholar, he entered on a course of theological reading and inquiry which led to important results. When he was about to be ordained at North Ronaldshay, where some of his friends thought he was in danger of being buried, his brother asked him how long he would like to remain in Orkney. ' Just six years,' he instantly and decidedly replied ; for, on full consideration, he had calculated on such a period for the completion of the studies he had projected for himself in his remote island home. And it so happened that, after he had spent about six years at North Ronaldshay, he was appointed minister of the new 'Extension' Church of Bridgeton, in the city of Glasgow.

In 1833 he was married to Miss Margaret Pitcairn, sister of the late Rev. Thomas Pitcairn, minister of Cockpen, who became first clerk of the Free Church General Assembly. Another brother of that lady, the Rev. David Pitcairn, at one time a minister in Orkney, went to the south of England and attained some eminence as a Christian author. Of several children, the fruit of this marriage, only one grew up, John Fairbairn, who, after spending some years in the Island of Java, ultimately settled in Australia, where he died only a few days after hearing of the death of his father. Mrs. Fairbairn died in childbirth, at Glasgow, soon after she and her husband had reached their new sphere of usefulness. Her infant, and another child, a fine boy of about three years of age, only a few weeks after her death followed her to the grave.

After faithfully performing the laborious duties of his Glasgow charge for about three years, Mr. Fairbairn was translated to the parish of Salton, East Lothian, which had been rendered vacant by the appointment of the Rev. Robert Hamilton to the Presbyterian chaplaincy at Madras. The predecessor of Mr. Hamilton in Salton had been the Rev. Robert Buchanan, now of the College Free Church, Glasgow, a churchman of the highest eminence in Scotland, and a man who for nearly forty years was the trusting and trusted friend of Patrick Fairbairn. Salton is also noted as having been for some years under the pastoral care of Gilbert Burnet, afterwards Bishop of Salisbury. That eminent dignitary left a considerable sum of money to found and support a library for the use of his successors in that Scottish parish, and for the education of a number of children of poor parishioners. Mr. Fairbairn took special delight in putting the Bishop's library into good working order, and probably derived more benefit from it than any of his predecessors. While he carefully prepared his pulpit discourses, and diligently discharged the numerous duties of a country minister, he was always a laborious

student, avaricious of time, and delighting in intellectual
toil.   He had already translated some works from the
German, for the well-known publishers Messrs. Clark of
Edinburgh, and was by this time meditating that original
work which was destined to give him a high place in British
theological literature.

Having from the very commencement of his ministry
belonged to the 'Evangelical Party' in the Church of Scotland, Mr. Fairbairn manfully supported his views in the
Church courts, though he did not aspire to the position of
an ecclesiastical leader.   At the Disruption of 1843 he had
no hesitation in joining the Free Church, and indeed was
the first of his brethren in the Presbytery to leave his
manse and face the hardships of the trying time.   He
found shelter for himself and his family, first in the neigh-
bouring parish of Bolton, and afterwards in the town of
Haddington ; but in spite of distance from his people he
visited them regularly, and fulfilled every duty of a diligent
pastor, while he still carried on his loved theological studies.
Of the Presbytery of Haddington, to which he belonged,
nine out of sixteen ministers had joined the Free Church ;
and he took a leading part in helping to form the new Free
Church Presbytery, and generally to advance the interests
of religion in the district.   But at that period of sharp
contention between rival Churches he showed no unworthy
bitterness of spirit.   With the late Dr. Cook of Haddington
and some other of his former co-presbyters he continued on
terms of friendship, though he differed widely from them
on certain points of theory and practice.

In 1845 he published, in one thick duodecimo volume,
his *Typology of Scripture*, a work which had occupied a

great part of his leisure for a number of years. It was subsequently published in two volumes, and reached some time ago a fifth edition. In its enlarged and improved form it is as free from imperfections as any work of the kind can well be, and it is now universally regarded as a standard theological treatise. The subject of the Old Testament types had never before been handled in a philosophical and satisfactory manner by any British or American theologian. It was reserved for the Free Church minister of Salton to produce a work upon it which, for critical insight, grasp of principle, and solid though unostentatious learning, was not surpassed, if even equalled, by any similar theological performance of the day. It is unnecessary to dwell upon the merits of a work so well known and so highly prized as the *Typology of Scripture.* It is one of those fresh and valuable contributions to our modern theological literature which is sure to keep its ground, and to be always in great request among students of theology. The writer of this sketch well remembers visiting, soon after its publication, Trinity College, Dublin, and seeing on the library table a copy of it, well worn, and apparently in high favour with the students. He could not help remarking, that while the richly-endowed Fellows of the College had done nothing of importance on the field of theology, there was at least one sterling theological work produced by a disendowed Presbyterian minister which they had the discernment to value and to introduce into their library.

In 1846, Messrs. Clark of Edinburgh published the first volume of an English translation of Hengstenberg's *Commentary on the Psalms.* Two other volumes subsequently appeared, completing the work. The translators were Mr.

Fairbairn and the Rev. John Thomson, an accomplished German scholar, now minister of St. Ninian's Free Church, Leith. Mr. Fairbairn had previously, when in North Ronaldshay, translated for the *Biblical Cabinet*, a foreign theological series published by the same eminent firm, *Steiger on 1st Peter*, and *Lisco on the Parables*. His knowledge of German, thus early and well exercised, was undoubtedly of good service to him as an earnest theological student. It introduced him to a vast and varied field of theology which must be traversed by every one in these days who would truly earn the name of theologian. But while he prized the excellences, he was well aware of the defects and dangers, of German theology, even of that large section of it which cannot fairly be called Rationalistic. Few of his countrymen have equalled him in making good use of German learning and its solid results, while rejecting what is inconsistent with sound doctrine or that reverence which is due to the word of God. In his *Typology*, and in most of his other publications, we find an excellent combination of German erudition with Scottish orthodoxy.

Towards the latter end of 1847, Mr. Fairbairn was invited to London to deliver a course of theological lectures in the newly instituted College of the English Presbyterian Church. On that occasion he first displayed his peculiar qualification for a theological chair, and may be said to have commenced his professorial career. His services were highly appreciated by the professors and students of the new College, and he always looked back with pleasure to this episode in his life. Professor Lorimer, and several of the ministers of the English Presbyterian Church who attended his lectures, speak at this day in the warmest terms of his learning and ability. They also testify to the great respect which they entertained for him, and the expectations they formed of his future eminence.

In 1851 he published, in one volume, his work entitled *Ezekiel, and the Book of his Prophecy*. This performance, in popularity, perhaps also in freshness and originality, ranks next to his *Typology*. In it the most difficult subjects are discussed with great ability and judgment. The principles of interpretation applied by the author in his exposition of the obscurest of the prophets commend themselves to the understanding of sober and philosophical critics. We do not know if a sounder and more profitable book on Ezekiel has been published in our times, and it is likely to keep its place in our modern theological literature.

In the course of 1851 and 1852, Messrs. Clark published in two successive volumes, Hengstenberg's *Commentary on the Revelation of St. John*, translated by Mr. Fairbairn. The work of translation in this instance was peculiarly delicate, the translator in some important matters not agreeing with his author; but the difficulties of the task were well surmounted, and a most important contribution to Apocalyptic literature was made accessible to the English public. It may also here be mentioned, that shortly before this time Mr. Fairbairn had published an interesting little work on the Book of *Jonah*, in which he took a more favourable than the common view of that prophet's character. Any complete list of his works would likewise include various lectures, pamphlets, and contributions to magazines, which proceeded from his pen chiefly about this period. A pamphlet on the real opinions of the leading Reformers about the obligation of the Sabbath was published by him,

so early as 1842, at the request of some of his brethren who
took a special interest in the subject. It was admitted to
be a very valuable contribution to the right discussion of
the Sabbath question ; but it has long been out of print.

In the autumn of 1852, Mr. Fairbairn was appointed
assistant to Dr. Maclagan, Professor of Divinity in the
Free Church College, Aberdeen. In December, only a
month after he had commenced his work in the college, he
met with the severest possible domestic bereavement. His
second wife, Mary Playfair, whom he had married before
leaving Glasgow, was seized with fever at Salton a few days
after giving birth to a daughter, her fourth child. On
hearing of her dangerous illness he hastened home from
Aberdeen ; but he had only the sad satisfaction of being with
his excellent partner during her last days on earth. Having
committed to the grave her mortal remains, he made the
requisite arrangements for the proper care of his motherless
children, and returned to his post. His duties, notwithstanding this heavy trial, were discharged during the whole
session with signal energy and success. His great sorrow,
through the grace of God, had only the effect of deepening
his sense of responsibility in the performance of the important work committed to his hand. By the General
Assembly of the following year he was appointed Professor
at Aberdeen in room of Dr. Maclagan, who had died before
his assistant entered on his duties. He always spoke in the
warmest terms of the happiness he enjoyed at Aberdeen,
notwithstanding his great bereavement and severe labours.
The remarkable kindness shown him by numerous friends
in that city made a pleasing and deep impression on his
memory.

In the summer of 1853, Professor Fairbairn visited the Continent in company with his friend John Elliot Wilson, Esq., Cranbrook, Kent. Mr. Wilson and he had become acquainted in 1845, through means of a correspondence in regard to some theological point touched on in the *Typology*. A correspondence, originating in the desire of the English gentleman to have some difficulties cleared up, led to a warm and lasting friendship between him and the Scottish theologian. It was some time before the two correspondents met; but their meeting only increased the strong affection which they had learned to cherish for each other. Mr. Wilson's admiration of the character and works of his friend was very great; and Professor Fairbairn, in his turn, learned to regard his English admirer with something much deeper than gratitude, even with the warm affection inspired by high accomplishments and singular Christian worth. The annals of friendship may be searched in vain for a more sincere and honourable union of hearts than that which was formed between these two men, who, after long living far apart from each other, were in a somewhat unusual way brought together.

The two travellers proceeded to Brussels and Cologne, then to Bonn, Coblentz, Mainz, and Frankfort, enjoying as they went along the splendid scenery of the Rhine. From Frankfort they proceeded by one long day's journey to Halle, in order to see its famous university. They were not much impressed either with the physical or moral aspect of the place, and unfortunately missed seeing its most celebrated professor, Tholuck, who was in the country. From Halle they went to Berlin, where they had an interview with Hengstenberg. This distinguished theologian, whose works

Professor Fairbairn had helped to make known in Great
Britain, did not favourably impress his visitors. Indeed,
his appearance, manner, and spirit greatly disappointed
them both. He looked more like an awkward and rather
morose student than an accomplished theological professor,
acquainted with the world as well as with his great science.
The questions put to him by his English translator he
answered curtly and imperfectly, while he had no questions
whatever to put in regard to the state of religion and the
Churches in Great Britain. But Hengstenberg had by this
time surrendered himself to those high Lutheran views
which greatly impaired his Christian usefulness, and lost
him the confidence of the Evangelical party in Prussia.
Having visited Potsdam, the travellers went to Hanover,
and thence to Cologne on their return to England.

In 1857, the same two friends made a tour in Switzer-
land, visiting on their way Paris and Strasburg. They went
on to Basle, Lucerne, Berne, Thun, Interlaken, Martigny,
Chamonix, and Geneva, greatly admiring the scenery, and
otherwise enjoying the delights of travel, mingled though
these were with the usual fatigues. At Vevay they had a
pleasant interview with Mr. Howson, now Dr. Howson,
Dean of Chester; and at Geneva they met with Dr. Stevens,
Rector of St. Andrew's Church, Philadelphia, who spoke of
Dr. Fairbairn's works as being greatly valued in America,
and acknowledged the benefit he had derived from their
perusal. Interesting notes of both these Continental tours
were written by Dr. Fairbairn, and are still preserved;
but no extracts can be given in a brief narrative of this
kind.

The Professor and his friend also made tours together at

various times in the Highlands of Scotland, in Wales, in Cumberland, and in Ireland. On one occasion they likewise visited the two great English universities. At Oxford they met with Dr. Jelf, who seemed greatly struck with Dr. Fairbairn's appearance, and courteously showed them the principal colleges and the library. They also breakfasted with the Rev. Edward A. Litton, who then first made the acquaintance of the Scottish professor, and afterwards contributed largely to the *Imperial Bible Dictionary*, at the request of its Editor. Their visit to Cambridge was also of a pleasant character. A Fellow of Christ's College, who was a friend of Mr. Wilson, conducted them over the principal buildings. During all these excursions, Mr. Wilson spared no personal effort to promote the enjoyment of one whom he regarded with the highest admiration both as an author and a friend.

While Professor Fairbairn filled with general acceptance his chair at Aberdeen, the University of Glasgow conferred on him the honorary degree of Doctor in Divinity. The University of Edinburgh, where he had commenced and completed his literary and theological studies, thus missed the opportunity of being the first to recognise in a special way the merits of her distinguished alumnus.

In 1856, when the Free Church College of Glasgow was instituted, Dr. Fairbairn was appointed by the General Assembly its first professor, and in the following year he was elected to the office of Principal. The Glasgow College, at first equipped with three chairs, and a year after with a fourth, was presided over from the very outset by Dr. Fairbairn with great ability. He brought his valuable experience gained at Aberdeen to bear upon the management of the new Institution, and soon had the satisfaction of seeing it in excellent working order. While he discharged his onerous and often unexpectedly increased professional duties with signal success, he gave much time and thought to the improvement of the buildings of the College, the foundation and enlargement of its library, the better endowment of its chairs, and the transaction of its general business. Perhaps no man in the Free Church could have performed so well the numerous duties that devolved upon him as Principal, or which he voluntarily undertook out of zeal for the success of an Institution which he helped so materially to found and form, and which will long be associated with his name. And while as Professor and Principal of the College he commanded the respect of all his colleagues, and endeared himself to his students as their accomplished instructor and zealous friend, he took a high position in Glasgow as a public man, ready to give his countenance and assistance to every religious or benevolent enterprise that engaged the attention of that great commercial city. His majestic presence and dignified bearing, coupled with readiness of speech and unaffected suavity of manner, were sufficient to win favour in any company, to grace any platform, and to aid the advocacy of any Christian cause.

In 1856, Dr. Fairbairn published his work on *Prophecy, viewed in its Distinctive Nature, its Special Functions, and Proper Interpretation.* This was intended to be a sequel or supplement to the *Typology;* and certainly it partakes in many respects of such a character. But though an able performance, full of sound and solid views based on philosophical principles of interpretation, it has not escaped the common fate of supplementary works of the kind. It has not been so popular as the *Typology*, but it undoubtedly deserves to be studied by all admirers of that excellent work. In 1858, its author also published a *Hermeneutical Manual, or Introduction to the Exegetical Study of the Scriptures of the New Testament*. This work contains many able discussions of difficult texts and subjects that meet the student of the New Testament; but, from its very nature, it is more of a text-book for a theological class than a work likely to attract the attention of the public. Though worthy of his reputation, it has never gained general favour.

A man of Principal Fairbairn's eminence could not fail to receive the highest honour the Free Church has to bestow. Accordingly, in 1864, he was elected Moderator of the Free Church General Assembly. His dignified conduct in the chair was universally admitted, while his opening and his closing address as Moderator were admirable in tone and sentiment. It may here be remarked, that while his favourite occupations were those of the scholar and the professor, he had an excellent knowledge of Church business, and took a fair share of the burden of ecclesiastical government. When he spoke in his Presbytery or in the General Assembly, he uniformly commanded the attention of his brethren, and his views were received with more than ordinary respect. The weight of his character gave him peculiar power in debate; and when he failed to convince, he never offended his opponents. In the great Union controversy, which lasted from 1863 to 1873, he found himself always in the same ranks with his revered friend Dr. Buchanan; but temperate in the advocacy of his own opinions, he did everything in his power to mitigate and

allay those unhappy contentions that for a time estranged
so many of his brethren from one another.

During many years of his residence at Glasgow, Dr. Fairbairn acted as editor of the *Imperial Bible Dictionary*, an
important work published by Messrs. Blackie and Son.
Even before he went to Glasgow as professor, it had been
virtually arranged that he should occupy that responsible
literary post.   But some years elapsed before he had actually to enter on his editorial duties.   The labour and
anxiety he underwent for many years in connection with
this great undertaking severely taxed both his intellectual
and physical energies.   He was assisted, of course, by a
staff of able contributors ; but not a few of these failed at
the last moment to send articles they had promised, and he
had of necessity to supply by a great effort their lack of
service.   None but a man of his high attainments in biblical
scholarship could have so promptly and adequately met the
varied exigencies that arose during the preparation of such
a work, and its progress through the press.   His arduous
labours in this undertaking came to an end in 1866, when
at length the *Imperial Dictionary* was completed.   The work
combines, in an almost unrivalled degree, sacred learning of
a high order with sound doctrine and an evangelical spirit.
Its admirable pictorial illustrations add greatly to its interest
and value.

Soon after this great work was off his hands, Dr. Fairbairn
was appointed to deliver in Edinburgh the third series of
' Cunningham Lectures.'   The first series, on the ' Father-
hood of God,' had been delivered by Dr. Candlish, and the
second series, on the ' Doctrine of Justification,' by Dr.
James Buchanan, one of the Professors of Theology in the

New College, Edinburgh. Dr. Fairbairn chose for his subject the 'Revelation of Law in Scripture,' and treated it in nine separate lectures, the first of which he delivered on the 3d March 1868. The whole of them, in terms of the trust deed founding the lectureship, were published in a single volume soon after their delivery. This work undoubtedly possesses high merit as a philosophical treatise on an important theological subject; but in its nature and style it is too abstract to be popular. It is not unworthy, however, of that excellent foundation which the Free Church of Scotland owes to the self-denying liberality of Mr. Binny Webster.

At the meeting of the Free Church Commission in March 1867, Dr. Fairbairn, Dr. Guthrie, and Mr. Wells of the Barony Free Church, Glasgow, were appointed a deputation to visit the Assemblies of certain Presbyterian Churches in America. These ministers, with their wives, sailed from Liverpool for America in the April following; but Dr. Guthrie, owing to serious indisposition, was obliged to disembark at Queenstown, and thus was unfortunately prevented from paying a long-expected visit to his numerous friends on the other side of the Atlantic. Dr. Fairbairn and Mr. Wells first visited the Assembly of the Old School and also that of the New School Presbyterians, and found both of these bodies hopefully negotiating that grand Union which has since been so happily consummated. They were received by their American brethren with great cordiality, and loaded with hospitable attentions. The learned Principal, whose name had travelled before him across the sea, and whose 'Jove-like presence' excited general admiration, was everywhere specially welcomed as a scholar of distinction. The

two deputies next visited the Synod of the United Presbyterian Church and the Synod of the Reformed (Dutch)
Church in the United States, and afterwards the Synod of
the Canadian Church not in connection with the Established
Church of Scotland.   They also took the opportunity of
spending a few days at Princeton, for the sake of seeing its
celebrated college, which has since risen into increased
prosperity under the vigorous presidency of Dr. M'Cosh.
Dr. Hodge, that prince of American theologians, was absent
at the time, but Dr. Fairbairn had afterwards the satisfaction of spending a day with him in Washington.

When the Committee was constituted for revising our
authorized version of the Old Testament Scriptures, Dr.
Fairbairn was naturally selected as one of the representatives
of the Biblical scholarship of Scotland.   He attended most of
the meetings of the Committee from the commencement of
its arduous labours to nearly the period of his death, and
bestowed upon his work much careful study.   It is understood that his services were highly valued by his learned colleagues.   On at least one occasion he was voted in a very
complimentary fashion into the chair.   The meeting-place of
the Committee, the celebrated Jerusalem Chamber, interested
him greatly, from its Presbyterian associations, though he
acknowledged that a room more convenient for the purpose
might easily have been selected.   Having at one time expressed a wish to resign his seat in consequence of the
growing inconvenience of his journeys to London, he was
entreated by his colleagues to change his mind ; and he, on
public rather than private grounds, agreed to co-operate
with them some time longer.   He expected that the revision
of our English Bible would be successful and ultimately

popular, but was not sanguine about its completion at a comparatively early date.

In 1871, the Principal received an unexpected expression of the extraordinary affection with which he was regarded by the young men who had studied at the Glasgow Free Church College. A sum of £200 was subscribed with enthusiastic eagerness by his 'present and former students' in order to present him with a full-length portrait of himself by an artist of acknowledged eminence. Mr. Norman Macbeth, A.R.S.A., was selected, and succeeded in producing a very fine picture as well as an admirable likeness. After it had graced the walls of the Royal Scottish Academy's Exhibition in Edinburgh, it was presented to Dr. Fairbairn in due form at a meeting of subscribers and friends held at Glasgow in the following November. The Rev. James Nicoll of Free St. Stephen's, Glasgow, acted as the spokesman of his fellow-students, and on handing over to their revered instructor the portrait in their name, delivered a very eloquent speech. The Principal, in his reply, adverted feelingly to the studies of his early life, the methods of study he had followed, and the great objects he had always endeavoured to keep stedfastly in view. He also spoke of the evening of life drawing on, and the necessity of increased earnestness in doing his work while health and strength remained.

The Rev. Robert Howie of Govan, who, along with Mr. Nicoll and the Rev. Archibald Henderson of Crieff, took an active part in the management of the necessary details, bears the strongest testimony to the feelings of love and veneration for Principal Fairbairn manifested by all his students when subscribing to this testimonial. The portrait, after being publicly exhibited in Glasgow, was hung up in the hall of the Free Church College, where it still remains, having been bequeathed by the Principal to that Institution.

At the commencement of the College Session in November 1872, Principal Fairbairn discharged the important duty of presiding at the induction of Professor Candlish and the ordination of Professor Lindsay, both of whom had been appointed to chairs in the Glasgow College by the preceding General Assembly. He preached from 2 Tim. ii. 2, and delivered a very appropriate discourse, in which he addressed his new colleagues in an affectionate and faithful manner. Taking the deepest interest in everything bearing on the prosperity of the Theological Institution over which he presided, he specially rejoiced, on this auspicious occasion, in the prospect of its undiminished efficiency.

Early in 1874, he published an elaborate work, in one volume, on the *Pastoral Epistles*. In a learned introduction, the authenticity of the epistles, recently assailed by many German critics, is ably and successfully vindicated. Then the Greek text is given with a new translation. But the most valuable part of the work is a commentary, or series of expository notes, displaying fine discernment, sound sense, and the varied results of genuine learning. In an appendix, some important points receive a fuller discussion than could find a place in the body of the work. This is really one of the best of the author's books, and ought to be one of the most popular. It is a very fresh and useful contribution to modern biblical literature ; and the present volume, which is full of the spirit of the Pastoral Epistles, will, it is expected, be ranged by its side in many theological libraries.

In a limited sketch like this, no details of Principal Fairbairn's private life or personal religion can find a place. But it must be stated that his house always presented a picture of domestic happiness and intelligent piety. In 1861 he was married to Miss Fanny Turnbull, a lady in every way fitted to add to his comfort and usefulness. The pain of former sad bereavements was gradually forgotten during the latter years of his life, than which, in a domestic point of view, none could be more tranquil and happy. While his time was largely spent in severe intellectual toil, and in the diligent discharge of arduous official duties, his inward spiritual life steadily increased, and he appeared to realize, with growing vividness, the preciousness of those great Christian doctrines he had done so much to elucidate and defend. And thus, when in the course of last year were held in Glasgow the remarkable series of evangelistic meetings which have been associated with the names of Messrs. Moody and Sankey, he took a deep interest in the religious movement that ensued, and publicly gave it his support. He presided over several of the meetings at which Mr. Moody was the chief speaker, and rejoiced in the success of the great evangelist's work. That work was especially commended to the support of not a few through the countenance given to it by such a wise and judicious man as Principal Fairbairn.

On the 16th April 1874, Dr. Fairbairn attended a great evangelistic Convention held in the 'Crystal Palace,' Glasgow, and delivered an earnest and valuable address; but, owing to the heat and excitement, as well as to some previous derangement of his system, he suddenly felt sick and unwell before the business was far advanced, and had

to leave the meeting. When he reached his house, he
went to bed, being prostrated by what may be called the
first serious illness of his life. He had always been a
remarkably healthy man, methodical and temperate in his
habits, an early riser, and accustomed to take long walks
before breakfast. Yet, while he had appeared to enjoy
perfect health and strength, there can be little doubt that his
constant devotion to study during a long course of years had
gradually developed an affection of the heart, which seems
to have been up to this period totally unsuspected. This
sudden and threatening attack, which confined him to his
bed for a few days, yielded to medical treatment, and all
serious danger was soon considered to be over. But he was
advised to spend a month or two of the summer in the
country, where he could tranquilly enjoy pure air and
necessary relaxation. Accordingly, accompanied by Mrs.
Fairbairn, his daughter, and a few other near relatives, he
went to Arrochar, Dumbartonshire, in the beginning of
June; and, being favoured with fine weather, he greatly
enjoyed his sojourn in that romantic locality. All around
him remarked that he seemed to be regaining completely
his former strength and spirits. The mellowed tone of his
conversation, and the finer traits of his character, brought
out, as it were, by affliction, also gave a new charm to his
society, and endeared him more than ever to his loved
domestic circle.

When at Arrochar, he returned to Glasgow for a single
day to preach in the evening, and preside at the ordination of Messrs. Gibson and Barclay as missionaries to
China. This service, though it broke in upon his needed
leisure, was quite congenial to his feelings; and he had

peculiar satisfaction in ordaining to the ministry two devoted young men,—one of them the son of his former colleague, Professor Gibson,—who had offered themselves as labourers in a difficult part of the Foreign Mission field. He delivered on this occasion a very beautiful and appropriate discourse from Ps. cxxvi., which has been published since his death in the *Christian Treasury*.

On the 30th of June he went up to London to attend a meeting of the Old Testament Revision Committee ; and on the Saturday following he paid a visit to his friend Mr. Wilson, which he greatly enjoyed. Of that visit Mr. Wilson writes : ' It was short, but never can be forgotten by myself or household. He bore evident traces of his recent illness ; but still more evident were the signs of deepening conformity to his Saviour's likeness, and of fellowship with his God.' Having completed his attendance on the Revision Committee, he returned to Glasgow on the 11th July.

The following week he went to Berwickshire to visit some of his relatives ; preached in the Free Church, Eyemouth, on the 19th ; and went to Greenlaw on the 24th, to assist his brother at his Communion. On the Sabbath he spoke at the Communion Table, and preached in the evening with great unction and power. Many were deeply moved by his words and still more by the spirit that breathed through all his ministrations. Leaving Mrs. Fairbairn and his daughter behind him, he returned to Glasgow on the following Tuesday, in order to be present at a meeting of the Board for the examination of students in Divinity, that was to be held in the course of the week.

On the Monday following, the 3d of August, he received intelligence of the serious illness of his eldest son in Australia. This painfully affected him ; but he endeavoured to bear the afflicting news as calmly as possible. Yet Mrs. Fairbairn, on hearing from him on the subject, immediately left Greenlaw, and joined him at Glasgow. On Thursday evening he conducted family worship as usual, and retired to rest about eleven o'clock. In little more than half an hour, a peculiar breathing gave indication of a sudden and fatal attack, which almost immediately ended in death. Without a note of warning, either to himself or his beloved partner, his spirit, in the solemn silence of midnight, suddenly passed away. Thus terminated, as by a swift translation, a truly noble life. Like Chalmers, Patrick Fairbairn was spared all abatement of mental strength, the feebleness of old age, the pain and struggle of the last conflict. In the fulness of his power and usefulness, yet not before his work was done, he was summoned to rest from his labours, and to enter into the joy of his Lord.

On the 13th August he was buried at Edinburgh, in the Grange Cemetery, which contains the precious dust of so many of God's honoured servants. Not far from the graves of Thomas Chalmers, William Cunningham, Thomas Guthrie, and many other eminent Christian worthies, his mortal remains are laid, in the hope of a blessed resurrection.

The death of this distinguished man was deeply lamented, not only by the members of his own Communion, but by many in all the Churches to whom his name and works were familiar. The writer of this sketch happened to be out of Scotland when the sad event occurred, and he can testify to the deep sorrow it excited among ministers in other lands, and of various denominations. Presbyterian and

Episcopalian admirers of the *Typology* vied with one another in expressing their regret for the loss which the Church of Christ had sustained by the death of its author.

Principal Fairbairn left a widow, three sons, and a daughter. His eldest son, as has been mentioned, died in Australia soon after his father's death. Two sons, Patrick and Thomas, and a daughter, Mary Ann, all by his second wife, still survive. Patrick is settled at Demerara; Thomas is at present in Shanghai. An interesting daughter, Jane, after growing up to womanhood, died at Glasgow in 1859, and was interred beside her mother in the family burying-ground in the Grange Cemetery, Edinburgh, where her father is now also laid. It may serve various useful purposes to inscribe the names of an eminent man's children in any account, however brief, of their father's life.

THE OFFICE AND DUTIES OF
A CHRISTIAN PASTOR.

CHAPTER I.

INTRODUCTORY.—THE RELATION OF THE PASTORAL OFFICE
TO THE CHURCH, AND THE CONNECTION BETWEEN
RIGHT VIEWS OF THE ONE AND A PROPER ESTIMATE OF
THE OTHER.

THE office of a Christian pastor obviously proceeds on
the assumption of a Christian membership or community, as the parties in respect to whom, and among whom,
it is to be exercised. It assumes that the flock of Christ are
not a mere aggregation of units, but have by divine ordination
a corporate existence, with interconnecting relationships,
mutual responsibilities, and common interests. It assumes,
further, that the Church in this associated or corporate
respect has a distinct organization for the management of
its own affairs, in which the office of pastor occupies a
prominent place, having for its specific object the oversight
of particular communities, and the increase or multiplication
of these, according to the circumstances of particular times
and places. There are other things of a collateral or subsidiary kind, not unimportant in themselves, and fitted to
exercise a considerable influence on pastoral relations :—
such as the internal constitution of the Church, or section
of the Church to which the pastorate belongs, its relation to

a superior governing power (whether of a presbytery or an episcopate), the understanding on which destination is made to a specific field of labour, or the tenure under which the appointment is held. Matters of that description cannot fail to tell with more or less effect on the exercise of the pastoral function, though they cannot be deemed of essential moment. For they may be, and have been, ruled differently in different portions of the Christian Church ; while still a pastorate, with substantially the same duties to discharge, and the same interests to prosecute, remains in each of them. Nothing more for the present needs to be assumed than the existence of the Church in separate outstanding communities, constituted with a view to the promotion of the great ends of evangelical truth and duty, presided over by persons destined to spiritual functions, and, in particular, set apart to the ministration of the word and the care of souls. This much, however, must be assumed, and assumed without any detailed proof or lengthened vindication. But as much depends upon the idea entertained of the Church for the idea that also comes to be entertained of the nature and ends of the ministerial calling, so that the one cannot fail to act and react on the other, a brief outline of the scriptural view of the Church (as we understand it) in its more essential characteristics, and of the false views which would either altogether supersede or injuriously affect the character of the pastoral office, may form an appropriate introduction to the line of thought and inquiry that lies before us.

I. *Scriptural idea of the Church, considered with respect to the nature and calling of the Christian pastorate.*—(1.) The Church in its primary and fundamental aspect is the kingdom of Christ, the spiritual society within which, as more peculiarly His own, He is acknowledged as the rightful Head, and served with a loving, loyal obedience. The members of it are the election of grace, the partakers of Christ's life and Spirit; and as such, His body, in which He more especially resides, and through which He acts for holy ends upon the world. There is therefore a pervading unity, an essential agreement in position, aims, and character among those who really constitute the Church, arising from their common relation to one head, and their mutual relation one to another, precisely as in the members of the human body, or in the subjects of a rightly-constituted and well-ordered kingdom. The Church, in this higher aspect, cannot be thought of but as an organic whole, bound up in living fellowship with Christ, He in it as the habitation which He fills with the manifestations of His presence and glory, and it again in Him as the root out of which it grows, and the pattern after which, in character and destiny, its members are to be conformed.

(2.) But the Church in this higher sense exists only *ideally*, so far as human perception or outward organization is concerned; *visibly* and *actually* it nowhere appears in the world, except as it may be in part, by successive stages, realizing itself among the members of Christian communities. This, however, it is ever doing; it is the very law of its growth. And so, what is usually termed the *invisible* Church, invisible as regards its component elements or actual membership to man's view, though perfectly known to God's, demands as its proper counterpart the *visible*. It demands this not as a circumstantial adjunct merely, a convenient or suitable adaptation, but as a necessary co-relation, the inevitable tendency and result of those spiritual instincts and divine principles which link the believing soul to Christ, the Church of the first-born on earth to the Church made perfect in glory. For, as the *internal* operation and life-giving agency of the Spirit come into effect through the *external* call and ministration of the word, thus, and no otherwise; so the one spiritual body of Christ has for its necessary comple-

ment a formally constituted corporate society.   In short, the
process of calling out of the world, and preparing for glory
the elect of God, realizes itself through the existence and
agency of a visible Church ; the visible is the nursery, and,
in a measure also, the image of the invisible.   Only in so
far as it is so can it be said to fulfil its divine calling and
appointment.   In each Christian community the offices and
ministrations, the government and discipline, should be such
as may through the Spirit most effectually serve to diffuse
the saving knowledge of Christ, awaken and sustain the love
of those who receive it, form, nourish, and draw forth the
spiritual and holy graces, which are the very life and glory
of the elect society that are there in training for the kingdom
and presence of God.   So that every individual, when as a
believer he connects himself with the membership of the
Church, should feel as if entering a society that holds of
heaven rather than of earth, a society in which all should
drop, as they enter, the selfishness and corruption of nature,
that they may mingle in the blessed harmony and communion of redeemed souls.

(3.) It follows from this relation of the visible to the invisible Church, as to character and calling, that everything
in the several sections of the Church on earth should be
framed and regulated so as in the most faithful and efficient
manner to carry out the revealed mind of Christ.   It ought
to be so, in a very special manner, with respect to the
Christian pastorate, to which belongs for all ordinary ministrations and results the highest place.   Christ Himself is the
Shepherd of the entire flock; and the pastors whom He promised to provide, for whom He received gifts on finishing
the work given Him to do,[1] are the under shepherds who
have to tend the flock in subordinate divisions, and distribute in due season the materials of life and blessing
committed to their hand.   It is *their* part to stand and

[1] Eph. iv. 11, 12.

minister in His name; to give themselves to the defence and
the propagation of His gospel; to cause His voice, in a
manner, to be perpetually heard and His authority respected;
in a word, to direct the operations and ply the agencies
which are fitted to bring those that are far off near to Christ,
and to carry forward their advancement in the life of faith
and holiness. Whatever private members of the Church
may, and also should, do toward the same end,—for where
all are taught of God, who should venture to think or to say
that he is charged with no responsibility for the good of
others?—yet those who are formally set as pastors and
teachers in the various Christian communities must, from the
very nature of their position and calling, have the chief
responsibility resting on them of doing what is needed to
enlighten, and edify, and comfort the souls of men.

(4.) And, finally, while all this has immediate respect to
the Church as a select body, and to the spiritual life and
wellbeing of those within its pale, it has also a real and important bearing on the world at large. For as the Church
is gathered out of the world, so it is called to be ever acting
on the world with regenerative and wholesome influence.
In this evangelistic and reformatory work the Church as a
whole, the Church individually and collectively, has the
charge committed to it; it is the candlestick which the
Lord has set up to diffuse abroad the light of heaven, or, to
refer to another metaphor of Scripture, the divinely impregnated and impregnating leaven, which is to work till
the general mass of humanity is leavened. But the pastors
and teachers of the Church have here also, by virtue of their
special gifts and calling, the foremost place to occupy; and
much must ever depend on their zeal and energy for the
progress that is made in the blessed work of reconciling the
world to God.

The views now presented contain nothing more than the
briefest possible outline of the nature of the Christian Church,

of the position assigned to the office of the pastorate in it, and the share which this must necessarily have in all the more vital and important functions which the Church has to discharge. But even such an outline can hardly be presented without conveying to our minds an impression of the lofty character of the pastoral office, and of the momentous interests which are entrusted to its keeping. It stands in close affinity with what lies nearest to the heart, and most peculiarly concerns the glory of God ; and high, assuredly, must be the honour, and large the blessing, of being counted worthy to take part in its sacred employments, if these employments be but faithfully discharged ; while, on the other hand, a fearful responsibility must be incurred by those who rush unprepared into the holy vocation, or manage in a slovenly and careless manner the concerns with which it charges them. But of this more hereafter : we turn now to other views of the Church, such as are either wholly inconsistent with a Christian pastorate, in the scriptural sense, or injuriously affect it.

II. *Views of the Church which are subversive of the pastoral office as exhibited in Scripture.*—The views which most palpably tend in this antagonistic direction are those which spring from a disposition to push to an extreme the more spiritual aspect of the Church. The reformers found it necessary to bring out very clearly and forcibly the distinction between the Church in this higher aspect, and the existing visible communities, compounds of light and darkness, purity and corruption, which claimed in the hands of the Papacy to be possessed of everything which entered into the idea of the Church. It was impossible otherwise to raise a testimony, such as the times required, against soul-destroying error. But the Reformation had not proceeded far on its course when a tendency appeared on the part of some to carry to an extreme the spiritualistic element, and make comparatively nothing of the outward and visible, consequently disparaging the organizations of scripturally-constituted Churches. And such views have their concrete representation still, in the Society of Friends, for example, the Quakers, who so isolate and exalt the internal agency of the Spirit, as to render it independent of all official appointments or formal distinctions. According to them, it is only when 'God raises up and moves among the assemblies of the faithful by the inward, immediate operation of His own Spirit,' certain persons to instruct, and teach, and watch over them, that any are called to do the work of ministers of the word; and the proof that they *are* called, is 'by the feeling of life and power on the part of the brethren which passes through them,' in connection with the ministration.[1] Hence, Möhler in his *Symbolik*, trying to expose the Lutheran doctrine respecting the visible and invisible Church, represents Quakerism as 'the consummation of Lutheranism,' because it carries fully out the maxim, which he takes to lie at the root of Lutheranism, that 'God teacheth man only inwardly.' In Quakerism, certainly, there is a very earnest endeavour to act in accordance with this maxim, though the endeavour is by no means either consistent in its working, or in its results successful. The Society so far yields to it as to discard all stated forms of worship from having a place in the divine service, to disallow the administration of sacraments, and to suffer the word of exhortation or the presentation of audible prayer only when the motion to do so proceeds from one who is conscious of a special call from above to the exercise. Not merely the *actual*, but the *perceptible* influence of the Spirit is required to constitute a right to impart spiritual instruction or guide the expression of pious feeling in their assemblies; so that it is not enough to say with the apostle, 'If any man speak, let him speak as the oracles of God,' but let him speak as a

[1] Barclay's *Apol.* Prop. x.

conscious instrument of God's Spirit, obeying the impulse of a higher power in his soul.

But with all this curtailment of the outward means of grace, with the view of enhancing and elevating that which is spiritual, much still remains, even with this peculiar class of spiritualists, to reach the point, that God teaches man only inwardly. For the formal basis, and to a large extent the material, of the instruction which man has to receive in divine things exists outside of him, and in so far as it works by way of enlightenment, must do so from without inwards. The incarnation of the Son of God, His atoning sacrifice, corporeal death, and resurrection, were all external things, connected on every side with the realities of sense and time ; hence in themselves they belong to another region than that of the individual consciousness, as does also the written word, in which they are presented to our belief and contemplation. There have been some, not so much, I believe, in this country as in America, who in the interest of the distinctive principles of Quakerism, the sufficiency of its inward light and direct action of spirit upon spirit, have quitted their hold of the historical Christ, and treated the evangelical record as an allegory. This was, indeed, a terrible sacrifice to make for the consistent maintenance of their spiritualistic principles ; it was, indeed, abandoning the substance of Christianity itself for the sake of an extravagant assertion of one of its characteristic features ; but, after all, it still fails to secure the desired emancipation of the soul from dependence upon the outward elements of instruction. For, interpret the written word as you may, it is in itself an objective in- strument, and, as such, the ground on which Quakerism, as well as every other Christian denomination, rests for the justification of its tenets and discipline. We know, indeed, —and it is the exaggeration of this truth which gives rise to the extravagance in question,—that the word may be read or proclaimed in the letter without being understood or received in the spirit. Yet that in no way prevents its being the common, or even the indispensable, handmaid of the Spirit's working, the means by which He may, without which He ordinarily does not, let in the light of salvation on men's souls, and conduct them in the way of peace. And if the word has such an end to serve, why should it not be statedly read in the assemblies of God's people? Why not preached and prayed over at every favourable opportunity? Why not embodied also in outward symbol, and with the solemnity of a covenant transaction impressed upon the heart and conscience? These are all, no doubt, outward things, and of themselves are incapable of either converting souls to God, or of building them up in righteousness; but so far they stand on a footing with the Bible itself; and the same principle which would discard the one might equally discard the other.

So, doubtless, the party in question would have acted if their spiritual instincts had not prevailed in some degree to counteract the tendency of their abstract principles. Yet the system, as a whole, has proved a palpable failure; it has been without living warmth or impulsive energy, scarcely able to perpetuate its existence, and exercising no assignable influence on the degeneracy and corruption around it. The fundamental mistake of its adherents, and of the few other sects who in principle coincide with them, lies in a misconception of the nature of the Spirit's work upon the soul. And the inconsistence alleged against Protestants generally by such writers as Möhler has this in common with it, that it imputes to them, without any just warrant, substantially the same view of the doctrine of the Spirit, and thence chiefly derives what it possesses of a plausible character. It assumes the action of the Spirit to be, according to Protestant ideas, so peculiarly and essentially inward, as to have no proper dependence on what are called the means and ordinances of grace; in which case it would be in ill accord with the complex constitution of man, and the known laws of human thought and feeling.   But, to use the words of Isaac Taylor, who in this speaks the common sentiments of Protestant divines,[1] 'if it be true that the agency of the Holy Spirit in renewing the heart is perfectly congruous with the natural movements of the mind, both in its animal and its intellectual constitution, it is implied, that whatever natural means of suasion, or of rational conviction, are proper to rectify the notions of mankind, will be employed as the concomitant, or second causes, of the change. These exterior means of amendment are, in fact, only certain parts of the entire machinery of human nature ; nor can it be believed that its Maker holds in light esteem His own wisdom of contrivance, or is it at any time obliged to break up, or to contemn, the mechanism which He has pronounced to be "very good."   That there actually exists no such intention or necessity, is declared by the very form and mode of revealed religion ; for this revelation consists of the common materials of moral influence, argument, history, poetry, eloquence.   The same authentication of the natural modes of influence is contained in the establishment of the Christian ministry, and in the warrant given to parental instruction.   These institutions concur to proclaim the great law of the spiritual world, that the heavenly grace which reforms the soul operates constantly in conjunction with second causes and natural means.   In an accommodated, yet legitimate sense of the words, it may be affirmed of every such cause, that the powers which be are ordained of God ; there is no power but of His ordaining ; and whosoever resisteth (or would supersede) the power, resisteth (or supersedeth) the ordinance of God.'

Such being at once the scriptural and the commonly received view among Protestants on the subject, it is manifestly erroneous to suppose that the internal action of the

[1] *Nat. Hist. of Enthusiasm*, p. 69.

Spirit on the souls of men must be of a perceptible kind, consciously distinct from one's own thoughts and volitions; equally so, that it must make itself known by communications apart from, if not superior to, those contained in the revelation of divine truth in Scripture; and still again, that it stands in any sort of contrariety to an ordained ministry and stated ordinances of worship. Any view of the Spirit's agency which runs counter to the use of such natural aids and appropriate channels of working betrays its own arbitrary and enthusiastic character. And it certainly is, as again remarked by Taylor, among the singular incongruities of human nature, that notions of spiritual agency, which, when viewed abstractedly, seem as if they could only belong to minds in the last stage of folly and extravagance, have been for generations maintained by a sect remarkable for the chilliness of its piety, for its contempt of the natural expressions of devotional feeling, and even for a peculiar shrewdness of good sense in matters of worldly interest.

Another religious party, however, has arisen much more aggressive than the Society of Friends (as these have been known in later times), and differing from them also to a considerable extent in regard to the work of the Holy Spirit, who yet so far concur with them in their views both as to the Spirit and the Church, that they equally set themselves against the function of an ordained ministry, and, indeed, any fixed Church organization. I refer to the Plymouthists, who perhaps approach more nearly to the parties that in the times of the Commonwealth were known by the names of *Seekers* and *Spirituals*, than to the Quakers of the present day;[1] but they may be classed with the latter in this respect, that they disallow the right of any one to teach or rule in the assemblies of the faithful, except such as are directly called and endowed by the Spirit to do so.   They therefore repudiate and denounce all kinds of ecclesiastical ordi-

[1] See Gillespie's *Miscellany Questions*.

nations, fixed appointments to office, powers and authorities conferred, or attempted to be conferred, through a human instrumentality ; nay, associate with these, especially with a regularly trained and endowed clergy, most of the corruptions in the Christian Church.   And along with these negative peculiarities, they hold it to be now, at this particular stage of the gospel dispensation, the special and primary duty of believers to stand forth as expectants of the near advent of Christ ; and, as such, to separate themselves from the mixed communities of Christendom, simply to recognise each other as united in the common bond of Christian faith and hope, and, when meeting together, to promote each other's edification by the exercise of such gifts of teaching or administration as the Spirit may be pleased to confer on any of their number.

It is of course quite easy, in the existing state of many of the Protestant Churches of Christendom, to take advantage of various corruptions and abuses for the purpose of giving some plausible colour and support to the views now indicated ; and there are not wanting currents of religious thought, phases of mind and character, which tend to foster the disintegrating, individualizing spirit, which finds its peculiar power and development in Plymouthism.   But without entering into the examination of these, looking only for a moment at the views themselves which this party wish to have regarded as emphatically scriptural, there are two fundamental errors which, on the ground of Scripture, may be charged against them, and which are entirely fatal to the pretensions raised upon them.   One is an error in respect to prophecy, which they unduly elevate ; and another in respect to history, which they unduly depreciate.   As regards the former, we lay down the position, that it is not now, nor ever has been, the insight furnished by prophecy into the Church's future which constitutes the ground of her polity, but present truth and duty.   Believers in Old Testament times, more especially when those times were verging to a close, were assuredly called to look and wait for a coming Messiah. Yet it was not this state of expectancy, or the changes which were to be introduced by it, but the past revelations of God, and the measure of truth therein unfolded, which gave birth to the ordinances of worship that were binding on the members of the old covenant, and determined the relative functions and modes of administration by which its affairs were to be carried on. The very last charge given by Old Testament prophecy to the people of God, was to observe the statutes and judgments introduced by Moses (Mal. iv. 4). Not, therefore, by separating oneself from these (as the Essenes did), but by the diligent and proper use of them, was the work of preparation for the events in prospect to be secured. And it is the same in New Testament times. There, the Church itself as an organized institution, with its gifts of grace and offices of ministration, took shape in connection with the incarnation and work of Christ in the flesh ; in this, a thing of the past, not in any announcement of His coming again in the future, is placed the ground and reason of all that properly belongs to it. And though intimations were given, both by our Lord and His apostles, of defections that should take place, and corruptions in doctrine and practice that should enter into His Church before He should appear in His glory, yet the call that is addressed to His people in connection with these is merely to resist the evil and witness against the abuse, but not to refuse the order or change the administration which from the first has carried with it the sanction of His approval and the promise of His blessing. For this a specific revelation from heaven would be needed, laying anew the foundation of a Church polity on earth, or warranting believers to withdraw from the foundation already laid. And believers only invert the established order and revelation of things, when they have recourse for the rule of their procedure in

such matters not to the historical past, but to the still un-
developed future.

But it is not thus alone that the historical element in the
constitution of the Church is made too little account of by
the parties in question.   For this Church, it must be remembered, did not come into existence as an entirely new
creation.   It was grafted, like Christianity itself, on the old
stock of Judaism; and as to external form and official organization, it had its preparatory type in the arrangements of
the Jewish Synagogue.   The narrative of apostolic labour
in the Acts and other incidental notices of New Testament
Scripture plainly implies as much ; and subsequent investigation has confirmed the impression beyond any reasonable
doubt.   The Christian Church, even when under apostolic
guidance and direction, did not disdain to borrow, in the
regard now under consideration, from existing institutions ;
and for any persons now summarily to discard what exists,
and attempt to model everything anew, with no object but to
afford scope for the exercise of spiritual gifts and operations,
is certainly to follow another course than that marked out
by apostolic precedent.   True, in one point there is, if not
a total, yet a comparative want of resemblance, between
the Jewish Synagogue and the Christian Church ; no one
in the former was ordained to the office of a regular and
stated pastorate ; and this circumstance has been laid
hold of, by the parties now immediately under consideration, for the purpose of disproving the necessity of such a
pastorate in the Christian Church. But the idea of the office
in a *general* form was undoubtedly there, namely, in the
joint eldership who were charged with the spiritual oversight of each synagogal community; only, from the relative
defect of the times as to spiritual light and privilege, this
idea never developed itself into a proper pastorate, or a
regular ministration of word and ordinance in the hands of
any single individual.   Such a development was necessarily

reserved for the gospel dispensation; which had scarcely entered on its course till a palpable advance was made in this particular direction, and a church was constituted in which a prominent place was given to the office of pastors and teachers, not, indeed, as formally distinct from that of the eldership, but with a special rise and enlargement of one of its functions.

In regard, however, to the right to hold and exercise the functions in question, there is a point that requires to be carefully guarded, which in regularly organized communities is apt to be somewhat lost sight of, sometimes is even entirely misapprehended; and the partial defect, or actual error, is not unfrequently turned to account by the spiritualists in disparagement of the pastoral office.   I refer to the relation of the office, as an institution of Christ, to the gift of the Spirit qualifying an individual for its discharge. What is of God in the matter *may* also be, and ordinarily *should* be, through man; and it is in the due co-ordination and harmonious working of the human and the divine that the will of Christ is properly accomplished.   The original planters of Christian churches, the apostles of our Lord, held directly of Him; in *their* ordination, human instrumentality had no room to work; as also in their qualifications for what was given them to do, not only spiritual, but supernatural endowments of a high order came into play.   But we are not thence warranted to infer that there should be the same direct intervention from above in subsequent and inferior appointments, any more than that because the word had the outward attestation of miracles in the gospel age, a like attestation might be expected for it after the Church had begun to take root in the world.   Even in the apostolic age, from the time that matters had become in some degree consolidated, respect was constantly had to the official position and instrumental agency of men.   St. Paul himself, who was not only called, but had occasion strongly to assert that he had been called, to the work of an apostle, 'not of man, nor by the will of man, but of God,' still submitted to be designated by the Church of Antioch, through imposition of hands, to a special mission (Acts xiii. 3) ; and both he and the other apostles associated with them the eldership of the church at Jerusalem, when they came together to determine the question about circumcision.   The decree issued was sent forth as the joint resolution of the Holy Ghost and the assembled heads of the Church on the subject (Acts xv. 28).   In all the churches, too, planted by Paul, we find him ordaining elders or presbyters for the regular administration of word and ordinances ; while the real authority to act in the name of Christ, and the excellence of the power in doing so with effect, he never hesitated to ascribe to God.   Why should any contrariety be supposed, in such cases, to exist between the divine agency and the human instrumentality?   In ministerial ordinations and appointments, the Church does not pretend, at least she *should* not, and when rightly constituted she *does* not pretend, to confer the gifts necessary to the rightful and profitable exercise of spiritual functions ; she simply recognises the gifts as already possessed in such measure as to warrant her, by a solemn act, to encourage and authorize the exercise of them in a particular sphere.   Wherever the matter is rightly gone about, the process is as follows :— the Church, through her ordinary channels of working, comes to obtain a certain number of persons, who are possessed of higher qualifications and spiritual gifts than belong to the general run of her members ; these, when she finds them willing to separate themselves to the work of the ministry, she puts into a course, or takes cognizance of them while they put themselves into a course, of training for the work ; and this being done to her satisfaction, the endowments of nature and of grace possessed by the individuals being in her judgment such as to warrant the hope of future usefulness, she sets her seal upon them by a formal act of ordination, appointing the individuals to the oversight of some particular portion of the flock of Christ. Viewed thus, which is the only proper light wherein to contemplate it, ordination to the work of the ministry, and other cognate offices, is only a becoming exemplification of the apostolic precept, 'Let all things be done decently, and in order.'

On the other hand, let the principle of the spiritualists be adopted, and perfect freedom allowed every member of the religious community to exercise the gifts he thinks himself possessed of, what effectual check is there against abitrariness and presumption? What confusion and disorder may not, for a time at least, come into operation? Here one, we can suppose, shall rise up claiming to have received the gift of teaching from the Spirit ; there another, asserting for himself the power of government ; and another claiming to possess the discernment of spirits, so as to be capable of assigning to each his proper place and character in the reckoning of heaven ; and whatever extravagance or delusion there might be in such assumptions, still, on the views of an idealistic and individualizing spiritualism, the claim must in the first instance be conceded, and only by and by rejected, if the teaching and procedure founded on it should be found to clash with the general sense of the community. But, meanwhile, what disturbance might be created? what unprofitable jangling, perhaps irreparable mischief, occasioned in the process? Such, indeed, that no religious community acting on the principle in question, and fairly carrying it out, has ever been able to perpetuate itself. Either some sort of constitutional government has been practically called into existence to temper and control the spiritualistic element, or the community has fallen a prey to its internal weakness and indiscriminate self-assertion.

Doubtless there were things connected with the first great

B

movements of spiritual life and action in the Christian Church which have a somewhat irregular appearance, not quite reducible to the method and order of constitutional government; as there have been also in times of convulsive energy and deep spiritual awakening. The parties against whom we now reason are in the habit of making their appeal to such things. That is, they would make what is peculiar and occasional the rule and warrant for ordinary administrations; and not uncommonly what was peculiar and occasional is exaggerated, made to appear greater than it actually was, by throwing into the background circumstances of a qualifying or counterbalancing kind. It is in accordance with all that we know of the Spirit's mode of operation in the Church, that when the position of affairs was so singular, and the exigencies of the Church in many respects so great, as they were at the commencement of the gospel, He would adapt His gifts and methods of working, in ways somewhat extraordinary, to the state of the times; thus giving special encouragements to believers amid their heavy struggles and embarrassments, and compensating, in a measure, for the want of resources which might at other times be within their reach. But things of that description, however expedient or even necessary at the beginning, might have proved disadvantageous afterwards; because tending to hinder the free and fitting development of the Christian life in its various capacities and powers of action. And it is again in accordance with all that we know of the Spirit's operations, that the natural should, wherever and so far as properly available, be turned to account, and sanctified to spiritual uses. In the case even of the apostles, at least of the more prominent and influential among them, the recognition of this principle can be without difficulty traced. For, amid all that surrounded them of the supernatural and miraculous, we still see nothing like a disparagement or suppression of their natural powers and susceptibilities; but,

on the contrary, a most real and valid consideration made
of them. By these, indeed, their relative places and spheres
of operation were to a large extent determined. In St.
Paul's case, especially, if we may not say he was called
to be the apostle to the Gentiles *because* he was possessed of singular mental powers, of Grecian culture, and
Roman citizenship, it is still clear that these formed no
mean part of the qualifications which rendered important
service to him in the prosecution of his high calling. Nor
was it materially different in regard to the outward support
of the ministry. During the earliest stage of ministerial
agency our Lord charged Himself, in a manner, with the
support of those who were engaged in it. He sent forth
His disciples on their first missionary tour without purse, or
scrip, or even change of raiment,[1] in order that, while He
was still present with them, and personally destitute of
material resources, they might have convincing evidence of
His willingness and power to bring all necessary provisions
to their hand. But at a later period, when on the eve of
taking His departure from them,[2] and preparing them for
what should be the future order of things, He indicated the
propriety of their adopting whatever means or precautions
lay within their reach : they were, henceforth, to serve themselves of the natural and the ordinary materials of suste-
nance or safety, so far as these might be at their command,
and could be made available. It was but to follow out the
spirit of this original revelation of the Lord's mind and will,
when the members of the New Testament Church provided,
through their free-will offerings, for the maintenance of those
who gave themselves to the work of the ministry, as well as
for the relief of the poor ; and when the principle was
formally announced by the Apostle Paul, that 'they who
preach the gospel should live of the gospel.'[3] If the
principle has been abused in later times by the institution

[1] Matt. x. 9, 10.   [2] Luke xxii. 36.   [3] 1 Cor. ix. 14.

of rich benefices, and the employment of simoniacal practices, the legitimate use, with its scriptural warrant and
obligation, still remains.

Other considerations, also, come in aid of those which
are furnished by the word of God, pointing in the same
direction. How, in a busy, and to a large extent hostile
world, can the interests of the gospel be expected to flourish
without a special class of officers charged with the responsibility of watching over them, and placed in a position which
may enable them to devote their time and energies to the
work? How, even in well-informed and orderly congregations, can the souls of the people be fed with sound knowledge, and their Christian efforts be rightly stimulated and
made to tell with proper effect on the state of things around
them, without the wise counsels and earnest application of
a faithful ministry? The dictates of common sense, and
the lessons also of past experience, concur in showing the
necessity of adhering in this respect to the method, which
has met the common approval of Christendom. It is well
to say that the members of Christian congregations should
each apply themselves, as God may enable them, to exhortation, and prayer, and active labours for the spiritual
instruction and wellbeing of others. No doubt they *should*,
and also *will* do this, if religion is in a healthful and
thriving state among them; but never, unless perhaps in a
few exceptional cases, can it be reasonably expected to such
an extent as to supersede the necessity of a regular pastorate.
It certainly has not done so in the past, and it seems less
and less likely to do so in the future. The circumstances of
the world, and of the Church itself, are manifestly of a kind
to call for the undivided efforts of as many qualified pastors
as there is the least probability of obtaining, and whatever
occasional help besides can be derived from the more zealous
and devoted members of particular congregations. It is not,
we may be well assured, the cause of righteousness, but the

interests of worldliness or sin, which would be gained by a general discontinuance of the pastoral office in the Church, or by the withdrawal, from those who fill it, of such temporal encouragement and support as may admit of the undivided application of their services to the work of the ministry.

III. *Views of the Church which, though not fatal to the existence, are injurious to the proper character of the pastoral office.*—It is quite possible, and has, indeed, been found greatly more common, to err both as to the idea of the Church, and the nature of the pastoral function associated with it, by pushing to an extreme the formal or visible aspects of the subject, than by going too far in the opposite direction. These may be so unduly magnified and dwelt upon as virtually to disparage and cast into the shade such as are of a more vital and spiritual nature ; as is done pre-eminently in the hierarchical system of Rome, and in other communions in proportion as they are leavened with High Church notions of the priesthood and the sacraments. The system (whatever elements of truth may be combined with it) is always fraught with danger to the spiritual interests of the individual believer; for the tendency here is to repress individualism, hence to weaken the principle of personal responsibility, and dispose men to substitute an easy and formal acquiescence in something done for them, in lieu of a work of grace wrought in them by the Word and Spirit of Christ. It does not, however, carry the same formal opposition to the subject more immediately under consideration, as the erring tendencies in the other direction ; for in the hierarchical Churches referred to there is also a pastorate, or cure of souls, only one of a materially different character from that recognised in the Reformed Churches, and, as we believe, sanctioned in Scripture ; a pastorate which is at the same time a priesthood, and is mainly distinguished by

the work of mediation which it has to perform in behalf of
those who are the objects of its solicitude. Under such a
system, everything necessarily partakes of a false tinge and
bias ; pastoral theology has to busy itself chiefly with offices
and administrations of a vicarious kind, ritualistic services
and sacerdotal offerings ; with these, at least, much more
than with any direct manifestations of the truth to the hearts
and consciences of men. But the extent to which this may
be done, and the danger which is in consequence brought
to the interests of vital godliness, will depend on the degree
in which the hierarchical element, with its accompanying
ceremonialism, is allowed to prevail.

It is in the Romish Church, with which indeed may be
included the several divisions of the Eastern Church, as
in this respect there is no material difference, that the
element in question has its most complete and systematic
development. And it has obtained such ascendancy there,
mainly because of the undue, almost exclusive regard that
it had to the external relations and formal services of the
Church as a visible Institute. Indeed, so far as any practical purpose is concerned, no other view of the Church is
ever brought into notice, or distinctly contemplated as possible ; and every effort is put forth to treat as entirely
theoretical and inconsistent the Protestant doctrine of a
spiritual or invisible, in connection with a visible Church.
' Protestants ' (says Bossuet in his *Variations*) ' insist that the
Church consists exclusively of believers, and is therefore
an invisible body. But when asked for the signs of a
Church, they say the word and sacraments, a ministry and a
public service. If so, how can it consist exclusively of the
pious ? And where was there any society answering to the
Protestant definition before the Reformation ?' So, also,
more recently Möhler in his *Symbolik*. After quoting
Luther's sentiments regarding the individual Christian as one
taught of God through the divine word and Spirit, and re-

presenting the Church as composed of such as have been so taught, he thus proceeds : ' It hence cannot be discerned why he should need the supplemental aid of a congregation invested with authority, from whose centre the word of God should be announced to him ; for by the assistance of the outward divine word alone, written in the depths of his heart, he hears His voice, and without an immediate organ. What, after all this, can the Church be other than an invisible community, since no material object in the visibility of the Church can any longer be conceived ? Yet,' he adds, ' Luther all at once admits, without its being possible to discover in his system any rational ground for such an assumption, the establishment of human teachers, and even the lawfulness of their calling. Hereby the Church becomes visible, recognisable, obvious to the eye ; so that the ill-connected notions of God, the sole teacher, and of a human teacher declared competent, and who cannot even be dispensed with, meet us again in such a way as to imply that the invisible is still a visible Church also.'

The whole that there is of plausibility in this line of attack arises from a kind of clever confounding of things that differ, treating the two aspects of the Church as set forth by Protestants with studied perplexity, as if they were to be understood in reference to precisely the same interests and relations. When contemplated with respect to the true scriptural idea, the Church is the living body of the glorified Redeemer ; and, as such, it is necessarily composed of those, and of those alone, who have been justified by His grace, and made partakers of His risen life. The signs of it in that point of view are not, as Bossuet insinuates, the word and sacraments,—no intelligent Protestant writer could so represent it,—but faith, holiness, perpetuity. These, however, from their very nature, are strictly inward and spiritual properties ; they depend simply on the reality of the soul's communion with Christ, and the regenerating grace of the Holy Spirit. But when the question comes to be, How usually is this life-giving work of the Spirit, and communion with the Son, begun and carried on in the experience of men? it is proper to reply,—Through the word and the sacraments, or the ministrations and ordinances of the gospel, which, in so far as they are scripturally maintained and dispensed, are of God, and if not the only, still are the ordinary channels through which the Spirit imparts the blessings of salvation to the soul.

In the Bible first, and generally also in the Protestant confessions, the work of our salvation is presented to our view as primarily a personal concern, a transaction which has to take place between the soul and God. And the determination of the question, whether this has really become an accomplished thing in our experience, must ever turn on the state of the heart toward God, whether or how far it has come to be alive to the concerns of salvation in Christ, and has surrendered itself to the power of His grace and truth. The great source of salvation, and the vital bond that connects us with it, being alike spiritual, the main stress neither *is* nor *could* by possibility be laid upon our relation to some external apparatus, or human instrumentality. These, at best, can be but the appointed means and channels. The boon itself reaches the soul only when by a spirit of faith there is the appropriation of a living Saviour, and a humble reception of His word of truth. If these really exist, no matter how they may have come into operation, or where; it is of no moment whether amid the solemnities of worship, or in an hour of silent communing with Heaven; whether through a message spoken in due season by an ordained minister of the gospel, or by a word dropped in the private intercourse of Christian fellowship by a believing brother; the soul *has* found the blessing; it has laid hold of Him who is the fulness of life and blessing; and its portion is, beyond doubt, with the Church of the first-born, whose names are written in heaven.

But are we on this account independent of the visible Church ? Do we owe nothing to its ministrations, and has it nothing to expect from us in return ? On the contrary, we should never, in all probability, have sought after the requisite state of mind, and the blessings associated with it, or known how to attain them, except from the advantages enjoyed in connection with the visible Church ; and as with the beginning, so with the future progress. The two, in short, stand related as a double and closely interconnected system of means ; the direct and immediate are repentance toward God, and faith toward the Lord Jesus Christ ; but in order to the production and development of these, there is in the hand of the Spirit another class of means, of a remoter and outward kind,—the ministrations, ordinances, watchful superintendence and oversight of the Church. Is not this in correspondence with what takes place in the natural sphere of things ? *There* also the prime, the essential thing is the secret implantation of a living principle in an organism fitted to receive and manifest its properties ; but this organism itself is linked to a system of external adaptations, through which the vital principle is brought into existence, nourished into strength, and carried forward to the proper maturity and perfection of its nature.

Thus the sought-for point of union between the visible and the invisible Church,[1] to use the words of Litton, ' lies in the administration of those means of grace by which, as instruments, the Holy Spirit works, continually replenishing the true Church with members out of the visible ; and those means are the preached word and the sacraments. To the visible Church it belongs to administer these ordinances ; for whatever be the state of heart of those to whom the ministry of the word and the sacraments is committed, these

[1] *The Church*, p. 368.

means of grace are efficacious not on account of, that is, not directly or primarily on account of, the human channel through which they pass, but by virtue of Christ's promise, and the faith of the recipient. To the visible Church, then, belongs the public administration of the means of grace ; and as it is by the instrumentality of these means that the true Church is gathered in, it is obvious that it is no more possible to sever the one from the other, than it is to sever the inward grace of the sacraments from the outward sign ; and that, in fact, as in the sacraments the outward sign and the inward grace are not two sacraments, but the two aspects, the inward and the outward, of one and the same ordinance, so the visible and the true Church are not distinct communities, but one and the same, regarded from different points of view.   The *true* Church depends for the maintenance of its existence on the *visible* Church ; and, in turn, the visible Church is supported by the true.   Thus a reciprocal action is ever going on : the visible Church, as such, dispensing the means of grace by which Christ works to the gathering in of His elect ; and the true Church, as such, upholding and perpetuating the visible use of those means by furnishing faithful recipients of them.'

I only add to this clear statement regarding the mutual bearings and relations between the true and the visible, or the elect and actual Church, that the distinction, we should ever remember, is of man's, not of God's making.   The two *should* correspond in number and extent, and *would* do so but for the corruption and hypocrisy of men, which are ever marring the efficiency of God's ordinances, and bringing imperfection and disorder into His kingdom.   The visible Church, as formerly stated, *ought* to be the community of saints, the brotherhood of faith ; so that in it, as in a mirror, men might see what the life of Christ actually is, and be ever deriving from it salutary impressions upon their hearts and consciences.   This can be but imperfectly done so long as the representation stands in the characters of single individuals or isolated families. There must be social organization, united action, collective results, otherwise nothing great, or general, or permanent can be reached; and the Church militant is true to her calling, and fulfils her mission, only in so far as she everywhere presents the aspect of a kingdom of righteousness, peace, and joy in the Holy Ghost.

With such views of the nature and calling of the Christian Church, we have no hesitation in rejecting as unscriptural and misleading any Church system which, on the ground merely of its historical position, its ecclesiastical polity, or hereditary claim to be the dispenser of salvation, would dispose men to look more to the external framework and formal administration of the kingdom of Christ than to its spiritual aims and inner life ; to be more concerned about preserving the right relation to a human instrumentality and a generally recognised order of things, than about their relation to the mind and Spirit of Christ ; in a word, to make salvation primarily and chiefly a matter of compliance with a prescribed ritual of service, and of interest in the ministrations of a divinely-constituted priesthood. Such a system, wherever it exists, and however it may be guarded, must always be perilous to the souls of men, since it necessarily tends to carnalize their views of divine things, to fix their regard more upon form than substance, and to turn the work of the ministry, in its higher functions, from an earnest treatment of the sublime realities of the gospel for the good of men, into a mechanical routine of observances which the stupidest of men could perform with equal propriety as the most intelligent and wise.

The evil, too, is all the greater, and the more apt to impose on the credulity of men, from its existing in the firmly-compacted system of Rome, where, with a certain measure of plausibility, an appeal can be made to an ap-

parently unbroken historical connection with the past, and
the claim is made, as of right, to the heritage of doctrine
and worship which has descended from the first fathers of
the Christian Church. Unquestionably a certain weight is
due to the historical element in determining the relation we
should occupy toward any particular Church, and the title
it may rightfully have to our allegiance. It should not be
without solid grounds that we set aside a claim which,
either in a national respect, or from personal ties, may press
itself on our regard. Still this historical element itself is
an outward thing ; it does not directly touch the vitals of
the faith ; and there are important considerations to show
that the outwardness belonging to it, whether as connected
with the Church of Rome or with any other visible Church
in Christendom, should be allowed nothing more than a
secondary place, and should yield, when necessary, to the
higher claims of truth and righteousness.

(1.) In the first place, the history of the past presents a
conclusive argument against the absolute force of any simply
historical claim, on the part of a Church or religious community, to our acceptance. For the Christian Church itself
started on its course with the peremptory denial of such a
claim. Christianity sprang out of Judaism, and when taking
root in the earth as an organized society or spiritual kingdom, though but a fresh exhibition and proper development
of what already existed in the synagogue, it had at the outset to cast off the authority of the synagogue, and pursue an
independent course. This consideration has been put forth
by the advocates of Protestant liberty in former times, by
Claude, for instance, in his disputation with Bossuet, and
has never met with a valid reply. Bossuet urged the inevitable tendency of the Protestant doctrine toward Indepen-
dentism, and asked what remedy it provided against ' that
intolerable presumption which must lead an individual to
believe that he can understand Scripture better than the

best Œcumenical Councils and the whole Church together.'
Claude objected to this alleged unanimity, the contrary
decisions of councils, such as that of Rimini; but passing
from that, he said there is 'an incontestable example; there
is the judgment of the synagogue when it condemned Jesus
Christ, and by consequence declared that He was not the
Messiah promised by the prophets.' This, he affirmed, was
an unquestionable fact, and it proved that one might do
without presumption that which had been pronounced to be
intolerable and presumptuous. Bossuet professes to have
seen at once the transparent fallacy of this argument, and
prayed for grace that he might show it to be so to those
who appeared greatly taken by it. 'When an individual
now,' he said, 'denies the authority of the Church, there is
no other external means by which God can avail Himself to
dissolve the doubts of the ignorant, and beget in the faithful
the necessary humility. In order to draw such an argument
from the conduct of the synagogue, it is necessary to affirm
that there was not on earth any external means, any sure
authority, to which one ought to submit. But who can say
that when Jesus Christ was on the earth? Truth itself then
visibly existed among men, the Messiah, the eternal Son
of God, to whom a voice from heaven gave testimony before
all the people: "This is my beloved Son, hear Him."
True, it was resisted, though infallible. I don't say that the
authority of the Church has never been contested, but I say
it ought not to have been so by Christians. I say there has
never been a time on the earth in which one has not been
sure of a visible, speaking authority, to which obedience
ought to be yielded. Before Jesus Christ we had the synagogue; when the synagogue was going to fail, Jesus Christ
Himself appeared; and when Jesus Christ withdrew, He left
His Church with the Holy Ghost. Bring me back Jesus
Christ; I no longer want the Church; but you must restore
to me Jesus Christ in person, and an infallible authority.'

Such, from a Papal point of view, will naturally appear a perfectly satisfactory way of viewing the matter, and unanswerably right ; and yet it is without any solid foundation, and entirely evades the real merits of the question. *First*, it lays stress upon the peculiar circumstances of the time, as if these formed the essential features of the case, and in a manner constituted it a principle of working. This, however, was to misjudge Christ ; for it was precisely *through* the circumstances in which He was placed, and His bearing under them, that we learn His will ; and whatever He did in the fulfilment of His mission, may in spirit be done over again by His people when placed in positions somewhat analogous. But, *secondly*, it totally misrepresents the action of Christ at the period referred to, for the purpose of destroying the parallel between *His* case and *ours*. When Christ personally appeared before the synagogue, truth did then, indeed, visibly exist among men ; but He did not stand upon what, as such, was due to Him ; neither then, nor at any other time during His sojourn on earth, did He press rights and prerogatives that were peculiar to Himself. When tempted by Satan in the wilderness, He took the part of an ordinary believer under trial, simply leaning as a child on the word of His Father in heaven. And when judged and condemned by the synagogue, He waived all His distinctive claims to honour and regard, and quietly carried His appeal heavenwards, committing Himself, as St. Peter expresses it, to Him that judgeth righteously.[1] If, however, we look from the Master to the disciples, whose case more nearly resembles ours, the light furnished is still more decisive ; for when it became necessary for them to take up a separate position, as the guides and leaders of the Christian Church, Christ was no longer visible on earth ; He had gone to the right hand of the Majesty on high, and to this invisible Head was their appeal formally made : ' We must

[1] 1 Pet. ii. 23.

obey God rather than man ;' or more exactly, 'Whether it be right in the sight of God to hearken unto you more than unto God, judge ye.'[1] *Thirdly*, when the advocate of the Romish Church speaks of the Church being left as Christ's substitute, the only remaining visible authority upon earth, he quietly assumes the very point at issue ; for what or where is the precise community so left ? Is it the Papal, or the Greek, or some particular branch of the Reformed Church ? The case now is greatly stronger for a liberty of choice among these, or a freedom to act in certain circumstances above them all, than at the commencement of the Christian Church. For *then* there was but one authority on earth with which, as a competing jurisdiction, the disciples of Christ had to do. But now there is Church beside Church ; the very face of Christendom wears a divided aspect. It therefore remains for all time a most instructive and monitory fact, that when the Church of the New Testament was entering on its history, those who guided its counsels had, in the face of existing authorities, to prosecute their course under direct appeal to heaven ; and that it was ' precisely those who refused to examine, who gave themselves up with implicit faith to the guidance of their Church, and relied absolutely upon the teaching of their priests and their learned men, who rejected and crucified the Lord of glory' (*Cautions for the Times*, p. 110).

(2.) There is, however, another, a *prophetical* ground for the line of procedure now under consideration, which serves greatly to strengthen and confirm that which is derived from the history of the past. For in the prophetic announcements made by Christ and His apostles, the plainest intimations were given of a coming degeneracy in the Christian Church, not only warranting but most urgently demanding a spirit of faithfulness on the part of true believers, and, in particular, of Christian pastors. It was not merely that single

[1] Acts iv. 19.

individuals, or even scattered communities, were to give
way to doctrines and practices inconsistent with the tenor
of the gospel ;[1] but that there were to be false prophets or
teachers arising and gaining ascendancy, a general growth
and prevalence of iniquity, what one apostle represents as
a gigantic system of harlotry,[2] carrying away multitudes in
the sweep of its abominations ; what another designates, by
way of eminence, *the apostasy*,[3] a huge and portentous back-
sliding from the faith and purity of the gospel in the professing Church, coupled with a defiant and persecuting spirit
toward those who should presume to question its authority.
With such pre-intimations respecting the future of the
Christian Church, interspersed also with the most solemn
charges and admonitions to watch against the evil, to resist
it, nay, to come out and be separate from it, though at the
hazard of property and life, is it not the height of presumption to quash all inquiry and consideration by pointing to
some ecclesiastical corporation, and saying : ' There it is,
the very Church which was of old planted by evangelists
and apostles ; hear it.' It may be so, we reply, as to local
possession or hereditary descent ; there may be in one sense
an unbroken continuity ; but those same evangelists and
apostles forewarned us that corruption was to mar their
handiwork, that it was to be infested by the spirit of error
and delusion, even as by a spreading plague ; and we are
expressly enjoined by them to consider whether the Church
which claims our homage be a Sardis or a Philadelphia,
the Lamb's bride or the whore, a Church which has kept
the faith and testimony of Jesus, or a Church which has
allied herself to the pride and carnality of the world. This
is necessarily a point for decision between Church and
Church ; and as those to whom the revelation of God has
come, we cannot escape from the responsibility of searching

[1] Matt. xxiv. 11, 12, 23, 24.   [2] Rev. xvii. 4, 5, xviii.
[3] 2 Thess. ii. 3–10 ; 1 Tim. iv. 1–3 ; 2 Tim. iii. 1–7.

for ourselves, and determining where the truth lies, and what part it calls us to take. For this purpose, among others, that revelation has been committed to writing, and handed down to us ; and as by it we shall ultimately be judged, so by it we must now be guided, as well in regard to our ecclesiastical as to our social and domestic relations.

Enough, however, for the present. It would be out of place to pursue the subject further here. Our object is not to enter into a full discussion of it, but to lay down a few fundamental principles upon it, with reference more especially to the responsibilities and calling of those who are either preparing for, or are actively engaged in, the pastoral office as the great business of their lives. As matters actually stand, divisions in the Church, even in its sounder portions, may be held to be inevitable. Christian prayerfulness and effort, it is to be hoped, will lessen their number, but still for many a day they may be expected to exist ; and aspirants to the ministry, as well as believers generally, have no alternative but to select a particular community in preference to others as that with which to associate themselves in the exercise of Christian privilege or the discharge of Christian duty. But certain difficulties of a practical kind necessarily arise out of this state of things touching one's relation to the pastors and members of other evangelical Communions, and the way and manner in which, with due regard to one's own position, Christ's great law of love may still be effectively maintained. A few reflections on this point may not unsuitably close these preliminary discussions.

IV. *The relation of Church to Church and pastorate to pastorate in connection with the great law of Christian love.*— It was, doubtless, clearly foreseen by our Lord that the imperfections in faith and knowledge which should attach to His people, and the entanglements amid which His Church should have to make its way in the world, would

c

have the effect of originating formal diversities in outward
fellowship and government, even where there might be a
substantial agreement on all the great things of salvation.
Yet, in imposing His specific law of love, Christ made no
account of these prospective differences. Contemplating
His believing people through all time as standing in essentially the same relation to Himself, He prayed that they
might be kept one in such a sense that the world might be
able to take knowledge of it,[1] and also charged them to love
one another simply as His disciples ; so to do it, that by this
very exercise and mutual interchange of love men might with
some degree of confidence discern them to be His disciples.

(I.) Now, amid the perplexities and embarrassments which
the present broken and divided aspect of the Christian
Church throws around the subject, especially for those who
are called to preside over its several and somewhat antagonistic communities, there is a consideration which it is
important to bear in mind, and which so far relieves the
difficulty. It is this, that the interchange of love from
disciple to disciple, and, of course, also from Church to
Church, while enjoined quite generally by our Lord, is not
necessarily uniform, and could not have been meant to be
altogether uniform, either in its strength or in its manner of
exercise. It admits of preferences both as regards individuals and as regards Christian communities. Those who
are connected with us by closer bonds, who hold more
intimate relationships to us than other men, are on that
account entitled to a more special place in our regard. The
providence of God has made them to us in a sense what
other men are not, and this calls for a corresponding degree
and exercise of affection. This implies, no doubt, a distinction in the fold of Christ, yet only a relative distinction,
and one for which we have the authority and example of
our Lord Himself. For while He loved *all* His disciples,

[1] John xvii. 21, 23 ; xiii. 34, 35.

there was one so peculiarly the object of His affectionate regard, that he is called ' the disciple whom Jesus loved.' Hence, as the charge of our Lord to the disciples was to love one another as He had loved them, it is perfectly allowable and proper for them to make distinctions in their love ; within the circle of one's own Communion there may be a circle narrower still, a select few with whom we find such congeniality of feeling, such harmony of spirit, such mutual conformity of gifts and graces, that we are instinctively drawn to them by the warmest affection. And if so in respect to the members of one Communion, much more in respect to that Communion as compared with others, with which we are not *visibly*, however we may be *really* and *internally* united, as partakers of one common salvation.

It never was the design of that grace which is exhibited in the gospel to interfere with the constitution of the human mind, or impose on it laws of working different from those which it naturally obeys. On the contrary, it adapts itself to these, and seeks to bring them into harmonious and healthful operation. But there is nothing more certain or uniform in regard to the emotional part of our natures than that we are formed for particular attachments, with affections that settle upon one object or class of objects with greater force and intensity than on others. We cannot, even though we might wish to do so, love all persons alike ; and it is no part of Christianity to oblige us to attempt it. To be without hatred or malice toward any, to be ready to repay evil with good, and show kindness even to the undeserving, this *is* an essential mark of a Christian spirit. But it were no mark of such a spirit to be without special attachments, or to confer no higher tokens of regard on some than we do on others. One not only *may* but *should* love one's own family otherwise than persons who live outside of it ; the bonds and obligations of grace concur with the impulses of nature to establish such a difference. And, in like manner,

it is at once natural and dutiful to feel more deeply concerned in the welfare of the particular communion to which
we belong, and to do more to promote its advancement in
all that is really good, than for others, though equally sound
and living branches of the true Church, only less intimately
known and related to us.

All this arises from the operation of that law of our
natures which requires that our feelings and affections, in
order to be strong, must be limited in their range of action.
If scattered over a multiplicity of objects, they necessarily
lose in intensity and force. It is therefore not to be regarded as any proof of sectarianism, or violation of this law
of Christian love, if we should think, pray, and labour more
for a particular Church, or for individual members of a
Church, than for others. Only care should be taken that
the good sought in this more special line may not be such
as to involve the manifestation of an unbrotherly spirit in
some other direction. The rights of Christian communities,
as well as of single believers, must ever be respected.

(2.) There is still another distinction to be made, and in
that another principle of direction to be found, in respect
to the exercise of Christian love ; which is, that we are not
called by it to countenance or show ourselves indifferent to
any error or delinquency into which, whether as individuals
or as Churches, they may have fallen. Love rather requires
us to give a clear and unequivocal testimony against the evil,
and seek its removal. It was, doubtless, through an infirmity, a defection from the gentle and forbearing spirit of
the gospel, that Paul and Barnabas fell out between themselves, since in the matter of dispute no vital truth was at
stake. But it was no infirmity, it was a noble proof and
exhibition of love, when Paul withstood Peter to his face at
Antioch for acting in a manner which tended to mislead
the disciples ; or when he rebuked the Churches of Galatia
for their weakness in suffering themselves to be withdrawn

from the simplicity of the faith, and the Corinthians for their party strifes, and abuse of supernatural gifts of the Spirit.

There may be sections of the Protestant Church so far removed from what we take to be the proper ideal of a Church of Christ in creed or government, that we could hold no direct or ostensible fellowship with them. Fidelity to the cause of truth and righteousness seems to require that, in that respect, we should stand aloof; love itself compels us to show, by the position we occupy, or the testimony we at fitting times deliver, wherein we conceive them to be in error; and openly to fraternize with them might naturally be construed into an indifference toward our points of disagreement. But if in such communities we meet with individuals who by their spirit and behaviour give evidence of being true disciples of Christ, holding by the great principles of His gospel, and living to the glory of His name, we should then fail in our duty if we did not eye them with affection, and declined to reciprocate the feelings of kindness and goodwill which they may exhibit toward us. The Master, as appears from their spirit and behaviour, has accepted them; who are we, that we should dispute the propriety of His choice, or disown the seal which He has put upon them? Though they will not follow with us, nor may we follow with them in what is peculiar to us both, yet in what is common, in what concerns the fundamental principles of the faith in Christ, the repression of iniquity, the advancement of righteousness in the world, it is in accordance with the spirit of the gospel that there should be brotherly recognition, harmony of thought and action.

How much may not be learned in this respect from the bearing and procedure of Christ Himself? The spirit of love which was exemplified in His course was not more remarkable for its depth and fervency in one direction than for its tenderness and forbearance in another. Himself the light of the world, in whom dwelt all the treasures of wisdom and knowledge, there was necessarily an immeasurable gulf between Him and those about Him as to the degrees of knowledge and spiritual discernment respectively possessed by them.   There would have been so even if the disciples had made the most diligent improvement of their privileges ; but as matters actually stood, the distance was much greater than it might have been.   In spite of Christ's endeavours to teach them, their notions of divine things continued to be crude ; their minds remained full of misapprehensions respecting the nature of His kingdom ; and indications were ever and anon appearing of the carnal tempers and sinful misgivings which cleaved to them.   Yet how meekly did Christ bear with them under all !   With how gentle a hand did He try to remove from their minds the clouds of darkness and prejudice which rested upon them !   How gladly did He avail Himself of the opportunities which arose to impart to them the truth as they were able to receive it !   And, again, how considerately did He hold His hand when He saw that they were incapable at the time of receiving more !   Altogether, we have here most valuable materials for our guidance, peculiarly valuable for the time and circumstances in which we live.   If the spirit of our Lord's behaviour is imbibed, it will dispose us, whenever we perceive the honest and childlike heart of faith, to bear with much that may appear weak and defective ; and to be more ready to convey instruction and dispense blessing, or should that be impracticable, to make due allowance for personal imperfections and failings, than in a feeling of actual or fancied superiority to boast it over others.   Were this but more generally done, were the truth, without being less firmly held, more frequently combined with the meekness and gentleness, the patient and considerate spirit of Christ, it might conciliate more hearts ; not the interests of the truth, but rather those which are opposed to it, would suffer by such line of behaviour.

CHAPTER II.

THE NATURE OF THE PASTORAL OFFICE, AND THE CALL TO ENTER ON ITS FUNCTIONS.

IT is only with some of the preliminary points bearing on the office of the Christian pastorate that we have as yet been occupied. We come now to the subject itself, which naturally falls into a few leading divisions. *First*, there is the *nature* of the pastoral office, with the consideration of what constitutes a valid call to its functions and employments. *Secondly*, the personal and social life befitting one who undertakes the responsibilities and duties of such an office. *Thirdly*, its proper work, comprising : (1) homiletics, or the composition and delivery of discourses ; (2) the employment of subsidiary methods of instruction and counsel ; (3) the devotional services of the sanctuary ; (4) the administration of discipline ; (5) supplemental helps and agencies, not strictly connected with the work of the ministry, but having, in certain respects, an incidental bearing on its operations or results. Under one or other of these divisions every topic of importance relating to the subject may be brought into consideration. And we take that first which naturally precedes the others in the order of discussion, the pastoral office itself, with the call to enter on its functions.

I. *The office viewed in relation to the persons in whose behalf it is instituted.*—This office has to do with the oversight and care of souls, and by its very name imports that ministers of the gospel are called to exercise somewhat of the same fidelity and solicitude in behalf of these, that shepherds are expected to do in respect to their flocks. The names usually applied in Scripture to the highest officers in the Christian Church carry much the same import, though each with some specific shade of meaning as to the primary aspect under which their calling is contemplated. Those names are πρεσβύτεροι and ἐπίσκοποι, presbyters and bishops, or elders and overseers, both alike involving the charge or duty of superintending and consulting for the good of the religious community. The more distinctive Greek term (ἐπίσκοποι), even in its primary or civil application, bore just this meaning. It denoted a class of persons appointed to the work of inspection and responsible government in towns or provinces subject to the parent state. And when transferred to a corresponding class in the Christian Church, it must have been meant to convey the ideas of watchful vigilance and authoritative control. If the term *elders* may be regarded as having originally borne respect to seniority of rank, as marked by advance of years, when it came to be used as an official designation, first in the synagogue, then in the Church. It denoted the heads of the religious community, the fathers of the spiritual household. Both terms, therefore, pointed rather to the exercise of authority, or to the ruling and governing power, than to any other ministerial function. They simply designated the men who were set over Christian congregations as the guides and guardians of the flock, who had to watch for its safety and welfare as those that must give an account. And of the same import also is another epithet employed—a description rather than a designation, ὁι ἡγούμενοι, the leading or ruling ones : 'Remember them that have the rule over you.' [1]

A form of expression, however, is occasionally used,

[1] Heb. xiii. 7.

which seems to point in the opposite direction, representing, as it does, the work and calling of ministers under the notion of a service, or, we may even say, of a servitude. Our Lord had Himself employed this language : ' Whosoever will be great among you, let him be your minister (διάκονος) ; and whosoever will be chief among you, let him be your servant (δοῦλος, *slave*) : even as the Son of man came not to be ministered unto (διακονηθῆναι), but to minister (διακονῆσαι), and to give His life a ransom for many.' [1] The Apostle Paul was peculiarly fond of this form of expression, and seems to have considered it more distinctly indicative of his apostolic or ministerial agency than any of those commonly applied to the presidents or overseers of particular Churches : ' Who, then, is Paul,' he asks, ' and who is Apollos, but ministers (διάκονοι) through whom ye believed, as the Lord gave to every man ?' [2] ' Christ Jesus our Lord hath enabled me, for that He counted me faithful, putting me into the deaconship,'[3] the ministerial employ.   And speaking yet again of the manner in which he conducted himself toward the Churches, he gave no offence, he says, in anything,[4] ' that the διακονία (the ministerial office) might not be blamed.'

It is the same thing still, only presented under another aspect, and with more immediate reference to the perform- ance of work not directly connected with the exercise of authority, though necessarily involving its possession, and its exercise also, in so far as circumstances might render it needful.   Whatever special exercise Paul had to render in his office as an apostle of the Lord Jesus Christ, it is clear from his epistles, that the light in which he chiefly delighted to contemplate his calling was that of a cure of souls ; it was his destination to minister to the perishing the bread of life, and bring them to the possession of a saving interest in Christ.   Therefore, when he seeks to magnify his office, it is more especially with respect to the preaching of the

[1] Matt. xx. 28.   [2] I Cor. iii. 5.   [3] I Tim. i. 12.   [4] 2 Cor. vi. 3.

gospel that he does so.   What he dwells upon is the commission he received from the glorified Redeemer to proclaim the unsearchable riches of His grace and goodness, and, in the fulfilment of this commission, the labours he underwent, the sufferings he endured, the efforts he plied, and the measure of success he obtained.   We can thus be at no loss to understand what kind of service or ministry it was that the apostle meant when he spake of his διακονία in the Lord ; in its more essential features it coincided with that which has to be discharged by every faithful missionary and minister of the word.   Having for its object not merely the bringing of sinners within the pale of salvation, but the constituting of those so brought into an organized society, it necessarily included the exercise of an *administrative* as well as of a *teaching* function ; yet the teaching more directly and prominently, as everything was to proceed in connection with the knowledge and belief of the truth.   This, in its entire compass, belongs to the ministry of the word ; which is, as Bucer notes, a *ministerium*, not a *magisterium ;* a service, not a lordship ; but a service founded on a divine commission, and holding at command a sacred authority, which it is permitted and even bound to employ whenever the interests of truth and righteousness may seem to require it.

In apostolic times the *primary* object of concern was the diffusion of the gospel, and the planting of churches consequent on its propagation ; the oversight and government of particular churches occupied but a *secondary* place.   The apostles gave hours to the one and only minutes to the other.   And though the same might be deemed fitting still, if the matter were viewed with reference to the calling of the Church generally toward the world, yet the proportion comes nearly to be reversed when the pastoral office is considered with respect to individual congregations.   This, indeed, is what is plainly implied in the instructions given concerning it in the later epistles of the New Testament.

The name itself of *pastor* is but once used there, namely in Eph. iv. 11, where the discourse is of the gifts provided and conferred by Christ for all official service and employment in the Christian Church, and where *pastors* and teachers are mentioned among the persons who were intended to share in the bestowal. If not the precise word, however, the idea involved in it, and the relative obligations and duties to which it calls, have expression given to them elsewhere ; as at Acts xx. 28, when St. Paul charges the elders of the Church of Ephesus to 'take heed to themselves, and to all the flock over which the Holy Ghost had made them overseers, and to feed (ποιμαίνειν) the flock of God, which He hath purchased with His own blood ;' also at 1 Pet. v. 2, where the exhortation to feed the flock of God is addressed by Peter as an elder in the universal Church to all the elders of particular congregations ; and for encouragement in the work points to the expected appearance of Christ as the chief Shepherd, who will give to His faithful servants the unfading crown of glory. It was the more natural for Peter to view the office in this light, as it was the one in which our Lord presented the calling and destination of the apostle, on the touching and memorable occasion when, after drawing forth the confession of his love, He gave to him the charge, ' Feed my lambs,' ' Feed my sheep.' [1] And standing as Peter did on that occasion, the representative, in a sense, not only of the select company of apostles, but of all in every age who should be called to ply the work of an evangelical ministry, it is but to enter into Christ's mind in the matter when they view the work in the light of a pastorate, and regard themselves as charged by Christ to care for and feed the sheep of His pasture.

It is what may be called the *interior* side of the office which this view of it most naturally suggests, its relation to

[1] John xxi. 15-17.

those who are already *within* the fold, nominally, at least, the members of Christ's spiritual household. It was under the same aspect that our Lord presented His own high calling, in that gospel which is pre-eminently inwards and spiritual in its representations. He there speaks of Himself as the Shepherd, who knows His sheep, and is known of them ;[1] who even came to lay down His life on their behalf, and who ever keeps them in the grasp of His almighty hand. Yet, while in such representations of Christ there was, in one point of view, a certain limitation, in another there was a wide comprehension, far beyond what at first might occur to the mind. If His eye excluded from the range of its vision those who should ultimately perish from the way of life, it at the same time included all who might at any period be brought into that way ; not the existing members merely of the fold, but one and all who in the future ages of the Church's history, and from whatever quarter, should come to have a place in it. Such intimate and comprehensive knowledge, however, is only for the Chief Shepherd Himself, whose eye can discern the things that *are to be* as clearly as if they already *were*. And interpreting His words by the light reflected on it from His own actual procedure, which is *our* pattern and rule, they tell us of a love He cherished, a compassion He displayed, a watchful and beneficent care He exercised toward many who for the moment were far off from His peculiar people, as well as those that were formally numbered in their ranks. All, in some sense, belong to His flock, as forming part of that creation-proprietorship which is His by inherent, indefeasible right ; only, in their natural state they are in the condition of *lost* sheep, and with multitudes the state of nature becomes the fixed and abiding one ; so that they cease to be reckoned of the flock in the stricter sense. But it is from the same lapsed and perishing mass that those

[1] John x. 14.

who became the true sheep have to be gathered ; all stand originally on one footing ; and hence the work of Christ is so many - sided, and bears in such diverse ways on the responsibilities and interests of the world at large. Directly and properly, it has a twofold object in view, aiming first at the recovery of those who had gone astray, and then at their establishment and growth in the life of holiness. To turn enemies into subjects, aliens into children, sinners into saints, this is its primary design ; and its further aim is to keep those who have been so reclaimed from falling away, and carrying forward their preparation for glory. As the Shepherd, therefore, by way of eminence, Christ in His pastorate as clearly goes forth to seek the lost, that they may be brought into the fold of safety, as He ministers to those who are already there what is required to sustain and nourish them in the life of holiness.

The relation in which ministers of the gospel stand to Christ puts it beyond a doubt that the pastoral office in their hands was meant to be a kind of reflex or copy of His, alike in respect to its general scope and aim, and the relative order of its ministrations. Here, also, the *evangelistic* was ever to go along with, and in a sense precede, the *evangelical;* or, as we may otherwise put it, the ministry of *reconciliation* must prepare for and accompany the ministry of *edification.* And this from the very nature and design of the office, since men are nowhere born members of the spiritual flock of Christ. They have first to be made such, and, when made, nourished with the sincere milk of the word. And amid the manifold variety of fields and circumstances in which the pastoral office has to be discharged by those who assume its responsibilities, it may sometimes be the one, sometimes the other department of the work which is entitled to the greatest prominence and application. But both must always to some extent be the object of the pastor's solicitude and endeavours.

Besides, while in any specific field of pastoral labour the direct objects of its assiduities should be ever *coming into being* as members of Christ's true flock, as well as *growing into maturity*, the whole together, pastor and flock, should exercise a diffusive and regenerative influence around. They should operate for good on the ungodly mass amid which they are placed, not by any means exclusively, yet with a more concentrated and sustained energy through the ministrations of the pastor himself. If the church to which he ministers is set as a light in the world, he should be as the lustre of that light, and should avail himself of every opportunity, and employ every means within his reach, to bring the truth to bear with power upon the hearts and consciences of sinners. In short, if the pastoral office more directly contemplates the good of particular congregations, and in these congregations the spiritual wellbeing and comfort of Christ's true flock, it has respect also to an intermingling or outlying portion, who have to be brought under the husbandry of the gospel, with a view to their becoming children of God and partakers of the blessing. Were it not for operations of this sort, constantly proceeding and successfully plied, there should soon be no flock, in the proper sense, to feed ; as, on the other hand, without due attention to the work of feeding, the flock when found should want its proper nourishment, and fail to grow up to 'the measure of the fulness of the stature of Christ.'

I shall advert presently to the relative importance and the mutual interconnection of those two departments of ministerial agency, and the methods best adapted for their successful prosecution. But whichever of them may be primarily regarded, whether it be the formation of a Christian flock, or the nourishment and growth of its members in their most holy faith, the work itself which the Christian pastor has to perform is always presented to our view in Scripture as *a service of love*, not as a *vicarious mediation ;*

it is a ministerial, not a priestly agency he has to ply ; and the results aimed at, of course, must be of a reasonable kind, such as may be expected to flow from an intelligent apprehension of the truth as exhibited in the word and ordinances of God, not what might be effected by any mysterious charm or magical operation.   In all that is said concerning the office, in the words either of our Lord or of His apostles, not a hint is dropped which would bespeak for the ministers of the gospel the character of a secret-loving, wonder-working priesthood.   And when, a few centuries after the gospel era, we light upon descriptions which present them in such a character, one cannot but be sensible of a huge discrepance between them and the representations of Scripture.   It seems as if an essentially new office had come into being, rather than the original office perpetuated with certain slight modifications.   Listen, for example, to Chrysostom's description of what he calls the glory of the Christian priesthood :[1] 'The priesthood, indeed, is discharged upon earth, but it takes rank with heavenly appointments, and deservedly does so.   For this office has been ordained not by a man, nor by an angel, nor by an archangel, nor by any created power, but by the Paraclete Himself, who has laid hold on men still abiding in the flesh to personate the ministry of angels.   And therefore should the priest, as standing in the heavenly regions amid those higher intelligences, be as pure as they are.   Terrible, indeed, yea, most awful, were even the things which preceded the gospel, such as the bells, the pomegranates, the stones in the breastplate, the mitre, etc., the holy of holies, the profound silence that reigned within.   But when the things belonging to the gospel are considered, those others will be found little, and so also what is said concerning the law, however truly it may be spoken : " That which was glorious has no glory, by reason of that which excelleth."   For when

[1] *De Sac.* iii. op. vol. i. p. 467.

you see the Lord that has been slain, and now lies before you, and the priest bending over the victim, and interceding, and all dyed with that precious blood, do you still reckon yourself to be with men and still standing on the earth? Do you not rather feel transplanted into heaven, and, casting aside all fleshly thoughts and feelings, dost thou not with thy naked soul and thy pure mind behold the things of heaven? O the marvel! O the philanthropy of God! He who is seated above with the Father is at that moment held by the hands of all, and to those that are willing gives Himself to be clasped and received; all which they do through the eyes of faith.' He then refers to the action of Elias on Carmel, declaring that of the Christian priest to be much greater; and he asks: 'Who that is not absolutely mad, or beside himself, could slight so dreadful a mystery? Are you ignorant that the soul of man could never have borne the fire of such a sacrifice, and that all should have utterly perished had there not been the mighty help of the grace of God?'

Such was what constituted, in Chrysostom's view, the peculiar glory of the Christian ministry; and he proceeds in the same magniloquent style to enlarge on the pre-eminent dignity and power connected with it in its prerogative to bind and to loose souls, to forgive or retain sins, to purge men through baptism and other rites from all stains of pollution, and send them pure and holy into the heavenly mansions. All that is, of course, priestly work; work in which the officiating minister has something to offer for the people, and something, by virtue of his office, to procure for them; benefits, indeed, so great, so wonderful, so incomparably precious, that the typical ministrations of the old priesthood, and the benefits accruing from them to the people, were completely thrown into the shade. Now, this is a view of pastoral work on which New Testament Scripture is not only silent, but against which it virtually protests. The service which it associates with the ministry of the gospel is one that employs itself not with presenting a sacrifice *for* men, but in persuading them to believe in a sacrifice already offered, and through that promoting *in* them a work of personal reconciliation with God, and growing meetness for His presence and glory. Hence the ministry of the gospel as set forth in Scripture has the revealed word of God in Christ for its great instrument of working ; and according as this word is received in faith, and brings forth in the lives of men the fruits of holiness, the end of the ministry is accomplished.

In such a service there is, no doubt, a priestly element, since it requires those who would perform it aright not only to deal with men on behalf of God, but also to deal with God on behalf of men, to accompany all their ministrations of word and doctrine with intercessions at the throne of grace. But it is a priestly element of the same kind as belongs to the calling even of private believers, who are bound to bear on their spirits before God the state of the unconverted, and entreat Him for their salvation. And no more in the one case than in the other is there anything of that distinctive characteristic of the priestly function which consists in formally sustaining a vicarious part, and doing for others what they are not warranted or called to do for themselves. The work of the Christian ministry, indeed, is more nearly allied to the *prophetical* than to the *priestly* office of the Old Testament ; and like it, too, it stands on a higher elevation ; for it is a nobler thing to deal directly with the spiritual realities of God's salvation, and by the varied exhibition of these to wield an enlightening and renovating influence on the souls of men, than to do the part of performers in a merely outward, however imposing, ceremonial. Peter and his fellow-apostles on the day of Pentecost displaying the banner which their Lord had given them because of the truth, and bringing crowds of penitent and willing captives to His feet, did a far higher service in

D

the eye of reason than if they had acted as ministrants at an altar where thousands of bleeding victims were presented, or were even for a whole lifetime sending up clouds of incense from golden censers in a temple. And the same may be said in a measure of every one who, like them, or like the apostle of the Gentiles, is enabled through divine grace to commend himself, by the manifestation of the truth, to every man's conscience in the sight of God. No ministry is comparable to this, because none is fraught like it with the elements of power and blessing.[1]

In regard, now, to the *distribution* of ministerial agency, as between that which is devoted to the work of reclaiming sinners and the work of edifying believers, the relations of time and circumstance must determine. Nothing definite respecting it has been indicated in Scripture, nor can it be done here. The actual state of matters differs so widely with one pastor as compared with another, and even with the same pastor in different localities, that the greater prominence will naturally be given sometimes to the one department of labour, sometimes to the other. If he has reason to think that many around are dead in sin, and in danger of sinking into perdition, he cannot but regard it as a much more pressing business to have such rescued from their peril, than that the others, who appear to be already safe, should be plied with encouragements and supports to continue in the path on which they have entered. On the other hand, if spiritual life seems to be generally diffused through the flock, to have this life quickened into greater

[1] So even Erasmus well remarks: 'The minister is then in the very height of his dignity, when from the pulpit he feeds the Lord's flock with sacred doctrine' (*Eccles.* L. 1). And referring to Paul's statement, that Christ sent him not to baptize, but to preach, Stillingfleet justly asks in his *Irenicum :* ' Shall we think that those who succeed him in his office of preaching are to look upon anything else as more their work than that ? '

activity, and drawn forth into more abundant fruitfulness, will naturally become the main object of his ministrations. But, in reality, the two aims of the ministry run very much into each other; and not unfrequently the means which are more immediately directed toward the conversion of sinners will be found of greatest service in strengthening the graces of believers ; as, inversely, what is intended to prompt some to the higher attainments of faith and holiness may react with wholesome influence on such as are still living in vanity and sin.

There is no difficulty in understanding how this should be the case. It always is owing to the dominion in some form or another of the flesh and the world, that those who have the root of the matter in them are impeded in their progress heavenwards, and are less active than they might be in the service of their Redeemer. But it is only the same thing in a yet higher degree which operates to the danger of those who are altogether estranged from the way of life ; and the means and appliances which are employed to rouse these out of their perilous security, cannot but have points of contact in the hearts and consciences of such as, though partakers of the divine life, are still but imperfectly subject to its power. It will even sometimes happen, that individuals of this class may feel as if services of the kind referred to had a special application to them, and they, more almost than any others, had need to listen to the warnings and admonitions which are addressed to the supine and godless. On the other side, things said concerning the faithful in Christ Jesus may strike a chord in the bosom of men far off from righteousness : for, when such hear of the privileges of true believers, of the desires and feelings awakened in their souls by the grace of God, of their blessed nearness to God Himself, their zeal in well-doing, hope in death, and meetness for eternity, how natural the reflection for those who are still living after the course of a present world, that all this belongs to a line of things to which they are entire

or comparative strangers, and that if they should continue
as they are, the shades of an irrecoverable death may overtake them ! It is an undoubted fact, that some of those
whose ministrations have been most blessed to the conversion of sinners, have also been most distinguished for the
deep spirituality and richly varied experience that have
characterized their services, though it cannot, perhaps, be
said to be quite common.

Indirectly, however, the same result is accomplished by a
ministry of this description, since the work of spiritual
nourishment and growth in the better portion of the community, in proportion as it is healthful and vigorous, will
ever be found conducive to the enlightenment and reformation of the classes which lie beyond.   If the members
generally of a Christian Church are full of faith and of the
Holy Ghost, if their conversation and their conduct are
deeply imbued with the earnest, generous, and blessed spirit
of the gospel, they will assuredly be to many around them
' as a dew from the Lord, as the showers upon the grass.' [1]
The careless and ungodly with whom they come in contact
will be constrained to feel that there is a reality and a
power in the life of faith which bespeaks its connection
with a higher world ; so that, as in the case of the Thessa-
lonian converts, the word of the Lord will be ever sounding
forth with convincing and refreshing power to others.   And
every successful effort that is made for the perfecting of
the saints is also a train laid for the breaking asunder of
spiritual bonds, and recovering from the snare of the devil
those who are led captive by him.

But, in such matters, much must always depend on individual temperament and personal gifts.   Some are more
peculiarly qualified by nature, as well as by the special work
of grace in their own souls, for producing convictions of sin ;
others for guiding those who have been convinced to peace

[1] Mic. v. 7.

in believing, and progress in the Christian life. And it is in accordance with the highest wisdom, that each should lay himself out chiefly in the kind of work for which his talent is the greatest, and should even seek for such a field of ministerial labour as may admit of its being employed to most advantage. If one may refer to the Puritan period for examples, it is plain that such men as Owen and Howe would find their most appropriate sphere in ministering to congregations which as a rule were not only settled in the faith, but were capable also of receiving and relishing the strong meat of the gospel ; although it were not easy to find more solemn and stirring appeals to slumbering consciences than appear occasionally in their extant discourses. It is equally plain, that the next two most distinguished Puritans, Richard Baxter and John Bunyan, both from their native cast of mind, and the spiritual training through which they passed, were more especially fitted for the work of rousing dormant consciences, and moving sinners to flee from the wrath to come. The effects in this line actually wrought through their instrumentality were certainly of the most marked description. And the account which Baxter himself gives in the *Reformed Pastor* of the reasons which prevailed with him to aim mainly at the conversion of sinners, and to prosecute this aim with the most intense eagerness, are well deserving of the serious consideration of all who are either looking forward to pastoral work, or are actually engaged in it :—

' Alas,' says he, 'the misery of the unconverted is so great that it calleth loudest to us for our compassion. He that seeth one man sick of a mortal disease, and another only pained with the toothache, will be moved more to compassionate the former than the latter, and will surely make more haste to help him, though *he* were a stranger, and the other a *son*. It is so bad a case to see men in a state of damnation, wherein, if they should die, they are remedilessly lost, that methinks we should not be able to let them alone, either in public or in private, whatever other work we have to do. I confess I am forced frequently to neglect that which should tend to the greater increase of knowledge in the godly, and may be called stronger meat, because of the lamentable necessity of the unconverted. Who is able to talk of controversies or nice unnecessary points? yea, or truths of a lower degree of necessity, how excellent soever, while he seeth a company of ignorant, carnal, miserable sinners before his face, that must be changed or damned? Methinks I see them entering on their final woe. Methinks I even hear them crying out for help, and speediest help. Their misery speaks the louder, because they have not hearts to seek or ask for help themselves. Many a time have I known that I had some hearers of higher fancies, that looked for rarities, and were addicted to despise the minister, if he told them not more than ordinary: and yet I could not find in my heart to turn from the observation of the necessities of the impenitent for the honouring of these, nor to leave speaking to the apparently miserable for their salvation, to speak to such novelists; no, nor so much as otherwise should be done to the weak for their confirmation and growth in grace. Methinks, as St. Paul's spirit was stirred within him when he saw the Athenians so addicted to idolatry, so it should cast us into one of his paroxysms to see so many men in great probability of being everlastingly undone. And if by faith we did indeed look upon them as within a step of hell, it should more effectually untie our tongues, than, they tell us, that Crœsus' danger did his son's. He that will let a sinner go to hell for want of speaking to him, doth set less by souls than the Redeemer of souls did, and less by his neighbour than rational charity will allow him to do by his greatest enemy. Oh therefore, brethren, whomsoever you neglect, neglect not the most miserable! Whoever you pass over, forget not poor souls that are under the condemnation and curse of the law, and may look every hour for the dreadful execution, if a speedy change do not prevent it!'

Considerations like these will undoubtedly weigh much with all preachers of the gospel, who are animated by the true spirit of their office, and alive to its great responsibilities. Yet there is no need, even when such is the case, that conversion should be always thrust prominently forward, as if it were the one concern the faithful pastor had to mind. It will often be *felt* in the tone and manner in which the particular subjects are handled, rather than *discovered* in the choice of the subjects themselves. For there is such a manifold variety in the states of unconverted men, their degrees of guilt, and the kinds of deceitfulness with which it is accompanied ; such endless diversities exist as to the temper and habit of their minds, the avenues by which the springs of thought and feeling may best be reached, and the appeals that may be most likely to carry their decision for a life of piety, that it is proper to bring into play a corresponding variety of means of moral suasion ; and nothing, perhaps, in the whole revealed counsel of God, if wisely handled, may be excepted from the things calculated to effect the desired end. At the same time, it is not to be doubted, that persons who have in a strong degree the bent of soul, and the gifts, natural and acquired, which are more peculiarly adapted to the work of spiritual conviction, will generally find the greatest aptitude and success in handling the topics which do most directly bear upon the object in view. The Spirit of God within men, and the teaching of their own experience, must be their principal guide. But as regards the work itself, the work of winning souls from sin to Christ, if any are successful in accomplishing it, whether by the use of a more extensive and varied or of a more limited range of materials, blessed are they, even above other faithful labourers in the Lord's vineyard. For the highest place of

honour there, and the noblest heritage of blessing connected
with its labours, must ever belong to those who have been
the instruments under God of saving souls from death, and
turning the disobedient to the wisdom of the just.   It was a
fine saying of Samuel Rutherford's, 'Heaven would be two
heavens for me, if souls given me as seals were found there.'

II. *The pastoral office viewed in respect to its higher relations.*—The preceding observations have had respect to the
nature and responsibilities of the pastor's vocation chiefly
on one side, in its relation to those in whose behalf it is
exercised.   But there is another and higher relation which
it also holds ; for, considered as the ministry of reconciliation, it is of the nature of an embassy, and implies a commission from Heaven ; considered as a cure of souls, it is
stewardship, and involves a sacred trust, of which an
account must be rendered ; considered, finally, as the
instrumental agency for regenerating souls and preparing
them for glory, it is a work of God, and requires the possession of gifts which He alone can bestow.   These are the
higher aspects of the pastoral office, its points of contact
with the sanctuary above ; and it is of importance, both for
obtaining a right view of the office itself, and for the pre-
servation of the right spirit in discharging its functions, that
it be looked at also in this higher relationship.

(1.) Considered, first of all, as a ministry of reconciliation,
and implying a commission from Heaven, the original charge
of our Lord to His apostles, to go and preach the gospel to
every creature, lays for it a sure and abiding foundation.
It was obviously impossible that those immediately addressed could do more than make a commencement in the
execution of such a wide commission.   The charge delivered
primarily to them must necessarily go down as a descending
obligation to future times, and is virtually laid upon all who
in a right spirit and a becoming manner undertake the

duties of the pastoral office. Hence the Apostle Paul, speaking not in his own name merely, but in that of all who, like himself, were sincerely preaching the gospel, says, 'We are ambassadors for Christ, as though God did beseech you by us : we pray you in Christ's stead, be ye reconciled to God.'[1]   And the ministry generally he calls ' the ministry of reconciliation,' as having for its more immediate and primary object the pressing upon them of God's message of love, the reception of which would close their alienation from God, and secure their entrance on a state of peace and fellowship.   Having such an aim, and an aim to be accomplished through so vast a field, it was indispensable that the message itself, and the right to deliver it, should turn upon no nice technicalities or ecclesiastical punctilios, but should be of a plain, broad, and reasonable character. And so, indeed, they are as presented to us in the word of God.   For, while the Church is there most distinctly and solemnly charged with the mighty task of reclaiming the world to the saving knowledge and love of God, she is trammelled with no minute forms and rubrics as to the specific mode of carrying it into effect ; she is left with a few simple directions and ordinances of divine appointment, to proceed as circumstances of time and place might suggest or require.   And the terms of the embassy to be put into the mouth of all her official representatives are just the great facts and promises of Christ's salvation.   *There* for all times and all lands is the sum and substance of the pastor's commission.   Not in any new or more special communication from heaven, but in that revelation which has been delivered to the Church by apostles and prophets, lies the burden of everlasting weal, with its fearful alternative of woe, which he goes forth to deliver in the hearing of his fellow-men, and press on their regard ; the only thing, indeed, suited to his purpose and to the necessities of those with

[1] 2 Cor. v. 20.

whom he has to deal.   So that the grand rule here is, as the apostle puts it, ' If any man speak, let him speak as the oracles of God ;' for therein alone is contained the revelation of Heaven's counsel to fallen and sinful men, and the only sure grounds on which they can hope for acceptance and blessing.

(2.) Considered more strictly, in the second place, as a cure of souls, the pastoral office involves a stewardship, a stewardship of most grave responsibility, for it has entrusted to it the oversight of treasures of inestimable value. The flock themselves are such a treasure, seeing that in every one of them there resides a soul capable alike of the highest enjoyment and of the deepest misery.   To be set in a position of official superintendence and ministerial agency in respect to these, is plainly to be invested with the highest of all earthly stewardships.   But add to this the consideration also of the means furnished for meeting the wants of the flock, the treasures of spiritual knowledge, and life, and blessing which, in *their* behalf, are placed at the pastor's command, that he may give to all their food in due season.   What a thought, to be constituted the dispensers of such imperishable treasures !   No doubt the treasures are in a sense common, open to the members of the flock, apart from any human instrumentality ; open to all who are willing to search the Scriptures, and, in accordance with the tidings they convey, to make personal application for them through the blood of atonement.   *There*, unquestionably, is the ultimate authority for everything that is either offered or received in the matter of salvation.   Still, it is through the ministrations of word and ordinance, as connected with the labours of the pastoral office, that usually the treasures of divine grace and truth are unfolded, and made practically available to the ever-varying conditions of men.   Hence the word of our Lord, spoken in answer to a question from Peter, but spoken with reference to all who might be called to pastoral work, 'Who then is that faithful and wise steward, whom his lord shall make ruler over his household, to give them their portion of meat in due season? Blessed is that servant, whom his lord, when he cometh, shall find so doing.'[1] In another passage they are likened by Him to persons who are provided by their Master with spiritual treasures, and should be ever bringing forth from them things new and old;[2] as also by St. Paul they are designated stewards of the mysteries, or hidden riches of God's wisdom,[3] which, as he again expresses it, are put like heavenly treasure into earthen vessels.[4] What an honourable position! And, at the same time, what a high calling! The special keepers and dispensers of Heaven's peculiar treasure! The living conduits of that divine word which God Himself delights to magnify above all His name !

(3.) The office has still again to be considered as a work, a work of God, by means of which those naturally dead in sin are made alive to God, and carried forward on the way to glory; a work, we may say, impossible, unless divine influences come in aid of its accomplishment. Every work calls for the application of powers suited to its nature; by such alone can it be successfully managed; and as this particular work belongs to the new creation, it can only be made good if the earthen vessels engaged in effecting it have 'the excellency of power,' which comes from God. Here, especially, the great truth holds, 'Not by might, nor by power (viz. of man); but by my Spirit, saith the Lord.' Hence, when unfolding the gospel commission to His disciples, and pointing as well to the duties as the trials connected with the work, Christ gave such express assurance to them, that He would be with them even to the end of the world,[5] and would obtain from the Father, in answer to believing prayer, whatever might be needed for the service

[1] Luke xii. 42, 43.   [2] Matt. xiii. 52.   [3] 1 Cor. iv. 1.
[4] 2 Cor. iv. 7.   [5] Matt. xxviii. 18–20.

required at their hands.[1] St. Paul also refers to this plenitude of spiritual gifts for pastoral duty, and the readiness of Christ to bestow them, presenting it as the immediate result of His personal glorification : 'When He ascended up on high, He led captivity captive, and gave gifts unto men.[2] And He gave some apostles (that is, the grace needed to fit them for doing the work of apostles), and some prophets, and some evangelists, and some pastors and teachers, for the perfecting of the saints, for the work of the ministry, for the edifying of the body of Christ.' It is not properly of the distinction of offices in the New Testament Church that the apostle is here speaking, but of the distribution of gifts in connection with the discharge of office, and of all kinds of ministerial service. So far as office was concerned, apostles and prophets might be both one ; and, indeed, the highest kind of prophecy proceeded only from Christ and His apostles. Pastors and teachers, in like manner, might be, and doubtless were for the most part in the apostolic Church, as well as now, officially one. But whether united in the same person, or existing and exercised apart, the work itself proper to the parties so engaged, having to do with divine operations and results, necessarily required divine help for its successful performance ; and it was then, and even is, one of the great ends of Christ's mediation in the heavenly places to bestow the requisite gifts on those whom He calls to the work. So that, as in their spiritual husbandry they are fellow-workers with God, they have in the promised supply of those gifts of the Spirit the link of connection between the human instrumentality and the efficient power.

Rightly viewed, therefore, the work of the Christian pastorate is a kind of continuation of the agency of Christ, carried on through the instrumentality of a divinely aided as well as humanly ordained ministry. It bespeaks, in every faithful discharge of duty, and every saving effect produced,

[1] John xvi. 23, xiv. 12, 13.   [2] Eph. iv. 8, 11, 12.

Christ's gracious presence, and mediatorial fulness of life and blessing. And at every step in his ministerial course the true servant of Christ will have reason to say, 'Not I, but the grace of God that is in me! Whatever fitness I may have for the work, and whatever good I may be the means of accomplishing in it, is the fruit of what I have received.' The thought on one side is humbling; for it calls the pastor to regard himself as simply an instrument, and to renounce all claim to the glory. Yet, on the other side, how elevating! since it places him in immediate fellowship with the Lord of glory, and sets the stamp of heaven on what would otherwise have been marked only by human impotence and corruption.

III. *The call to enter on the pastoral office; what properly constitutes it.*—The view which has just been given of the higher aspects of the pastoral office, while throwing around it a certain elevation from the connection it thus appears to hold with the spiritual and divine, serves at the same time to aggravate the difficulty of the question, what should be regarded as constituting a proper call to the office? and how may particular individuals ascertain whether it has actually been received? Contemplated even on its human side, with respect simply to the oversight, responsibility, and anxious labour connected with it, there is much, undoubtedly, that is fitted to inspire awe, and awaken earnest inquiry and solicitude, in the mind of any one who desires to have his path cleared regarding it. But how much more when the higher relations of the office are taken into account; when it is seen to touch at so many points on the special gifts and operations of Godhead! How may it, in such a case, with certainty, or even with some measure of probability, be concluded that the requisite qualifications and conditions for the office meet in any one?

There are cases ever and anon occurring, in which no

difficulty of this kind exists ; the question, in a manner, solves itself ; for the experiences of the individual soul carry along with them a self-convincing and determining power. 'There are decisive hours in which a man feels the germ of a new vocation bursting forth in him ; a world all at once opens to his mind, and, seized with a passion imperious as the very voice of God, he takes upon his conscience the engagement to pursue the work, which is henceforth to be the end of his life.' So a late editor of *Pascal's Thoughts* (Faugere) says of him, and men of like religious impulse ; and what was true of Pascal, as the thinker and representative of an earnest religious party, has its exemplification also in persons with reference to the work of the ministry. The operation of divine grace upon their souls, coupled perhaps with something in the native bent of mind, has been such, so marked and peculiar, that they feel moved with decisive energy to give themselves to this sacred calling. Of such, therefore, there is no need to speak here ; the point is virtually settled already.

With respect, however, to others who have not the advantage of such marked experiences in their mental history, the way to a right determination of the question may be considerably smoothed, by taking properly into account the relation which the special calling of a pastor has to the general calling of a believer. It is a fundamental principle in Christianity, that there is nothing absolutely peculiar to any one who has a place in the true Church. Among its genuine members there is room only for relative distinctions, or for differences in degree, not in kind. It is a consequence of the vital union of true believers to Christ, by virtue of which there belongs to all alike the same spiritual standing, the same privileges and prospects, and, as a matter of course, the same general obligations of duty. If every sincere Christian can say, 'I am one with Christ, and have a personal interest in all that is His,' there can manifestly be no *essential* difference between him and other believers; and whatever may distinguish any one in particular, either as regards the *call* to work, or the *capacity* to work in the Lord's service, it must *in kind* belong to the whole community of the faithful, or else form but a subordinate characteristic. The ministry itself, in its distinctive prerogatives and functions, is but the more special embodiment and exhibition of those which pertain inherently to the Church as Christ's spiritual body. And the moment any one recognises himself to be a living member of this body, it thenceforth becomes, not his right merely, but his bounden duty, to consider what part of its collective responsibilities lie at his door, or what department of its common vocation he should apply himself in some specific manner to fulfil. Bring the principle here laid down into connection with the Christian ministry under any one of the aspects already presented, and you will readily perceive that fundamentally the ministerial vocation links itself to that of the simple believer; they differ only as a development may differ from the germ, or a higher and more intensive from a simpler and commoner mode of operation.

Let the ministry, for example, be considered in respect to the testimony it has to bear, or the message it has to deliver, in the name of God before men. This is certainly a very prominent part of the ministerial calling; and yet it is by no means peculiar to those who have been formally destined to the office. There are, we may say, various gradations belonging to it. In the highest degree it belonged to the Lord Jesus Christ, who came into the world, as He Himself says, to bear testimony to the truth by revealing it, and as so revealed sealing it with His blood. His apostles next, as His immediate representatives and delegates to the world, were sent forth to declare authoritatively, and for all time, the truth which He had partly taught them, and partly revealed to them by His Spirit, that there might be a sufficient and infallible testimony concerning it with the Church. But has not the Church also, the community of believers as such, to take up what has thus been delivered, and bear it forth to the world ?   It is of the Church, as composed of those who know and believe the truth, that our Lord has said, ' it is the light of the world;' [1] and the apostle, that ' it is the pillar and ground (or basement) of the truth.' [2]   To this Church there has been given a banner, that it might be displayed because of the truth ; [3] and it is the duty of every faithful member, in his own place and sphere, to witness for that truth by word and deed.   Here, in fact, lies the very essence of the trial and triumph of their faith, which consists in standing practically as well as doctrinally to the testimony for the truth of God ; and for holding not their lives dear to them, that they might faithfully acquit themselves of this obligation, the martyrs of the Church obtained at once their name and their crown.   When, therefore, a ministry is appointed for the special purpose of unfolding the testimony of Christ, and pressing its overtures of grace and love on the acceptance of men, it is not to be regarded as something altogether by itself; it is only a more full, regular, and systematic exhibition of the testimony which the Church is called, individually and collectively, to maintain and make known.

The same remarks may in substance be applied to the διακονία, or active service, which is required of the pastor for the behoof of others.   Christ Himself, as formerly noted, gave the first and highest exemplification of it in New Testament times.   From Him it devolved on the apostles, who were severally required to give proof of their apostleship, by their readiness to serve after the pattern of their Master, and whose respective places in His kingdom were to be determined by the comparative amount of humble, earnest, and devoted labour undergone by them.[4]   Yet it

<hr />

[1] Matt. v. 14.   [2] 1 Tim. iii. 15.   [3] Ps. lx. 4.   [4] Matt. xx. 25–28.

does not rest there, nor with those who, subsequently to the apostles, might be called to bear office in the Church. The members of the Christian Church are also called, according to their opportunities, to serve :—in prayers, in alms-deeds, in works of righteousness, in strivings against sin, in bowels of compassion, in brotherly admonitions, in ministrations of knowledge among the young and ignorant, and visits of kindness, or acts of beneficence among the distressed and destitute. The measure of what people *can* do in such things is the measure of their obligations ('she did what she *could*') ; and in so far as any professing Christian neglects or comes short of them, he does so in violation of the claims and responsibilities under which he is placed by his relation to Christ. All have *some* gifts to be used in His service, and for the good of their fellow-men, only 'differing according to the grace that is given to them ;' and, as a rule, they should be both most fully possessed and most fruit-fully exercised by the Church's pastors, because in them the calling and obligations of the spiritual community naturally find their highest exemplification.

Nor is it otherwise in respect to the higher aspects of the ministerial office, its connection with the sanctuary above ; for wherever the Christian really exists, that connection must exist also. The Church collectively is the habitation of the Spirit ; so is the individual believer. The works which, as a believer, he is called to do in order to make his calling and election sure, must be works of God ; and for one and all of them he needs the illuminating and strengthening agency of the Holy Spirit. No Christian parent within the private walks of domestic life can fulfil his obligations in regard to the godly upbringing of his children ; no Christian philanthropist, yearning over the miserable and degraded multitudes around him, can discharge the labours of love, which the mercies of God in Christ impel him to undertake in their behalf; no solitary individual even, warring in his

E

personal experiences with the solicitations of the flesh and the powers of evil in the world, can resist, and stand fast, and do the will of God,—except by receiving gifts of grace to qualify him for the work, and to render the work itself serviceable to the end toward which it is directed. In short, all who would move in the Christian sphere, and in any of its departments would serve their generation according to the will of God, *must* stand in living connection with the heavenly world. Their calling as the Lord's servants warrants them to expect, and, if they succeed in that calling, their success proves them to have received, grace for spiritual work ; in which respect, therefore, they are vessels of honour fitted for the Master's use, and partakers of the blessing.

Such, then, being the case in regard to the Church as a whole, the question as to a man's personal vocation to the Christian ministry is merely an application of the general to the particular. It narrows itself to the point, whether he has reason to consider it to be the will of God, that in addition to the ordinary obligations resting on him as a believer, he should undertake the special obligations, cognate in their nature, yet more arduous and exacting in their discharge, of the Christian pastor. It is not, strictly speaking, whether he is to enter into another sphere, or assume a relation altogether different to the Spirit and the cause of Christ ; but whether he would have himself more closely identified with this cause, and for the sake of it cultivate more earnestly the higher gifts and endowments of the Spirit than is done even by the major part of genuine believers. In a word, the question resolves itself into the consideration, whether he has the capacity and the will, the faculties of nature and the endowments of grace, which, if duly cultivated and employed, might reasonably be expected to render him more serviceable to the interests of righteousness in the *peculiar* service of the ministry, than in the *common* service of the Christian life.

When the matter comes to be examined in this light, there will very rarely be found much practical difficulty among earnest inquirers in arriving at a proper conclusion on the subject. It may very readily be otherwise if the correct relation of the Christian ministry to the Christian community is wrongly apprehended or virtually ignored, as indeed is not unfrequently the case. It is not unnatural for the mind, when first turning its thoughts in this direction, to look at pastoral work in too isolated a light, as having, all in a manner peculiar to itself, little or nothing in common with that which enters into the calling of members of the flock. By striking too low an estimate of this general calling, or for the time leaving it out of view, the mind gets perplexed with difficulties regarding its right to intermeddle with the higher vocation. The way cannot but appear to some extent relieved of those difficulties if it is distinctly understood that the primary and fundamental obligations are the same for the true believer as for the Christian pastor. In both cases alike the soul that is properly enlightened about the things of God, and earnestly desirous to fulfil aright its part concerning them, will feel that it has substantially the same gracious privileges to handle, the same principles of life to follow out, the same vital connection with the Spirit to maintain. And with this for a starting-point, it has merely to consider whether it may not be warranted, or even bound to go on to what further is involved in the destination and duties of the pastorate.

It is clear, then, that all just and proper inquiries on this point must proceed on one assumption ; they must take for granted the personal Christianity of the inquirer as the essential basis and prerequisite for all that belongs to a living and divinely-constituted ministry. He who has not yet been called of God to the common work of a believer cannot possibly have a call to the distinctive work of a pastor. One who is himself a stranger to grace can be in no proper condition to act as a chosen vessel and instrument of grace ; he cannot even cordially enter into and sympathize with the objects toward which the ministry of grace is directed. The connection between the common and the special in this respect was forcibly put by the well-known Mr. Robert Bruce, in relation to his own case : ' I was first called to my grace before I obeyed my calling to the ministry : He made me first a Christian before He made me a minister.' And then, as to the necessity of the personal work of grace for the proper exercise of the ministerial calling : ' If the Spirit be not in me, the spirit of the hearer will discern me not to be sent ; but only to have the *word* of the commission, and not the *power.*' It is therefore indispensable that those who would have any satisfaction as to their call to the ministry, and any blessing in the work when actually engaged in it, should have some reasonable evidence of their own interest in the salvation of Christ, and personal surrender to the claims of the gospel. ' We believe, and *therefore* speak ; ' such is the divine order.

But even when evidence exists of a work of grace in the heart, there may still be defects and hindrances which practically serve to place a barrier in the way, the absence of which must also be presupposed as an indispensable condition to a real call. For, considering the position which a pastor has to occupy, the amount of intellectual and exciting labour he has to undergo, and the share which public discourse must have in his ministrations, there are various things of a natural kind which may act as virtual disqualifications,—obstructions raised by the hand of God in providence against this particular way of serving Him,—such as physical inability, nervous temperament, defect of voice, feebleness of intellect, incapacity for continued study, want of literary acquirements, and other things of a like nature. Disadvantages of this sort may create difficulties which it is impossible to overcome, or which may at least

stand in the way of any reasonable prospect of the individual to whom they belong serving God more accept-
ably, or yielding more benefit to the interests of religion,
by devoting himself to the work of the ministry, than by
occupying a sphere in private life. Here, therefore, there is
room for calm and thoughtful consideration, sometimes for
friendly counsel and advice, as well as for earnest prayer ;
since, in such cases, neither personal desire nor what are
called providential openings can be regarded as sufficient
grounds of action. 'What some call,' said John Newton
justly, 'providential openings, are often powerful temptations; the heart in wandering cries, "Here is a way opened
before me;" but perhaps it is not to be trodden, but rejected.'
It is impossible, however, to lay down any definite rules
which would be generally applicable ; for the disqualifying
circumstances themselves exist in such various forms and
degrees, and the spheres of ministerial labour also differ
so widely in the comparative demands they make alike
for bodily and mental qualifications, that gifts quite in-
adequate to some, or even to most situations, might yet
suffice for a fair amount of acceptable and useful labour in
others. There can be no doubt that, however desirable a
happy constitution of body and mind may be, however
necessary superior powers in both respects for filling the
more arduous and prominent positions in the Church, yet
comparatively moderate talents, and talents accompanied
with marked bodily weaknesses or defects, when thoroughly
sanctified and diligently used, have been honoured to do
much effective service in the more retired fields of Christian
labour. The first-called labourers in the Lord's vineyard
were manifestly of very diverse grades in respect to those
natural qualifications of mind and body. In variety and
fulness of mental powers, as well as general culture, none
of them appear to have approached the Apostle to the
Gentiles ; while he, again, laboured under certain bodily

ailments or defects ; and Peter, James, and John seem to
have considerably surpassed the other members of the
apostolic band. Yet the Lord had work for them all. He
did not reject the weaker on account of the stronger ; they
too had their proper place, though a somewhat humbler
one, in the field of apostolic agency. On matters of this
description, therefore, I go no further than to suggest the
wisdom of prayerful consideration and friendly advice,
coupled with a readiness to submit to the application of
those tests which in well-constituted Churches are employed
to ascertain whether candidates for the ministry possess the
gifts which, in ordinary circumstances, may warrant them
to count upon some measure of success in pastoral work.

But supposing no hindrance should present itself on the
preliminary points now indicated ; supposing one has to all
appearance become a partaker of the grace of God, and,
along with a fair measure of natural talent, to possess also
a competency of other qualifications, there yet usually is
room for a certain regard being had to considerations of
a circumstantial kind, considerations arising mainly from
one's training and position in life, which may of themselves
go far to exercise a determining influence. Such, undoubtedly, and of the most decisive character, were the circumstances which marked the early career of the apostles and
many others of the original heralds of the gospel, who, from
their historical position with reference to Christ, or to the
movements of His kingdom, were singled out as by the
finger of Heaven for the work of the ministry. Those circumstances were, no doubt, in many respects peculiar, and
nothing like a formal repetition of them can now be looked
for ; yet, at the same time, what then took place may in
principle, however in point of form diversified, occur at *any*
time, and is in a manner sanctioned for *all* times. There
has often been since, and there may quite readily be expected in the case of particular individuals, such a direction

or concurrence of things in providence as may be sufficient
to constitute a distinct call to the Christian ministry ; nay,
even to do it when the individuals themselves might have
some cause for hesitation or doubt. In proof of this, and
as affording a most striking exemplification of the principle
in question, we can point to the case of one of the greatest
men who have filled the pastoral office in later times, that,
namely, of John Calvin. It was some time after he had
embraced the Reformed cause, and had published the first
edition of his *Institutes*,—a clear and lucid exhibition of
Christian faith and practice even in that form, but a brief
and imperfect production compared with what it ultimately
became. He had not, however, as yet resolved to devote
himself to the work of the ministry ; and was on his way
from Italy, where he had been on a visit to the Duchess of
Ferrara, to some place in Germany suitable for the further
prosecution of his studies. He took Geneva on his route,
intending only to spend in it a night or two, as he has himself informed us in the Preface to his *Commentary on the
Psalms*. But his arrival becoming known to Farel, who
was at the time labouring in Geneva, and who burned with
an incredible zeal for the propagation of the Protestant
faith, that Reformer determined to secure, if possible, the
co-operation of Calvin in the great work, and went to him
with an earnest entreaty that he would remain where he
was. Calvin endeavoured to excuse himself, and said he
could not yet think of attaching himself to any particular
community; but was desirous of continuing his studies some
time longer, yet with the intention of making himself useful
to the Reformed cause, wherever he might for the time
reside. On this Farel betook, as Calvin expresses it, to
execration, and addressed him in the following strain :—
'Now I declare to you in the name of Almighty God, since
you are taking your studies only for a pretext, that if you do
not give us your help in this divine work, God's curse will

rest upon you, as you are seeking not so much Christ's glory as your own.' This speech, Calvin states, struck such a terror into his soul, that he durst not carry out his original intention; he felt constrained to abide in Geneva, 'as if God had by an immediate hand arrested him in his course.' And I need scarcely add, the result showed how wisely he had interpreted the leadings of Providence, and in the entreaty and remonstrance of Farel had heard the call of Heaven to undertake the responsibilities of the public ministry of the gospel.

The circumstances which determined the wavering mind of John Knox in St. Andrews were not very unlike those now referred to in the case of Calvin. He, too, had at first declined the solicitations made to him in private, 'not considering,' as he said, 'that he had a call to this employment,' till by the unexpected and earnest address of Rough, in the name of the congregation, his reluctance was overcome, and he threw himself heart and soul into his great work. Both of these eminent men, indeed, had been educated with a view to the priesthood in the Romish Church, one of them (Knox) had actually been admitted into priest's orders; but their reception of the Reformed faith broke up existing relations, and virtually cancelled them as to the future vocation of both; and it was the special direction and ordering of God's providence in respect to them which forced on them the question, whether they should not give themselves to the work of the ministry, and helped them to arrive at an affirmative decision regarding it. In a more quiet and unobtrusive manner a similar decision may be rightfully come to still, under the guidance of circumstances essentially the same in kind, though less marked in character. The solemnly expressed wish of pious parents, the tuition and training of early years, the bent and habits of mind in advancing youth, the circumstances of the times, the opening prospects of usefulness, though none of them sufficient apart, yet when more or less combined, may exercise a legitimate influence, and, with minds already alive to the truth of God, and anxious to know how best to promote its interests, may practically be held as providential indications respecting the path of duty.

It is possible, however, and in the present day, perhaps, only too common, to allow more place than is justly due to such incidental considerations and external influences. Persons facilely yielding to them may be led at times to assume the responsibilities of a work for which they are but poorly furnished, and in which they are not likely to accomplish much for the real ends of the ministry. Others also, who may have been chiefly influenced by considerations of a circumstantial kind, though not unduly influenced, nor destitute of qualifications for the work, may possibly in the course of time have doubts stirred in their minds as to the reality of their call to the pastoral office, dreading lest perhaps things of secondary moment weighed more with them in the matter than they should have done. It is therefore of importance that there should be in the minds of those engaged in the office, or preparing to engage in it, a clear apprehension of the more inward and spiritual grounds essential to a proper call, such grounds as ought to exist in every case, even where the voice of external providences has seemed to give the most certain sound, and should be known for a light and refuge to the conscience. The subject in this point of view has been very admirably presented in a sermon by Mr. Robert Traill of London, on ' Winning Souls,' which is well entitled throughout to a careful perusal. It formed originally one of the Cripplegate lectures or ' Morning Exercises,' and is to be found both there and in Mr. Traill's collected works. On the special point under consideration, he says :—

' Take heed to thyself, that thou be a *called* and *sent* minister. This is of great importance to success. He that can say, " Lord, Thou hast sent me," may boldly add, " Lord, go with me, and bless me." It is good when a man is serious in this inquiry. . . . These things may satisfy a minister's conscience that Jesus Christ hath sent him.'

' (1.) *If the heart be filled with a single desire to the great end of the ministry*—the glory of God in the salvation of men. Every work that God calls a man to, He makes the end of it amiable to him. This desire sometimes attends men's first conversion. Paul was called to be a saint and an apostle at once. And so many have been called to be saints and ministers together. If it be not so, yet this is found with him whom Christ calls, that when he is most spiritual and serious, when he is most under the impressions of holiness, and he is nearest to God in communion with Him, then are the desires after the serving of Jesus Christ in the ministry most powerful. And the sincerity of his desire is also to be examined ; and when it is found, it greatly adds to a man's peace ; when his heart bears him witness that it is neither riches, nor honour, nor ease, nor the applause of men that he seeks after, but simply Christ's honour in the saving of men.'

' (2.) It helps to clear a man's call, that there hath been *a conscientious diligence in all the means of attaining fitness for this great work*. That love to the end, which doth not conduct to the use of the appointed means, may justly be suspected as irregular, and not flowing from the Holy Ghost. Even extraordinary officers seem not to have been above the use of ordinary means. Old dying Paul sends for his books and papers.'

' (3.) *A competent fitness for the work of the ministry* is another proof of a man's call to it. The Lord calls no man to a work for which He doth not qualify. Though a sincere, humble man, as every minister should be, may and should think little of any measure that he hath, whether compared with the greater measures of others, or considered with regard to the weight and worth of the work, yet there must be some confidence as to this competency for clearing a man's call. What such competency is, it is not easy at all times to determine ; singular necessities of the Church may extend or intend (contract) this matter of competent fitness. But in general there must be, first, a competent knowledge of gospel mysteries ; secondly, a competent ability of utterance to the edifying of others. This is aptness to teach, required by the apostle in 1 Tim. iii. 2, and that a minister be able by sound doctrine both to exhort and to convince the gainsayers.'

These considerations, stated with singular brevity and discretion, have respect to the question, What constitutes a proper call to the ministry, even if it should be only a matter in contemplation, not yet finally resolved on ? But for those who have actually entered on the spiritual vocation, other considerations will naturally present themselves along with these, particularly the accompaniment of their ministrations with tokens of the divine blessing, or the apparent absence of these. This cannot but form an element in the judgment of serious and thoughtful minds, although they ought to exercise great caution in their search for signs of blessing, and should be careful to include among these other fruits of spiritual labour than known cases of conversion to the faith. Yet results of *some sort*, definite, spiritual results, ought certainly to be looked for ; and very much in proportion to their number and distinctness will be the measure of satisfaction which one has in reflecting on the course that has been pursued. On the other and more elementary view of the subject, its relation to those who are inquiring beforehand whether they can discern in their state the evidences of a divine call, both the proper points and the proper order and connection between them are indicated in the passage given from Traill. The primary and most essential point of inquiry, beyond doubt, has reference to the state of the heart, whether it really beats in unison with the great end of the ministry. Without this there can be no proper adaptation to the work, nor any just expectation of blessing in its discharge ; since always in such a case the needful correspondence is wanting between the aim of the Divine Pastor and that of the under-shepherd. Most fitly, therefore, is the heart's desire toward the work placed first ; and only if the pulse beats truly here can healthful life and energy be looked for in the several functions.

Still, if of pre-eminent importance, this is not alone to be regarded, especially not in an age like the present, in which society has advanced so far in knowledge and civilisation, and Christianity has become allied to so many fields of literature and general information. At such a time no one can be reckoned ordinarily qualified to hold the place of a Christian pastor, unless he has shared in the general culture, and become possessed of such intelligence and re-sources as may enable him to command the respect of the people to whom he ministers. Where these do not in good measure exist, or where there is any marked natural impedi-ment over which the individual can exercise no control, even his desire to the work must give way, as anciently in the case of David, who did well in *desiring* to build the temple of the Lord, and was greatly blessed even for having such a desire, while yet, on account of special circumstances in his past history and condition, he was restrained from carrying the purpose into execution. A competent fitness, therefore, is justly named by Mr. Traill as another element in a minister's qualifications which requires to be taken into account, though in itself necessarily a somewhat variable element, and depending not a little on times and circum-stances.

And, unquestionably, there should also be included, as subsidiary to the fitness, and indispensable both to its acquirement and exercise, the still further element mentioned, of a conscientious diligence in the use of means for the improvement of all natural and spiritual qualifications. No one, whatever be his native talents or his religious experience, if he duly considers the greatness of the ministerial work and the incalculable results that depend on it, can have any reasonable doubt that he should avail himself of every advantage within his reach to give his faculties the finest edge, as it were, and best preparation for the work. Any manifest negligence in this respect, or manifest slighting of the means of intellectual and spiritual progress, would bespeak either an indifference to the calling, or a want of wisdom in going about the things that concern it, which must augur ill for future success. And the contrary result may be in like manner anticipated, where, along with the requisite gifts, there is manifested a laudable and steady endeavour in the way of improvement. It is justly said by Bishop Sanderson,[1] 'Where the Spirit of God hath manifested itself to any man by the distribution of gifts, it is but reason that that man should manifest the Spirit that is in him by exercising those gifts in some lawful calling. Do not say, because you heard no voice, that therefore no man hath called you. Those very gifts you have received are a real call, pursuing you with a restless, weary importunity, till you have disposed yourselves in some honest course of life, wherein you may be profitable to human society, by the exercising of some or other of those gifts.' Though spoken of the Christian calling in general, this is specially applicable to the calling of a minister of the gospel, and indicates well the proper connection between the possession of gifts suitable to the work, and the obligation to give oneself to its duties. But as the possession of such gifts is a call to particular lines of duty, so is it also to prayer and application for their proper cultivation and improvement. And it is a good advice on this point in the same discourse: 'Remember

[1] Sermon 3d, *ad clerum.*

these abilities you pray or study for are the gifts of God, and as not to be had ordinarily without labour, so not to be had merely for the labour ; for then should it not be so much a gift as a purchase. It was the error of Simon Magus to think that the gift of God might be purchased with money ; and it hath a spice of his sin, and so may go for a kind of simony, for a man to think these spiritual gifts of God may be purchased with labour. You may rise up early, and go to bed late, and study hard, and read much, and devour the fat and the marrow of the best authors ; and when you have done all, unless God gives a blessing to your endeavours, be as thin and meagre in regard of true and useful learning as Pharaoh's lean kine were after they had eaten the fat ones. It is God that both ministereth seed to the sower, and multiplieth the seed sown : the principal and the increase are both his. If, then, we expect any gift, or the increase of any gift from Him, neither of which we can have without Him, let us not be behind, either with our best endeavours to use the means He hath appointed, or with our faithful prayers to crave His blessing upon those means.'[1]

So much for the nature of the pastoral office, and the call to enter on its functions. The formal or ecclesiastical authority to enter on its discharge in any particular place, is a matter that scarcely calls for consideration here, as it is a branch of Church polity or government. But as regards the subjects of appointment to particular charges, it will, of course, be understood that if they have the right spirit and qualifications for the office, they will desire that in this respect also everything should be done in a becoming manner, and so as to promote a good understanding between the pastor and the people of his charge.

[1] See also Vinet's *Past. Theology*, p. 72 sq.

CHAPTER III.

THE PASTORAL AND SOCIAL LIFE OF THE PASTOR.

I T is not unusual to speak of the *profession* of a minister of the gospel as we do of that of a lawyer or a physician ; and were it simply a profession in the sense that these others are, our next subject of consideration, after having discussed the nature of the office itself, would be the different modes of operation, or lines of duty, through which its important ends are to be reached.   But there is an easily recognised distinction between the ministerial calling and a profession in civil life.   The one cannot, like the other, be contemplated as a thing by itself, apart from the state and character of the individual.   From its very nature, it is but the more peculiar embodiment and exhibition of the characteristics of the Christian community, a kind of concentrated manifestation of the views and principles, the feelings and obligations, which belong in common to the Church of Christ.   And as the Christianity which should pervade and distinguish the membership of this Church is emphatically a life, so the Christian ministry, in which it may be said to culminate, must be regarded as in the first instance a life, and secondarily as a *work*.   It has to do primarily with a condition of being and a course of behaviour, and only afterwards with the ministrations of service.   Not only must the two co-exist together, but they must stand related to each other in the manner now indicated ; the life from the first takes precedence of the work, and throughout must hold the place of pre-eminent importance. In the Sacred Scriptures our attention is frequently and very forcibly fixed upon this point. Thus in the Sermon on the Mount, when our Lord was speaking of those in His kingdom who should occupy the position of spiritual guides, He said, 'Whosoever shall do and teach these things, shall be called great in the kingdom of heaven,'[1] giving, it will be observed, marked precedence to the doing, even in the case of those whose distinctive place was to be that of teachers in the kingdom. In another passage of the same discourse, the absence of the doing, or rather its converse, the working of iniquity, is represented as the special ground of the condemnation which shall be pronounced on those who have falsely aspired to the rank of prophets and wonder-workers in Christ's name.[2]

The stress laid upon the pastor's life and behaviour is one of the most striking things found in the instructions given through Timothy and Titus in the pastoral epistles. They are themselves charged to be most careful and exemplary in this respect, while labouring to plant or build up the churches : as in this to Timothy, 'Take heed to *thyself*, and to the doctrine ; continue in them : for in doing this thou shalt both save thyself and them that hear thee ;'[3] and to Titus, 'in all things showing thyself a pattern of good works,'[4] making this, as it were, the sure ground of all your proceeding, looking to it as an indispensable element of success. Not only so, but in the delineations given of the qualifications that should be sought in those who were appointed to fill the office of presbyter or *episcopos* in the several churches, nearly the whole have respect to character ;[5] so that out of thirteen or fourteen different qualities mentioned, only one has distinct reference to the gift of teaching ;[6] virtually implying that character was the most essential thing, and that if matters were but

[1] Matt. v. 19.   [2] Matt. vii. 23.   [3] 1 Tim. iv. 16.
[4] Tit. ii. 7.   [5] 1 Tim. iii.   [6] Tit. ii.

right there, others would in good measure follow as a matter of course.   And how much it was St. Paul's own practice to let example go before, and give weight to all his ministrations, appears from the general tenor of his life ; in particular, from his addresses to the elders of Ephesus, and to the church of Thessalonica,[1] in which he points to the blameless, self-denying, and godly life he maintained, as the clear evidence of the sincerity of his heart, and the seal of His testimony as an ambassador of God.

Turning from the light of Scripture on the subject to the subject itself, a variety of considerations readily present themselves, lending confirmation to this view of the fundamental importance of the pastor's personal state and behaviour, in relation to the objects of his ministry.   First of all, it is itself one of the most effective means of teaching ; it is one side of the gospel in a living and embodied form, a form which, if sound and true, will, in accordance with the proverb which places example above precept, give forth deeper impressions than what is heard from the lips.   As the pastor is the official representative of the flock, he ought to be, all men expect him to be, a typal Christian.   There are thousands even in Protestant countries who seldom think of looking higher for their ideal of Christian perfection.   The saying of Massillon is at least partially true of them, 'The gospel of most people is the life of the priests whom they observe ;' or, as Philip Henry more happily expressed it, 'Our lives should be the book of the ignorant.'   More than other men the pastor is encompassed by influences which tend to encourage and stimulate him to the cultivation of what is pure and good.   For religion is more peculiarly the business of the Christian minister than it is of ordinary believers ; his daily occupations, unlike theirs, bring him into immediate contact with divine realities ; his position, with the proprieties naturally belonging to it, forms a kind of

[1] Acts xx. ; 1 Thess. ii.

F

safeguard against temptations to which they are frequently
exposed ; and as his proper business is to labour that others
may be good, consistency alone obliges him to strive to be
such himself.   It is inevitable, therefore, that men's expectations should generally be directed toward the minister as
the one in whom there should be seen the brightest exemplification of the spirit and character of the gospel ; and
if this expectation is in any competent measure realized,
the interests of religion and morality will be effectively
promoted ; if otherwise, they cannot but sustain material
damage.

Besides, not the *nature* merely, but the *practicability* also
of the Christian life finds its natural and appropriate illustration in the exemplary walk and deportment of the pastor.
The excuse is thereby in a measure cut off, which is so apt
to present itself to worldly men when they hear the spiritual
demands of the gospel, that these are but the devout
speculations of the closet, scarcely to be looked for as
realities amid the scenes and employments of every-day
life.   Let the realization of these, then, be actually witnessed ; let the man, who is God's more peculiar agent in
setting forth the requirements of a gospel obedience, be
himself an example of the spirit and behaviour they enjoin ;
and though still the thought may too readily be entertained,
that what is possible and becoming in the pastor is too high
for the observance generally of the flock, yet the visible
reality in him, if in a good degree conformed to the proper
standard, will go far to work in men's minds an impression
of the practicable nature of the Christian life.   Indeed, as
it will usually be impossible otherwise to convince them of
the practicability of such a life, it will be still more impossible to convince them of our sincerity in urging them to aim
at it, or of being ourselves persuaded that the earnest pursuit of it is of real moment to their well-being.   A minister's
testimony in favour of a godly life, if not borne out by his

own example, can only have its fitting counterpart in a people
holding the truth in unrighteousness, and for the most part
is but too likely to have it.

Even in those lines of action which are less directly connected with spiritual and moral ends, but in which also an
appreciation and advocacy of these is to some extent involved, a heartfelt regard to the good, and a practical exhibition of it, have ever been deemed essential to complete
success.   Thus Milton, writing in respect to the sphere of
things in which he came so near to the realizing of his own
high idea, nobly says : ' I was confirmed in this opinion,
that he who would not be frustrate of his hope, to write
well hereafter in laudable things, ought himself to be a true
poem ; that is, a composition and pattern of the best and
most honourable things ; not presuming to sing high praises
of heroic men or famous cities, unless he have in himself the
experience and the practice of all that is praiseworthy.'[1]   In
a sphere more nearly approaching the one before us, that of
the civic orator, if we turn to the thoughtful, judicious pages
of Quinctilian, we shall find him very distinctly and repeatedly insisting on the necessity of personal worth.   He even
throws it into the definition of an orator, saying, *oratorem
esse virum bonum dicendi peritum*,[2]—first himself good, then
skilled in the faculty of speech ; a notable description.
And again, ' Not only do I affirm that he who would be an
orator *ought* to be a good man, but that he shall not become
an orator unless he is a good man,' stating his reasons at
some length for the assertion, urging, especially for the
higher species of eloquence, the necessity of moral honesty
in him who pleads for the right, and vindicating Demosthenes
and Cicero from the charges sometimes preferred against
them of a defective *morale*.   Of Demosthenes himself we
have a testimony to the same effect in Plutarch, who tells
us, in explanation of the great regard which the orator had

[1] *Apology for Smect.*   [2] *Inst.* L. xii. 1.

for the public influence of Phocion, that 'he knew a nod or a word from a man of superior character is more regarded than the long discourses of another.'

An unhappy yet most striking illustration of the soundness of this judgment may be found in the case of one of the most highly gifted men of modern times, whose pleadings in the cause of reform chiefly failed of their end from his own sad need of personal reformation. Fox had everything to make him the resistless opponent of public abuses, the most effective and triumphant advocate of what is just and right in the government of the country, *except a moral life;* and this vitiating element counteracted the force of all his oratory. 'Both principles and practices tending toward arbitrary power and national degradation, were (to use the words of Foster[1]) progressively gaining ground during the much greater part of the time that he was assailing them with fire and sword ; yet the people could hardly be induced to regard him otherwise than as a capital prizefighter, and scarcely thanked him for the fortitude and energy he devoted to their service. He was allowed to be a most admirable man for a leader of opposition ; but not a mortal could be persuaded to regard that opposition, even in his hands, as bearing any resemblance to that which we have been accustomed to ascribe to Cato—an opposition of which pure virtue was the motive, and all corruptions whatever the object. The talents and the long and animated exertions of this most eloquent of all our countrymen failed plainly because the people placed no confidence in his virtue ; or, in other words, because they could never be persuaded to attribute virtue to his character. They did not confide in his integrity. Those who admired everything in his talents regretted that his name never ceased to excite in their minds the idea of gamesters and bacchanals, even after he was acknowledged to have withdrawn himself from such society.

[1] *Review of Fox's Memoirs.*

. . . We wish the greatest genius on earth (Foster concludes), whoever he may be, might write an inscription for
our statesman's monument, to express in the most forcible
and strenuous of all possible modes of thought and phrase,
the truth and the warning, that no man will ever be accepted to serve mankind in the highest departments
of utility, without an eminence of virtue that can sustain
him in the noble defiance,—Which of you convicts me
of sin?'

But if such be the case in respect to those who would
head a reform in the merely economical and political sphere,
how much more must it hold with the spiritual guides and
reformers of the people !   How inevitably must *their* efforts
in the cause of righteousness fail, if their own spirit and behaviour obviously fall below the mark !   Not only should
they have the *reality* of the goodness they undertake to
press upon others, but the *appearance* of it also should be
so vividly impressed on their aspect and demeanour as to
raise them above all suspicion of the contrary.   In proportion as any one recedes from this living exemplification of
the spirit of the gospel, he becomes disqualified for the
effective proclamation of its truths ; and if instead of a simple
deficiency there is a visible contrast, the result must be in
the last degree disastrous.   ' This,' says Baxter,[1] ' is the
way to make men think that the word of God is but an idle
tale, and to make preaching seem no better than prating.
He that means as he speaks, will surely do as he speaks.
One proud, surly, lordly word, one needless contention, one
covetous action, may cut the throat of many a sermon, and
blast the fruit of all you have been doing.'   He therefore
justly notes it as a palpable inconsistence and grievous mistake in those ministers who study hard to preach exactly,
but study little, or not at all, to live exactly ; who spend
most of the week in studying how to speak two hours, and

[1] *Reformed Pastor*, c. i. sec. 8.

scarcely spend an hour in studying how to live all the week. Such conduct in the case of a popular preacher once met with a just reproof from a blunt English farmer, in the cutting remark, ' Sir, you light a bright candle on Sundays, and put it out all the week.'

These are all considerations of grave moment, and are more than sufficient to establish the fitness, the necessity even, if any real good is to be accomplished, of the ministers of the gospel being themselves practical examples of its truths and principles. But there are other, and one might almost say higher, considerations still to enforce the same conclusion ; for, without being themselves under the power of the truth, they cannot adequately manifest the truth to the consciences of others ; they cannot do it as Christ requires it to be done ; and whatever talent or learning they may throw into their ministrations, there must still be wanting elements for which no amount of talent or learning can compensate. The kind of preaching, it must be remembered, which the Spirit is promised to bless for much spiritual good, is not the bare manifestation of the truth, but the truth made instinct with the life of Christian experience, quickened and intensified by feeling. It is the truth reflected from heart to heart from a soul already penetrated and imbued with its spirit, to other souls either wholly estranged from it, or less sensibly under its power. Let the same work which is done, or the same word which is spoken, by one from whom they pass lightly off, with little seeming apprehension of their importance, be done or spoken by another with the warmth and earnestness which bespeak a heart all on fire with the mighty interests involved, and that which in the one case falls on comparatively listless ears, will in the other awaken a response in every surrounding bosom. It is the action of the sanctified on the unsanctified soul, the expression of the truth from a conscience thoroughly alive to its teaching, which in the hands of the Spirit is the great means of conveying deep and salutary impressions of it to consciences that are still slumbering in ignorance or sin. And more especially for the purpose of maintaining such a living, spiritual agency has the preaching of the gospel been appointed to form a standing ordinance in the Church.

And then there is the progressive nourishment of the soul in the life of faith, the conducting of those who have already believed onwards to the higher experiences of grace, and a more enlarged acquaintance with its blessings. 'A minister,' it has been justly said,[1] ' may have piety, and yet not the quality of piety for this task. He may preach awakening sermons on such subjects as the value of the soul, the un- certainty of life, the terrors of the coming judgment; he may enlarge forcibly on the various branches of Christian prac- tice ; he may reiterate in every variety of form the doctrine of justification by faith ; and yet but inadequately fulfil this part of his commission. To exhibit the Saviour Himself to the eye of faith, and not a mere doctrine concerning Him ; to expose the devices of Satan, and unravel the windings of that labyrinth, the human heart ; to enter into the exercises of Christian experience; to conduct the flock into the interior recesses of the sanctuary, where the hidden manna of the gospel lies concealed, where Jesus manifests Himself to His people as He does not to the world, and the Spirit bears witness with their spirit that they are the children of God, and so to promote growth in grace by unfolding the rich privileges of the Christian calling,—this is to feed the flock, this is to make *full* proof of one's ministry. And who is sufficient for these things ? Assuredly none but he who through the Spirit's grace has penetrated into the mysteries of the life of faith, and knows the truth in its reality and power.'

Further, if a personal acquaintance with the things of the

[1] Sermon by Mr. Litton.

Spirit, and a consistent exhibition of them in the walk and conduct, be necessary to secure the proper aptitude to teach, they are equally necessary to secure the requisite conditions for the copious effusion of the Holy Spirit. Whatever importance may justly be attached to the clear and comprehensive exhibition of divine truth, it is not to be forgotten that everything ultimately depends on the presence and power of the Spirit. And though the Spirit in His regenerative and sanctifying agency does not exclusively bind Himself to any specific channel for the presentation of the truth ; though He distributes to every one severally as He wills, and sometimes communicates saving energy through instruments with which the element of personal holiness is little if at all connected, yet such is by no means His wonted method of working, nor is it what in any case we are properly warranted to expect. According to the ordinary law of the Spirit's operations, there is a close correspondence between the personal state of the agent and the measure of blessing that is made to accompany his exertions in the service of God. No one, as formerly stated, who is himself a stranger to faith, and the godly behaviour of which faith is the living principle, can have any just right to minister in holy things, much less to look for the seal of divine acceptance and effective co-operation in his work. And it stands to reason, that if the minister's soul is itself somewhat like a dry and parched region, the wilderness around shall not through his instrumentality be refreshed with the streams of grace. On the other hand, both reason and experience justify us in expecting that those whom the Spirit will most distinctly own in the husbandry of the gospel, whose efforts He will crown with the richest harvest of blessing, are such as have become true participants of grace, and know much personally of its saving operations. For the most part, they are made instruments of good to others in proportion as they are conscious to themselves of the love and practice of the good.   Truly spiritual and earnest ministers of the gospel will ever be able to distinguish in this respect between one part of their ministrations and another ; as Brainerd, for example, when pressing on those actively engaged in the Lord's service the importance of their possessing the more special influences of grace, strikingly said, ' These wonderfully assist them to get at the consciences of men, and, as it were, to handle them with their hands ; while, without them, whatever reason and oratory we make use of, we do but make use of stumps instead of hands.'

Yes ; and as an elevated spiritual frame is required to fit us instrumentally for the greater results of the Spirit's working, so this alone can properly dispose us to ask and look for the larger effusions of His grace.   There is a close connection between the measure in which the Spirit is given, and the degree of desire and faithfulness with which He is sought.   And it is the soul which has experienced much personally, that will ever be the best prepared for seeking much believingly for others.   He who has himself known only the small drops of divine grace and power, will hardly be in a condition to expect, or even earnestly to pray for, the richer showers of blessing on the field of his labours. And if there are to be Pentecostal times for the Church, we must look for Pentecostal experiences going before in the hearts of the ministry.   And these, I may add, manifesting themselves in an engrossing eagerness of desire and intensity of active effort for the salvation of men.   In whom but in such spirit-replenished souls could we expect a picture like the following, the life-picture of the Apostle to the Gentiles, to be in any measure reproduced ?   ' Though I be free from all men, yet have I made myself the servant of all, that I might gain the more.   And unto the Jews I became as a Jew, that I might gain the Jews ; to them that are under the law as under the law, that I might gain them that are under the law ; to them that are without law as without law (being not without law to God, but under the law to Christ), that I might gain them that are without law. To the weak became I as weak, that I might gain the weak : I am made all things to all men, that I might by all means save some. And this I do for the gospel's sake.'[1] It is this high-strung concentration of soul, through the larger gifts of God's Spirit, which most of all qualifies a man for doing great things in the more peculiar work of the Spirit. One master-passion animates and controls his movements ; and whatever he has of genius or talent, of time, of sympathy, of love, of skill in adapting himself to circumstances, and turning to account the opportunities which present themselves, all are laid under contribution to the one great end, and with an impressiveness of manner, a fulness of soul, which goes far to secure what it seeks to have realized. This one thing I desire, this one thing I do, seems to breathe in all he says and does.

On every account, therefore, it is of importance that the personal state and character of the pastor, his possessing and exercising the principles of a divine life in a higher degree than common, should be taken, in a manner, as the postulate of all that should otherwise characterize him, and be anticipated from his labours. And if the following portraiture, drawn by an eminent Dutch divine (Vitringa), of the proper ideal of a Christian minister be too high to warrant the expectation of its being fully realized amid the difficulties and temptations of a present life, it is at least what should be constantly aimed at ; and the more it *is* realized, the ampler will be the reason for expecting a blessing on the work done in the Lord's vineyard. 'The faithful servant of Christ, says he, the teacher of the gospel, is a man of sound mind, burning with zeal for the glory of God and the salvation of men, one taught by the Holy Spirit, experimentally acquainted with the ways of God ;

[1] 1 Cor. ix. 20–23.

one who seeks not the things of men, but men themselves; not his own things, but the things of Christ; of chaste and unadulterated manners; by his example teaching the virtues of piety, modesty, gentleness, zeal, prudence, gravity; one who, like a candle set upon a candlestick, gives light to all who are in the house, to all who are desirous of salvation; both showing the way of life, and on gospel terms dispensing the blessings of grace and peace. Whithersoever he goes, *there* is light; wherever he turns his steps, there is salvation; when he opens his lips, there is the salt of grace; everywhere beloved, respected, and not less the means of imparting consolation to others, than a solace to himself.'

It is the sacred influence which attends this personal piety, the felt power it breathes, the moral weight it imparts to everything said and done, which renders a pastorate much distinguished by it, more attractive in its ministrations, and in its results more beneficial, than another deficient in this, though bringing to its aid much ampler resources of human talent and learning. 'Read the biographies of those eminent labourers who in modern times have adorned the different communions of the Church of Christ, whose memory is blessed, and whose works to this day do follow them, and you will find that, without exception, they were men whose closets witnessed the close communings, the importunate pleadings, of a life hid with Christ in God; who, abiding near to the fountain of grace, and drawing from it rich supplies according to their need, went forth to their ministerial duties with their hearts enlarged by the love of God, and lips speaking out of the abundance of the heart' (Litton).

For those who are at all read in such biographies many instances will readily occur in proof of what has now been stated. But a better instance, perhaps, could scarcely be selected than that of Mr. Robinson of Leicester, especially when placed beside the case of one who yielded a noble testimony in its behalf, one immensely superior to the other in talent and eloquence, though far from equal in the point now under consideration.   I refer to Mr. Robert Hall, who at the time of Mr. Robinson's death was pastor of a Baptist Church in Leicester, and shortly after it, at a meeting of the Bible Society in the place, pronounced a generous and eloquent tribute to the memory of the deceased.   As a writer, Mr. Robinson could not be compared with Hall ; he is now chiefly known as the author of a series of *Scripture Characters*, a work which was once extensively read, and undoubtedly contributed in the earlier part of this century to revive the spirit of genuine piety.   In present times one is rather disposed to wonder at its former popularity; for, while it abounds in sensible reflections, and never fails to point to the great principles of the gospel as the living root of all godliness and purity, there is a flatness in the tone, and a commonplace character usually attaching to the style of representation, such as might be thought to argue no great power in the work, or any peculiar fascination about its author.   But turn to the delineation of Hall, drawn when the knowledge of the man's person, and the memory of his life and labours, were still fresh upon the minds of all, and, even making some allowance, as evidently requires to be done for the excitement of the occasion, it cannot be doubted that in the subject of the panegyric there had been witnessed one of the most eminent examples of ministerial attractiveness and power ; that a sway had been wielded by him, and moral effects produced, such as might well have excited the envy of the most gifted intellect.   ' His residence in Leicester,' said Hall, 'forms an epoch in the religious history of this country.   From that time must be dated, and to his agency under Providence must be ascribed, a decided improvement in the moral and religious state of this town and its vicinity ; an increase of religious light, together with the general diffusion of a taste and relish for

the pure word of God.   He came to this place while it was
sunk in vice and irreligion ; he left it eminently distinguished
by sobriety of manners, and the practice of warm, serious,
and enlightened piety.   He added not aqueducts and palaces,
nor did he increase the splendour of its public edifices ; but
he embellished it with undecaying ornaments ; he renovated
the minds of the people, and turned a large portion of them
from darkness to light, and from the power of Satan to
God. . . . The loss which the Church of Christ has sustained by the extinction of such a luminary is great ; the
loss to this populous town and neighbourhood irreparable.'
Certainly he must have been no ordinary man of whom such
things could be said, even with the abatements which must
be made on account of the impressions of the moment.
And if not the only, beyond all doubt the main element of
success lay in the deep-toned, consistent, elevated, and, we
may say, full-orbed character of Mr. Robinson's life and
ministry.   Piety the most sincere, charity the most enlightened and active, a zeal in doing good that grudged no
sacrifice or toil, a steadiness of aim that never deviated
from its purpose, the greatest kindliness of manners coupled
with the most blameless rectitude and sobriety of life : such
were the prominent characteristics of his life and behaviour.
' Religion with him was not an occasional feeling, but an
habitual element ; not a sudden or transient impulse, but a
permanent principle, a second nature, producing purity of
intention, elevation of mind, and an uninterrupted series of
useful exertions.'   And as a necessary consequence, ' no
one could hear him without feeling persuaded that it was
the man of God who addressed them ; their feelings toward
him were not those of persons gratified, but benefited ; and
they listened to his instructions, not as a source of amusement, but as a spring of living water.'   The example of such
a man, and it is but one of a numerous class, should be
viewed at once as an instruction and encouragement for all

who in pastoral work would be found occupying the higher places of the field. It shows how much depends on the spiritual healthfulness and vigour of the individual engaged in it ; and how much may be accomplished where this exists in any degree of perfection, even though there is nothing like the charm of genius or the force of commanding intellect. The greatest care and solicitude, therefore, should be applied by all in this direction, the more so as here a certain completeness is requisite ; and a single palpable blemish, or inconsistence, will go far to undo the effect of many an excellence. Some things will do it more readily than others, because more obviously indicative of a frailty, or weakness, which it is hard to reconcile with a felt apprehension of the great realities of the gospel, and a hearty surrender to its obligations ; such as an irritability of temper, apt to fire at trifling offences, or fret at petty annoyances ; an intermeddling disposition that is fond of prying into other people's affairs, or giving heed to the gossiping tales of the neighbourhood ; a proud carriage, that looks with indifference or hauteur on those who should be treated with tenderness and regard ; a want of disinterestedness and generosity, seeing that an obvious selfishness in pressing his own material comforts and advantages, to the neglect of those of others, seems like a contrariety to the whole design and spirit of his office. Let every one who would lay a good foundation for honour and usefulness in this office sedulously watch and pray against these and such like imperfections in temper and conduct, avoiding, as he would his deadliest enemy, whatever might serve to prompt the question in those among whom he ministers, ' Thou that teachest another, teachest thou not thyself?'

I have said that in general the minister's office is itself a monitor, guarding him against moral dangers to which others are exposed, and stimulating him to the personal cultivation of that goodness which it is his business to press on the

regard of others.   Perhaps I should add, that there are certain failings to which his office does present temptations
somewhat peculiar, and in respect to which he will do well
to take heed.   In particular, there may be a temptation, if
in the discharge of his office he has won the acceptance
of his people, to self-elation, impatience of contradiction,
jealousy of fame, fondness of applause, and at times, it may
be, of offensive dogmatism of manner.   So long as men
have difficulties to struggle with in their work, opposition to
meet, or little apparent success in their labours, the circumstances of their position at least cannot be said to afford
much provocation to the indulgence of such selfish humours ;
but it is otherwise when a prosperous current of affairs sets
in ; when the pastor finds himself at the head of a thriving
and numerous congregation, moving in a circle of admiring
friends, often receiving the breath of popular applause, and
by many sought unto for advice in perplexing and critical
affairs.   In such circumstances be assured it requires special
grace, grace sustained by constant watchfulness and prayer,
to keep the even balance of the mind at once open to the
encouragements of the position, and ready to check the
risings of every fractious or petulant feeling.   The great theme
he handles, it may possibly be thought, the gospel of salvation through the Lord Jesus Christ, should be of itself sufficient to guard against the danger to which he is exposed,
since it has so much to do with human weakness and corruption, and presents so many calls to deep abasement of
heart in all who cordially receive it.   No doubt it should
do so ; but another tendency in the preacher's position, the
tendency to handle the topics of sin and salvation with
reference to others rather than himself, and in handling
them, to think more of the mode in which he deals with
them than with the subjects themselves, will, unless carefully watched, serve in a great degree to neutralize their
influence on his own temper and disposition.   If he suc-

ceeds in preventing it, it will only be by taking pains to press home upon his own heart what he is often preaching to others, examining himself often in the mirror of the divine word, and charging upon his soul the considerations that should beget the meek and lowly spirit which shone so brightly out in the Master whom he serves, and should never be wanting in those who minister in His name.

Substantially the same thoughts are suggested, though more immediately with respect to preaching itself, in the following passage from a late German professor, from whom, considering his controversial keenness and severity, one would scarcely have expected it : ' Even the most beautiful and sacred things which flow from human lips may in time become mere phrases. It is a part of human weakness and defectiveness, a curse, as it were, accompanying the divine blessing, that the very richest gifts of speech are the most in danger of being used in the service of vanity, since they lead one to take pleasure in them, to tickle by means of them, and thus to glorify oneself, rather than to serve God and one's fellow-men. Or the words, being through frequent use deprived of their soul, become at last as sounding brass. To this danger the clergyman is more than others exposed. As he is required by his vocation so often to hold up the word of God to others, and to have always at hand and give expression to those truths and ideas which are most of all suited to move, startle, and penetrate men's hearts, it is only too apt to be the case, that these truths lose for him their terribleness, so that their force and effect on his own heart is neutralized or weakened, and the constant direction of his attention to others keeps him from watching himself ; so that while he works on the hearts of others he neglects his own, and lets the weeds in it grow up unheeded.' (Hupfeld, quoted in *Bib. Sacra* for October 1866.)

Enough, perhaps, has now been said on the subject of the pastor's life generally, considered with respect to the lead-

ing features by which it should be distinguished, and the
bearing, as so characterized, it is fitted to have on the success of his labours.   But there are various matters of detail
connected with it, which partly also stands to the life itself
in the relation of means to end, on which a few practical
hints may not be out of place.

1. First, it is essential both for maintaining such a life as
we have been endeavouring to describe, and for the efficient
discharge of the duties of his office, that the pastor secure
for himself a certain amount of privacy and retirement.   He
must know to be alone, and, in a measure, love to be so.
Vital godliness generally may be said to require this ; as it
necessarily involves a habitual recalling of the mind from
external things to those which concern its proper well-being,
and its relation to a spiritual and eternal world.   The life
of the soul not only cannot *thrive*, it cannot for any length
of time *exist*, without the habit of at least occasional abstraction from the busy scenes and avocations of the world, in
order to a more distinct recognition of the realities and
interests which lie beyond, and from which it mainly draws
its inspiration and power.   But in a still higher degree must
this be predicated of the pastor, whose calling it is, not
simply to maintain the divine life for himself, but also to
minister to its formation and growth in the souls of others.
It will be next to impossible for him to do this unless he
be much alone ; not as if he shunned society, or placed any
virtue in solitude, but because he needs the opportunities
it affords to counteract the distracting tendency of earthly
things, to have faith strengthened with its proper nourishment, and his ministerial resources supplied with suitable
materials of wisdom and knowledge.   No doubt he has
much also to learn from society, especially from personal
intercourse with the members of his flock ; *there* he will
find, if he knows how to get at it, a book which it much
concerns him to study, and from which he may derive many

G

valuable suggestions, both for himself and his ministry. As regards the poorer members of the flock more particularly must this course be followed, were it only to know how to reach their understandings and hearts ; for, as has been justly said, ' He only can think as they think who often hears them speak their thoughts. It is utterly impossible for a clergyman to preach down to their level who is not in their confidence.'[1] Yet such intercourse can only supplement, it can no way supersede, the advantages to be derived from systematic retirement. The pastor's favourite resort must be his study ; in it he must find what shall be more peculiarly his home ; for in the employments to which it calls him, he has what tends most directly to promote his self-culture, and feeds the fountain whence is to flow light and refreshment to others. If ever any minister of the truth might have fitly dispensed with such quiet hours for thought and meditation, it assuredly was the Captain of our salvation, who knew what was in man, and possessed, besides, the treasures of all divine wisdom and knowledge ; yet in this respect also He set His people an example. How long a period of preparation, culminating in a season of entire withdrawal from the world, and earnest communings with the things of the Spirit, preceded the commencement of His more public ministry ; and even amid its busiest scenes of energetic action, how eagerly did He seek for the lonely hour to refresh His soul with holy contemplation and sustained fellowship with Heaven ! With ordinary pastors, however, there are reasons for such seasons of retirement which could have no place with Jesus; and without them, as part and parcel of his regular course of life, no pastor, whatever may be his gifts and acquirements, can reasonably expect either to maintain in healthful vigour his own spiritual being, or throw into his ministrations the variety, the freshness, and the power which ought to characterize them.

[1] Alford, *Essays and Addresses*, p. 8.

True, perhaps some may be disposed to say, especially such as are actually engaged in pastoral work, and well when it can be carried into effect ; but the question is, how to secure the time requisite for the stated return of retired thought and spiritual occupation at home, so much being taken up with the calls of out-door duty, and interruptions from various kinds of business. Practically, this proves with many ministers of the gospel to be the great difficulty ; but in a very considerable proportion of cases, by far the larger number indeed, I have no doubt it comes very much from a prior defect on their part, from the want of a fixed purpose to obtain the requisite time as necessary to success, or the want of orderly, systematic procedure in arranging with a view to its attainment. Everything, in a manner, depends upon these two points : fixedness of purpose as to the object itself, and methodizing one's own time, or secur-ing the co-operation of others, so as to effect its accomplish-ment. Where these scarcely if at all exist, one comes to be much at the mercy of accidents ; and it may well-nigh be said of the more peculiar vineyard of the pastor, as was said by the Psalmist of another sort of vineyard : ' The boar out of the wood doth waste it, and the wild beast of the field doth devour it.' There is no regulative principle, no girdle, as it were, to bind together the scattered energies of his mind for specific action ; and so time on every hand runs to waste ; intermeddlers of all sorts are allowed to do with it what they will. Not that I would recommend a rigid and unbending adherence to a particular method of working, which, amid the ever-changing circumstances of pastoral life, could not be retained in even one of the quieter spheres of labour without giving frequent occasions of offence, and missing often the fitting time for the discharge of pastoral work if it is to be done with effect. Exceptions, therefore, ought readily to be allowed ; but still they should be known to *be* exceptions ; the minister should be generally understood to have a method and an order, from which he may be expected to depart only for some valid reason. And when such an understanding as this prevails, people for the most part will be found to respect it ; they will rarely intrude upon their minister, or expect to see him among them, when his plan of life requires him to be alone. Even if they should at times be disposed to complain that he is not even seen more frequently among them, they will not usually do it so as to disturb his equanimity, if they are well assured that he is really engaged in that kind of employment which is congenial to his office, and tends to fit him for its important duties.

2. A second subject for consideration, naturally growing out of the one just noticed, is the proper distribution of that portion of his time which the pastor may usually allot to the retirement of the study. A reasonable latitude must here be allowed, and to a large extent each individual must judge for himself. Several things of a somewhat specific and formal description used not unfrequently to be recommended to persons preparing to enter on a regular pastorate, such as keeping a registry of the acts and experiences of each day, or a summary of such at more distant intervals, of the course of study pursued, the modes of ministerial action adopted, also the feelings, purposes, behaviour of which the pastor has been conscious to himself from time to time, so that he may both preserve a more distinct recollection of the past, and may have materials beside him for future guidance and caution. Undoubtedly, there are advantages to be derived from such personal records, especially as connected with particular periods of life and experimental efforts ; but there are also doubtful tendencies which it is apt to foster, unless kept within definite limits, and managed with brevity and prudence. Discretion and experience must be the chief guides. Right-minded, humble, and earnest men will by degrees find out what is the wisest

course for them to pursue, the one best adapted to their own mental idiosyncrasy, and the circumstances in which they are placed. The good and profitable for one may not be so for another.

Leaving matters of that sort, then, as neither requiring nor admitting of any precise and uniform rule, the chief appropriation of the hours which the pastor devotes to solitude should unquestionably be given to meditation, prayer, and study. The exact distribution of time to each must be regulated by circumstances. It may, however, be laid down as a general principle, that the whole of a minister's labours should be intermingled with meditation and prayer. He should never be simply a man of learning or study ; for this itself may become a snare to him ; it may even serve to stand between his soul and God, and nurse a spirit of worldliness in one of its most refined and subtle forms. If he be really a man of God, experience will teach him how much, even for success in study, he needs to be under the habitual recognition of God's presence, and to have the direction of His Spirit. It will also teach him how little he can prevail, with the most careful preparations and active diligence, in regard to the great ends of the ministry, without the special aid of the Holy Spirit ; how, when left to themselves, his most zealous efforts and best premeditated discourses fall powerless to the ground ; yea, and how often, amid the comparatively quiet and orderly events of ministerial employment, he will himself err in counsel, and do what he shall have occasion to regret, unless he is guided by a higher wisdom and sustained by a stronger arm than his own. Continually, therefore, has the true pastor to give himself to prayer ; his study should also be his *proseuché*, in which he daily holds communion, not only with the better spirits of the past and present through the written page, but with the Father of spirits, in the secret communications of His grace and love.

There are also, it should be noted, special subjects and occasions in respect to which the pastor may justly feel that he is called in a more peculiar manner to seek the direction and blessing of Heaven. The purpose, for example, of instituting any new agency for the good of the congregation, or the spread of the gospel in its neighbourhood, everything of such a nature should be projected, planned, inaugurated with earnest prayer, both for guidance as to the instrumentality to be employed, and for the wished-for results on the measures that may be put in operation. Discouragements and perplexities in the work of the ministry form another special call to humble waiting upon God, it being always one great design of troubles of that description to bring the pastor to a deep sense of his own insufficiency, and to a closer dependence on God. The extent to which this effect is produced will usually be the measure of his profiting by the dispensations. But most of all should he exercise himself unto prayer in connection with his work as a preacher of the gospel. In the selection of the topics whereon to address his people, in the specific mode or aspect in which he should present particular truths to their heart and conscience, in the frame of his own spirit while delivering the message of salvation to his fellow-men, in the impression actually made by what is delivered on those who hear : in one and all of these the earnest pastor will find what should draw him as a suppliant to the throne of grace. How much often depends on a particular vein of thought being opened, on a certain illustration being employed, sometimes even on a single word of appeal to the conscience ! How much also upon the general tone and bearing of the speaker, or *the unction* with which all is done ! And what so likely to help in every respect to what is desired, as the spirit of habitual communion with the sanctuary above ? Let the pastor, therefore, like Milton, accompany all ' with devout prayer to that Eternal Spirit who enriches with all

utterance and knowledge, and sends out His seraphim with
the hallowed fire of His altar to touch and purify the lips of
whom He pleases.' What more than this contributed to
raise the genius of Milton himself to its singular elevation,
and has given to his productions a character of sacredness
and majesty that assimilates them to the lofty strains of a
Hebrew prophet ?

But prayer, it must ever be borne in mind, however
valuable as an auxiliary, will fail if it is taken as a substitute for other resources ; if it is allowed to supersede the
proper application to study. The same apostle who, for
himself and other evangelical labourers, speaks of the
necessity of 'praying always with all prayer and supplication,' has such exhortations as these : 'meditate upon these
things;' 'give thyself wholly to them.' So that to make
the exercises of devotion an excuse for neglecting continuous and stated application to study is to depart from the
course prescribed in Scripture, as well as to set at nought
the well-ascertained results of experience. Both extremes
are to be avoided as alike unwise and unscriptural. Study
should be accompanied and blessed by prayer, otherwise it
can never reach its end. On the other hand, prayer should
be fed and sustained by study, otherwise the spirit of devotion itself will languish, and both prayer and preaching
will become monotonous and languid. Proofs of this are
not far to seek. There are many who, at the outset of their
career, gave promise of much acceptance and usefulness
in the work of the ministry, but who by relaxing their
diligence in study have come ere long to exhibit a wearisome
flatness in their services, or in their thoughts and illustrations to move in a kind of circle, the same rounds of ideas
perpetually returning, clothed not unfrequently in the same
words. It is even worse when freshness is attempted. 'I
have been cured,' said Richard Cecil, 'of expecting the
Holy Spirit's influence without due preparation on our part,

by observing how men preach who take up that error. I have heard such men talk nonsense by the hour.'[1]

It is perfectly possible, of course, and perhaps not uncommon, to go to the opposite extreme, to study to excess, if not to the neglect of prayer, at least to an undue curtailment of more active labours and employments, and even, it may be, an impairing of the healthful tone and vigour of the frame. There is a certain amount of application in this particular line which may be overtaken with profit ; but if more is attempted than the constitution is able rightly to bear, nature will be sure to have its revenge, and a loss, not an additional gain, will be the result. The more immediate consequence will probably be, that the mind being overtasked will perceptibly lose its freshness and power, will feel unable for the sustained thought and application which it was wont to possess ; it can neither so well remember what it reads, nor so promptly and energetically use the materials of knowledge it has acquired. And what also not uncommonly, though somewhat more remotely happens, the nervous system falls into disorder, imaginary evils brood over the mind, and even the most ordinary duties are felt to be a burden. When such things begin to make their appearance, the studious pastor should hear in them a call to seek a period of rest, or to give a portion of his time to work less directly mental.

[1] I have referred only in one respect to the disadvantage attending an early settlement in a large city charge ; but other things also should be taken into account. In particular, the country is a far better field for the free and natural development of one's faculties, and getting fairly alongside the common feelings and sympathies of mankind. There is a much easier access there to men's understandings and hearts than when encompassed by the conventionalisms and formalities, not to say corrupt manners, too often found in city life. And in nine cases out of ten, a man's powers of thought and speech will be more likely to take their native direction, and reach their proper healthfulness and vigour, in the one sphere than in the other.

In regard to the subjects of study, there can be no doubt as to what should occupy at least the primary place. For a Christian pastor there is nothing in that respect to be placed beside the word of God ; that word itself, and the literature bearing on its history and elucidation. Whether his more direct object may be to qualify himself for the effective ministration of the gospel, or to become a well-read and able theologian, the close, exact, and continued study of Scripture is alike necessary. For any department, indeed, of ministerial service, whether as connected with the pulpit or the press, to be mighty in the Scriptures is to have the most fundamental qualification for doing it with success. But on this it is needless to enlarge ; it is rather to be taken for granted, as a point upon which there can be no reasonable dispute with those who understand and appreciate aright the things of God.

The difficulty rather lies in the practical direction, in getting such command of time, and bringing to the task so much resolution and energy, as will avail to keep up habits of study in any particular line. When a person, still comparatively young, and after, perhaps, no very long experience in evangelistic work, comes to have devolved on him the responsibilities of a regular pastoral charge, he will usually find his weekly preparations for the pulpit absorb all the time he has to spare for study ; and if he can only manage to investigate and handle Scripture so as to acquit himself with some measure of profit and satisfaction in his official duties, it will be nearly as much as he can seriously aim at. Work of this description undoubtedly has the first claim on his attention ; it will always demand the larger share of his time and application ; but in a great many cases it need not, in the long run at least, engross the whole, if there were only a wise economy and proper distribution of time, and what is perhaps fully as essential, the selection of some definite line of inquiry for more careful and prolonged examination. I of course except those who from the first commencement of their pastoral labours are set down in a large town, and charged with the oversight of a numerous and intelligent congregation. In such a case there is probably not one in fifty who possesses either the physical energy or the mental resources to do more than meet the immediate requirements of official duty. Scripture and everything else will have to be studied almost exclusively for the purpose of obtaining the requisite materials for public discourse. And along with this necessary contraction of the field of study, and living, as one may say, from hand to mouth, there naturally springs up also the habit of simply working for the occasion; so that when the occasion makes no demand, nothing of any moment is done, and there is no development of the powers of the mind, or systematic multiplication of its resources, except in connection with the stated labours of the ministry. Independent literary exertion is scarcely possible.

Take the case, however, of a person who is called to a sphere of labour, which may be described as of manageable extent or moderate compass; one which may afford scope enough for pastoral activity, and yet not so large but that, after the preliminary difficulties of the work have been mastered, there may be found some time to spare for independent study. Well, to turn this time to best account, it will usually prove of no small service to have the attention directed into a specific line of meditation or research, for the purpose of being somewhat minutely and fully acquainted with the things which belong to it, or of becoming comparatively at home with it. Where no selection of this sort is made, there is the want of a precise object whereon to concentrate the powers of the mind, and awaken its interest. The historian Gibbon, who may here be pointed to as an example, after having completed the first half of his great work, where he at first thought of concluding his labours, states that he then, as one relieved from toil, began to luxuriate over the wide field of ancient literature, but that he soon found such unrestrained and aimless liberty to grow distasteful to him ; so that ere long he came 'in the luxury of freedom to wish for the daily task, the active pursuit, which gave a value to every book, and an object to every inquiry ; ' and forthwith resumed the prosecution of his design. Now, whether one may have any approach to the mental calibre of Gibbon or no, whether also there may or may not be the intention of committing the result of one's labours to the press, still the selection of a particular subject or line of inquiry for more special and careful consideration will always bring along with it this advantage, that it engages the active interest of the mind, provides it with a theme to prosecute in seasons of comparative leisure, a resource to fall back upon in circumstances of discouragement, or, as Gibbon puts it, a pursuit which will impart a value to the books one reads, and furnish an object for specific inquiry.   Where such is altogether wanting, the reading is apt to become desultory, and the information obtained, being without any definite aim or connecting bond, is like random seed which yields no adequate harvest.   But, indeed, without some special study to nourish his intellect and sustain his thoughts above every-day concerns, the pastor, especially the country pastor, is apt to sink into common-place.   Besides, both for the improvement of the mind itself, and for one's own position and character, it is always an advantage to be well informed upon some particular branch of sacred learning, more so than to have a wider range of knowledge, though less exact and thorough in its character.   In the very process, also, of becoming an adept in some one department of inquiry, the mind necessarily gathers a great deal of collateral information, for every subject has its points of contact with many others ; and if there should be acquired real depth of research and maturity of view within a limited range, this will ensure a considerable degree of enlightenment over a much wider field.

It appears to me, therefore, a wise and beneficial thing for those who have some real taste for study, and the resolution to carry out a plan after they have got a settled position and had time to look about them, to make choice of some particular subject, or class of subjects, for their more peculiar consideration ; one that they shall be ever returning upon and labouring at till they acquire in regard to it a comparative mastery. The Bible itself presents a considerable variety of departments which might severally be chosen for such a purpose, each having associated with it a more or less extensive literature. There is, for example, the text of Scripture, viewed with respect to the authorities on which its correctness is based, or to the languages in which it was originally written, with the various and characteristic shades of diversity which they assumed in different ages, or in the hands of different penmen. Then there are the several classes of writings in the Bible, each indicating, on the part of the human authors, a distinctive cast of mind, and requiring a certain affinity with the same in those who would apply successfully to their elucidation : such as the historical books of the Old Testament, which not only relate to what may be called the kernel of all history, the development of God's kingdom in the world, but touch also incidentally on all the more prominent kingdoms of antiquity, and the manners and customs of former times ; the poetical and didactic books, which exhibit the forms of spiritual thought, and the devotional, spiritual, and moral results which sprang from the revelations and institutions successively given to the people of God ; lastly, the prophetical, which connected the past with the future, and laid open the more secret counsels of Heaven for the instruction and warning of men. In the New Testament, again, we have the Gospels, the

Epistles, the Apocalypse, each forming so many great divisions, and calling for a characteristic mode of treatment, as well as for prolonged study to become thoroughly acquainted with the materials which past diligence and research have accumulated for their elucidation. In addition to these, and more or less connected with the teaching of Scripture, how many other fields of investigation present themselves! Archæology, or Jewish and Christian antiquities, monumental theology, chronology, patristic and medieval phases of thought and action, the writings and labours of the Reformers, the Puritan development of theology, the controversies with infidels and heretics, the lives of eminent divines and missionaries, etc.; any one of which, if systematically prosecuted, might afford ample scope for profitable and interesting employment. Take up any one of them to which a sense of its own importance, or the drawing of natural inclination, might induce you to give the preference, and you will find that the deliberate effort to master its details, and obtain an intimate acquaintance with its different bearings, will serve at once to give an impulse to your studies, and enable you to make a profitable use of many fragments of time which would otherwise slip unimproved through your hands.

With this recommendation, however, let me couple the earnest advice, that no independent course of study be pursued in such a manner, or to such an extent, as to interfere with the regular discharge of pastoral duties, or suitable preparation for them. These should on no account be jostled out of their proper place ; and if things which, however important in themselves, are still in their relation to the pastor's own responsibilities but of secondary rank, come to usurp the time and application which are due primarily to them, dissatisfaction will inevitably arise, and the blessing of God may not improbably be withheld from the employments which are allowed to impoverish the flock.

The spirit of vital godliness in the first instance, and then a proper estimate of the nature and ends of the pastoral office, will alone be adequate to preserve in the mind the proper balance between the respective claims that press on it, and save it from running to extremes.

3. To refer now to that part of a minister's time which is not appropriated either to the occupations of the study or to the formal duties of the pastorate, he is undoubtedly entitled to find in it enough for purposes of daily relaxation, with seasons also of occasional recreation on a larger scale. Interludes of this sort are indispensable to his physical health, and the general freshness and elasticity of his frame. In the *kind* of occupations or entertainments, however, selected for this end, care should ever be taken to avoid what is unbecoming the gravity which befits the ministerial character, and what may tend to indispose the mind to serious employments. The sports of the field, therefore, hunting, shooting, and such like, are justly proscribed by the spiritual sense of the religious community, as too distinctively worldly in their nature, and in their tendency ministering too powerfully to animal excitement, to comport well with what should be the predominant state of feeling in those who are the keepers of souls. Even entering into parties which are formed for the purpose merely of going a pleasuring, if done at all, should be done with prudent foresight and consideration, as such things are exceedingly apt to degenerate into improper levity and frolicsomeness. For the most part, the safer and more becoming method of filling up the time devoted to relaxation will be to spend it in the quiet occupations of the garden, or in walking excursions and friendly visits, which can be managed without the slightest violation of decorum, and can be taken either alone, or in the company of a very few, and these quite congenial spirits. In matters of this description it were absurd to prescribe for others, or even for oneself, stringent

and imperative rules. One *must* be guided to a large extent by circumstances. Yet there are always limits which the thoughtful and well-balanced mind, which is duly alive to the interests of salvation and the powers of the world to come, though still without moroseness, will not fail to prescribe to itself.

As for diversions, exhibitions, and scenes which are in their very nature of a questionable kind, the safe path for a minister of the gospel will be to stand altogether aloof from them. It is not for him, who has to deal with his fellow-men on the great themes of mercy and of judgment, to be mingling in parties or frequenting places where he has to debate the matter at the threshold with his own conscience; and the advantage which he might derive from occasionally seeing what is transacted in them for the amusement of the mere lovers of pleasure, would be greatly more than counter-balanced by the extent to which his character and position should be compromised. In regard to all this class of things it is a good rule of Mr. Cecil's, that if a worldly man should meet a godly minister in them with the salutation, 'I did not expect to see *you* here,' it is a pretty sure sign that the minister is not in his proper place. For whatever licence the men of this world may often take to themselves, and however disposed to say one to another, What is the harm in such and such things? they have usually a quick enough discernment of the incongruity between questionable indulgences and a Christian profession, when exemplified in the conduct of those whose calling is more peculiarly associated with the spirit and obligations of the gospel.[1]

[1] A former dignitary of the Irish Episcopal Church (the Bishop of Limerick) has the following sensible remarks on the subject under consideration, in a charge to the clergy of the diocese : 'I do not see,' he said, 'how a clergyman, consistently with the sacredness and separation of his character and office, consistently with the vows which he has made at his ordination, can pursue the sports of the mountain or the

What are called *mixed companies* stand in a somewhat different position, for in the majority of cases it is impossible for the pastor altogether to avoid them. The boundary line here is not an absolute one between the lawful and the forbidden ; it perpetually varies with the circumstances of place and time ; and nothing but the fear of God, an enlightened conscience, spiritual tact and discretion, can be our guide regarding it. It can never beseem a minister of the gospel [to court worldly society for its own sake ; but neither ought he entirely to shun it. The example of our Lord speaks distinctly upon this point. He entered frankly into the society of those around Him, as conscious of certain relations He had to maintain, certain duties He had to fulfil toward them ; and so, within moderate limits, should the ministers of the gospel. But in so doing, they should endeavour, like their Master, to preserve the attitude of persons rather complying with occasions presented to them, than seeking for themselves a natural gratification, and watching the while for opportunities to do good to those with whom for the time they are brought into contact. It is a happy talent to be able, in the company of men of worldly ambition or loose morals, not only to keep one's own soul from sinking to a level with theirs, but also to exercise a restraint on their dispositions, and raise the tone of thought and conversation to something like a proper

field ; can be found at the card-table or in the ball-room. In avowing these sentiments, I avow the sentiments which, from the earliest ages of the Church, have been maintained alike by the old Catholic bishops and Fathers, and by the most distinguished and illustrious Churchmen of modern times. In these sentiments I have lived ; in these sentiments I hope to die ; and at the close of life it will be to me a crown of rejoicing, if, through my humble instrumentality, any of my reverend brethren shall be induced to become like-minded, and to consider, even in their most unguarded hours, what gravity and recollectedness are at all times and in all places demanded of our sacred order.' (Quoted in his *Life of Paley*, by Rev. E. S. Wayland, p. 38.)

pitch.   But it is a talent not easily acquired ; since it requires a combination of properties that may always be expected to be somewhat rare ; and for the most part it will
be found by experience to be but a limited good which a
minister can accomplish through his presence in mixed
societies.   Let him beware lest the cause of godliness
rather lose than gain by it.   For there is truth in what is
remarked by Vinet :[1] 'A man who is seen everywhere cannot inspire a respectful consideration.   The judgment
which is formed of a pastor who is seen in all companies
is not likely to be very favourable.   He will be accused of
not feeling his duties, and not appreciating the necessity of
solitude.   Society multiplies occasions for doing good, but
it yet more multiplies occasions for doing evil.   And there
are some men whom the pastor ought not to see at his own
house or elsewhere.   St. Paul counsels Timothy to turn
away from all men whose life is evil, and especially from
those who have the appearance of that piety of which they
have denied the power,' 2 Tim. iii. 5.

I add only further, that in all situations and in all companies, the pastor should never forget his office ; he should
bear in mind that he has a high calling to fulfil, and should
aim at preserving in his demeanour a dignified simplicity.
General gravity of behaviour must ever seem appropriate to
one who has such heavy responsibilities resting on him ;
but it should be natural, not affected or put on for the occasion ; it should be accompanied and relieved by a genuine
simplicity.   If this is wanting, the other will only be regarded as an official mannerism, and will not gain the respect
of the world, while it will effectually mar the freedom of his
access to the confidence and affection of his people.   If all
expect decorum, they not less desire simplicity in the air
and deportment of their minister.   Even people of finesse,
themselves living in an artificial state of society, will admire

[1] *Pastoral Theol.* p. 118.

H

simplicity in him, if only it is not coupled with rough-ness, or rendered offensive by low manners and a vulgar familiarity.[1]

4. A word may suffice for the pastor's more public rela-tion to the commonwealth ; for the less he meddles with the simply political contests and movements of the day it will usually be the better both for himself and for his work. So many ministers of the gospel, both in Established and Nonconformist Churches, have embroiled themselves in unseemly strife, and become visibly secularized in spirit by labouring too much at this oar, that if not an utter abstinence, at least a cautious reserve in respect to it, is the manifest dictate of wisdom. There are questions and measures so far political that they come to be legislated on in Parlia-ment, but which are intimately connected with the religious and moral well-being of the community. As regards these, ministers of the gospel have an obvious duty to discharge as members of the commonwealth ; they should endeavour to arrive at a sound judgment concerning them, manfully declare their views, and on fitting occasions try to influence aright the views of others. It is another thing, however, to enter actively into the political arena, make speeches in political meetings, and direct the machinery of elections. This they had better leave to others, who find their proper sphere in such troubled waters. It is in a higher sphere that *their* peculiar strength lies ; and so long as they keep to it, the sentiments they express, and the part they quietly but firmly take in the things which concern the wise ad-ministration and good order of the country will have their weight, without imperilling the interests of their office by making themselves the tools of designing men.

5. Lastly, in respect to the domestic relations, everything in the pastor's family should be in proper keeping with his

[1] On the subject of gentlemanly, as opposed to vulgar manners, I may refer to the excellent letters of Dr. Miller of Princeton.

place and calling ; of incalculable importance it is that it should be so.   As he should be himself a typal Christian, so his home should be a kind of pattern household.   St. Paul in several places lays special stress upon this, and points to the state of the pastor's family as an evidence whether or not he is qualified to preside over the household of God. With the state of his family his personal comfort and use-fulness are inseparably bound up ; and if there is palpable disorder and irregularity at home, it is impossible that in his public capacity he can wield the influence and secure the respect which it is proper for him to possess.   How many ministers of promising parts, and as preachers of the gospel apparently destined to excel, have been rendered comparatively ineffective in their pastoral relation by the disorderly condition of their households, or the scandalous misconduct of certain members of their families !   Perhaps a want of firmness at first, on the pastor's part, in checking the evil at its commencement, a connivance at things which ought instantly to have been repressed, a tendency too much indulged to let domestic affairs be overshadowed by the concerns of public duty, perhaps also a want of sympathy in respect to the high ends of the ministry on the female side of the house, opening the door to foolish companion-ships and improper worldly compliances, have, one or other of them, contributed to foster a spirit of insubordination and licence in the family, which grows till it becomes altogether unmanageable, and recoils with disastrous effect on the pastor's position and usefulness.   Here, therefore, the great-est pains should be taken, the most vigilant oversight main-tained, and, I may add, the most prayerful anxiety exercised from the outset, that the whole of his domestic and family affairs should be managed with discretion, so as to second, not to impede, his labours in the gospel.   It becomes him to be the more concerned about this, as here he is to a large extent dependent upon others ; he cannot stand alone ; nor can matters go well with him, unless along with fidelity and prudence to discharge his own part aright those who stand so near to him have corresponding measures of the same for the discharge of theirs. Most of all is it important, that if he be married, he should not be unequally yoked ; that his partner in life should be a person of genuine faith, Christian discretion, and active zeal ; for, if such, she may not only maintain order and decency in the household, but also by her example and influence render most effective service to the moral and spiritual interests of the flock. In some fields of pastoral labour, of course, the minister's wife may be able to accomplish more than in others ; but in nearly all, she may prove a valuable handmaid ; and, speaking generally, the proper relations here may not inaptly be represented, as they were by a German pastor at the Evangelical Alliance Meeting in Berlin (1857), when he said that the pastor was not to be considered as A, and his wife as B, but rather that he was A¹ and she A², meaning that her place and influence, when of the proper kind, come so near to his, that they are to be contemplated as lying in the same plane, and hers only second in magnitude and value to her husband's.

I cannot bring my remarks on this subject to a close without expressing again my deep conviction as to the vast importance I attach to the personal and social life of the pastor for the success of his mission as a servant of Christ. Even in a somewhat general respect the influence of a well-educated, exemplary married clergy has been of great benefit to society, and is acknowledged to have been so by persons who are not disposed to concede anything to them on the score of mere official position. Thus Mr. Lecky, in his *History of European Morals* (vol. ii. p. 354), speaks, though with a slight qualification, yet in very strong terms regarding it : ' Nowhere, it may be confidently asserted, does Christianity assume a more beneficial or a more winning form, than in those gentle clerical households which stud our land, constituting, as Coleridge said, "the one idyl of modern life," the most perfect type of domestic peace, and the centres of civilisation in the remotest village. Notwithstanding some class narrowness and professional bigotry ; notwithstanding some unworthy but half-unconscious mannerism, which is often most unjustly stigmatized as hypocrisy, it would be difficult to find in any other quarter so much happiness at once diffused and enjoyed, or so much virtue attained with so little tension or struggle.' And in regard to the pastor's wife : ' In visiting the sick, relieving the poor, instructing the young, and discharging a thousand delicate offices for which a woman's tact is especially needed, his wife finds a sphere of labour which is at once intensely active and intensely feminine, and her example is not less beneficial than her ministrations.'

This is true ; but the truth in it rises in importance when it is viewed in the bearing it necessarily has on what should ever be the great scope and aim of the pastoral calling. It is in reality the *personelle* of the pastor, what he is as to individual qualifications and character, that gives the tone to his work, and determines at once the nature and the effect of his ministrations. As water cannot rise above the spring from which it issues, neither can the acts themselves of a ministerial career, nor the results accomplished by them, be found to reach higher in spirit and character than his from whom instrumentally they proceed ; usually they may be expected to fall considerably beneath it. The services he conducts in the sanctuary must to a large extent take their impress from the preacher, and be in thought, in feeling, in utterance, the reflection of *his* style of Christianity. And both in these and in the more private labours of the pastoral life, it ever is the living image of the man which makes all what it properly is : not so much what is said or done on any particular occasion, as what he is in personal attainments and worth whose name it bears. If he demeans

himself as becomes his office ; if his feelings and habits as a
man, his endowments and bearing as a minister, are such
as to place him on the proper vantage-ground ; if all that is
seen and known of him is of a kind fitted to suggest the man
of God, as well as the official representative of a Church of
Christ, then an air of sacredness will attach to his ministerial
course, and the testimony he delivers for truth, righteousness, and mercy will come forth with an authority and an
impressiveness which cannot fail to command the respect
of all, while it will sink more deeply into the hearts of some.
But make the contrary supposition ; conceive a pastor but
poorly qualified for his high trust, so that in office alone he
seems to rise above many in his flock ; or conceive him
possessed of a fair measure of qualifications, and on various
accounts entitled to the esteem of his people, but these accompanied by certain marked deficiencies or palpable failings in his character and work, how impossible in such a
case must it be for him to get the position he ought to
occupy ! And how inevitably will the heterogeneous or
disturbing elements about him intrude upon men's minds
like a qualifying *but*, interfering with the impressions that
might otherwise have been produced, or taking back again
a portion of the good that may have been received.

If, turning from the interests of religion generally, we
think of those which concern our own Communion in particular, fresh reasons will discover themselves in support of
what has been said. On this more than anything else of
an instrumental kind the Free Church depends for her well-
being and prosperity ; indeed, the one may be safely tested
and gauged by the other. She has received, it is true, a
banner to be displayed because of the truth, a testimony
which *ought* to draw toward her the hearts of those who
have learned to know and prize the truth. Doubtless this
will more or less be the case ; yet not as apart from the
personal and official qualifications of her pastors. People

generally, even good Christian people, will take their impressions and form their opinions in a great degree from this ; and if, on the basis of her testimony, this or any other Church should fail to raise up a ministry that is adequate to her own wants and those of our age and country, her testimony will infallibly cease to carry the respect which it ought to command.   May all aspirants to the ministry lay this seriously to heart, and strive in earnest to make good what it requires at their hands !   It is pre-eminently a noble work to which they are giving themselves ; a work which cannot fail to yield a rich harvest of blessing in their own experience, as well as to those among whom they minister, if only it is prosecuted in the right spirit, and by men who are themselves the living examples of what they preach. But this is the indispensable condition of success ; and in proportion as it fails, there will also be a failure in the true mission and glory of the Church.

CHAPTER IV.

THE MORE SPECIAL DUTIES OF THE PASTORAL OFFICE.

SECTION I.—*The Theory and Practice of Preaching.*

IN proceeding now to consider the special duties of the pastoral office, we cannot hesitate to assign the first place to the work of preaching, the preparation and delivery of discourses on the great subjects of God's revelation to men. This forms more peculiarly the vocation of the Christian pastor; other things, though important in their proper place, are still but subsidiary in comparison of it. As the purpose of God is to save men by the knowledge of the truth in Christ, so by what the apostle calls 'the foolishness of preaching,' that is, by the simple, faithful, earnest proclamation of the truth, the great end of the ministry must chiefly be carried out. It is only by their coming to know and believe the truth that men consciously enter into the kingdom of God; and every step they may afterwards take in the discharge of its obligations, or in the personal experience of its blessings, must be in connection with realizing views of the things which belong to the person and the work of Christ. Whatever, therefore, is fitted to aid in bringing men to the possession of such views, is on that account entitled to a minister's attentive consideration; but he should ever regard the preaching of the gospel as the means more especially appointed by Christ, and in its own nature best adapted for bringing the truth effectually to bear upon the hearts of men, and maintaining its influence in Christian congregations.   So that preaching, as justly stated by Vinet,[1] 'is essential to the pastorate, which apart from this cannot reach souls, and cannot present the truth in its most regular and general forms.   This,' he adds, 'is the glory of our Reformation, that it has restored public preaching to the Church ; it may even be said to the Catholic Church.   Surely that was a noble movement by which the priesthood passed from a simple celebration of rites (which had become a species of magic) to science, to thought, to speech and aggressive action.'

I. *Points of agreement in essential qualities between preaching and public speaking in general.*—Preaching, as it is now understood, being only a particular kind of public discourse, necessarily has certain things common to it with oratory in general, but which must rather be presupposed here than formally considered.   Not, however, as if they were of little importance ; on the contrary, I quite concur in the statement of Mr. Rogers,[2] that the eloquence of the pulpit 'has never, I should rather say seldom, been assimilated so far as it might have been to that which has produced the greatest effect elsewhere, and which is shown to be of the right kind, both by the success which has attended it, and by the analysis of the qualities by which it has been distinguished.' It will be well, therefore, for those who are bent on attaining to such excellence in this respect as they may be capable of reaching, to make themselves acquainted with the great principles of public speaking as an art, as these have been unfolded by the masters of eloquence themselves, or by those who have made them the subject of special study. Here the ancients still continue among our best guides, not merely from the admirable specimens of oratory they have left behind them, but also on account of the careful study they gave to the subject, and their clear enunciation of all

[1] *Past. Theology*, p. 73.   [2] *Essay on Sacred Eloquence.*

the more important elements of success. There is scarcely, I believe, anything of moment, nothing certainly entitled to much consideration, which will not be found both lucidly stated and largely illustrated in the rhetorical treatises of Aristotle, Cicero, and Quinctilian. Such works, however, of modern date as Campbell's *Philosophy of Rhetoric*, Whately's *Rhetoric*, also Blair's *Lectures on Rhetoric*, may be consulted with advantage. That I may not altogether omit what relates to this more general, though in itself most fundamental branch of the subject, I shall endeavour as briefly as possible to indicate a few leading points.

(1.) First of all it is to be borne in mind, that nature here, as in other things, constitutes the foundation. It does so in two respects, both as to the measure in which success in public speaking may be possible, and as to the particular method or style through which it may be attained. Whatever the labour and cultivation of art may do, it must have certain aptitudes or capacities of a natural kind to build upon. That the first parts belong to nature (*primas partes esse naturæ*) is freely allowed by Quinctilian,[1] even when he is urging most strenuously the necessity of laborious application. In personal appearance, in freedom, flexibility and compass of voice, in strength of reason, retentiveness of memory, warmth of feeling, quickness and vivacity of thought, one man naturally excels another ; and the greater or less degree in which any individual may possess these respective qualities, cannot fail to bring along with it a corresponding advantage or defect in respect to the higher measures of success. 'Some,' says Cicero,[2] 'possess them in so eminent a degree, they are so adorned with the gifts of nature, that they seem to have been not so properly born, as fashioned by the hand of God for consummate orators ;' while there are others in the precisely opposite condition, so hesitating in their speech, so harsh and grating in their

[1] *Inst.* xi. 3.   [2] *De Oratore*, L. i. c. 25.

voice, so lumbering in their mental action or uncouth in their bodily movements, that no amount of application could be conceived adequate to make them tolerable public speakers.   But even where there is such combination of properties as may be said to constitute a natural aptness for the work sufficient as a foundation for oratorical culture, that nature must still determine the *kind;* and to set up before one's view a model as to method of discourse, or manner of speech and address, which should oblige one to go against the grain, would only be to lose that which *might* have been attained, to desert nature where it *could* achieve something for an ideal excellence which lies hopelessly out of reach.

(2.) A second point to be borne in mind is the improve-ableness of nature in the powers which actually belong to it, if only there is applied to their cultivation persistent and well-directed effort.   None speak more strongly on this point than those who have themselves risen to the highest degrees of excellence in the art of speaking, or have given finer examples of it to others.   The traditions respecting Demosthenes,[1] his partial failures at first only rousing him to more resolute endeavours, his laborious practice of elocution by the sea-shore, his frequent resort to the depths of a soli-tude where no voice but his own could be heard, and no passing objects could be seen to distract the eye of his mind, or interrupt the intensity of its application,—such things, as well as the character of his surviving speeches, tell of the earnest and long-continued study which bore him to the peerless elevation which he ultimately reached. Cicero, too, after he had gained some distinction as a pleader in the Forum, so far from being satisfied with this early success, or thinking that he had already approached the limits of perfection, put himself under the direction of pro-fessed rhetoricians, both at Rome and afterwards when

[1] Quinct. L. x. 3.

sojourning at Athens and in Asia Minor, giving himself, as Quinctilian expresses it, to be in a manner formed and modelled anew.[1] And his own advices to others are in perfect accordance with the course he had himself pursued, as may be seen, for example, in the 2d Book of his *Treatise on Oratory*, where explicit directions are given upon the subject, and the result of judicious and persevering application is represented as almost incredible. Preachers must expect no exemption from this law of nature, though few may be able to bestow such pains and application in conforming to it as the persons just referred to. As public speakers they have powers to cultivate, faculties to improve and exercise, and that both in respect to the proper treatment of the subjects they have to handle, and the way and manner of presenting their ideas, so as best to convince the understandings and impress the hearts of their audience. However easy it may be with certain natural advantages on their side to reach a respectable mediocrity in these respects, perfection, or even an approach to perfection, in any one of the properties going to constitute the really effective public speaker, is necessarily reserved for the painstaking and the diligent.[2]

(3.) The dependence of successful public speaking on an

[1] L. xii. 6.

[2] It should be remembered also, that whatever help one may sometimes get from others, self-culture, self-application must chiefly be looked to. So it certainly was with Demosthenes, so with one of the greatest of American orators. 'I owe my success in life,' said Clay, 'to one single fact, namely, that at the age of twenty-seven I commenced and continued for years the practice of daily reading and speaking upon the contents of some historical or scientific book. These offhand efforts were made sometimes in a corn-field, at others in the forest, and not unfrequently in some distant barn, with the horse and the ox for my auditors. It is to this early practice of the great art of all arts that I am indebted for the primary and leading impulses that stimulated me forward, and have shaped my entire subsequent history.'

appropriate style, is a third point requiring careful thought and application; style, I mean, not simply with regard to the choice of words or the structure of sentences (which may admit of many varieties), but as a fitting expression of the speaker's own cast of mind, as exercised on the class of subjects of which he discourses, and with a view to the specific end he aims at in handling them. Diligence and care in this respect Cicero calls the most efficient and controlling factor in speaking aright (*optimum effectorum ac magistrum dicendi*),[1] though Cicero himself, it must be admitted, carried the matter to excess, and in aspiring after that fine modulation of words and wealth and harmony of diction in which he became so great a master, he often impaired the naturalness and strength of his language by the too artificial, elaborate, and prolix structure of his sentences. The line that is really the most fitting and appropriate for a particular speaker will always be found involved in some difficulty, calling for wise discrimination in the individual, with a certain delicacy of feeling and propriety of sentiment; nor in anything will a false taste more readily discover its mistake, or prove more certainly fatal to success. It is also beset with this peculiar difficulty, that while one's style must to a large extent be formed on the model of written productions, there are qualities of style which may be perfectly proper, sometimes may add grace or dignity to the printed page, which would inevitably appear stiff or affected if transferred to the oral discourse. One thing requires especially to be kept in view by the public speaker, whatever may be the particular theme or the kind of audience with which for the time he has to do; he must cultivate lucidity and directness of speech; for it is not with him as with an author, whose readers may hang for a considerable time over his pages in order to catch the full drift of his meaning, or obtain an adequate appreciation of

[1] *De Oratore,* i. 33.

the felicitous manner in which it is unfolded. The public speaker must be understood as he goes along ; every sentence, every word he utters should find its way to the understandings of his hearers as soon as it passes from his lips ; in so far as it does not, it necessarily fails of its aim. But in respect to other qualities, such as regard to emphasis, comparative ease or tension, pathetic tenderness or rugged energy, elegance, terseness, epigrammatic point or careless simplicity, there is room for almost endless diversity ; and *which* of these to adopt, and *when*, demands not only a discriminating judgment with respect to each particular part and species of discourse, but also a just estimate of one's own powers in relation to the things required. Hence, all sensible critics recommend here much tentative and experimental action ; a cautious gauging of one's personal powers and resources ; a study of the most approved exemplars of thought and style, in their different kinds ; and, above all, the habitual practice of composition, whether for public discourse or merely for private exercise and improvement. *Scribendum ergo* (says Quinctilian) *quam diligentissime, et quam plurimum ;* [1] and this all the more, as he also urges, if we have much to do in extempore speaking, since without regular habits of study and experience in written composition, it is sure to degenerate into what he calls *inanem loquacitatem et verba in labris nascentia*, frothy talk and lip oratory.

(4.) Then, fourthly, there is the intimate connection between the things spoken and the action or bearing of the speaker, a point which the commonest hearers as well as the greatest rhetorical authorities are competent to judge of, and alike regard as of highest moment ; for the one class instinctively feel what the other intellectually discern. Thousands can judge of the propriety or impropriety, the defects or advantages of a speaker's voice and motions,

[1] L. x. 3, 7.

which together make up action, for the comparative handful
who can intelligently judge of the merits or demerits of the
discourse he delivers.   People are affected, not simply, often
not so much, by the thoughts presented to their minds, as
by the manner in which they are presented, the tone, the
gesture, the whole aspect and demeanour of him who is
seeking to gain a hearing for them.   So that, as is perfectly
known, a second or even third rate discourse, if set forth by
an appropriate and becoming action, will prevail more than
the most exquisite composition, which is accompanied in
the delivery by an unsuitable or defective manner.   The
judgment of Demosthenes on this point is well known ; and
Cicero speaks with scarcely less decision ; for he represents
action as having a sort of dominant power in speaking
(*unam in dicendo actionem dominari*).[1]   And he justly
notices that in that respect there is nothing so readily
marked, nor so apt to take a firm hold of the memory, as
that which occasions offence.   It is what every one per-
ceives ; it seems to thrust itself on the observation of all,
and cleaves to their remembrance whether they will or not.
There is therefore a double reason for attending to the
matter, since an appropriate and well-regulated action adds
immensely to the force of what is spoken, while anything
unbecoming, awkward, misplaced, or ineffective inevitably
palls upon the taste of the hearers, and hangs like a clog
upon one's efforts to produce effect.

(5.) Yet, with all the attention that should thus be paid
to the cultivation of native talent, of style, of action, and the
pains that should be taken on every hand to avoid obvious
blemishes and defects, there is still another point that may
be said to overtop the whole, and the more difficult to be
reached in practice, that to be attained in any competent
degree it is necessary that all the rest should be cast into
comparative forgetfulness ; it is the surrender of the heart

[1] *De Orat.* i. 28.

to the subject in hand, the power of letting oneself out into it. The soul of eloquence may be said to lie here; and without some measure of it, though there may be ever so finely constructed sentences, close and correct reasoning, graceful elocution, there cannot be the quickening impulse and persuasive speech which rivet the attention of the audience, and stir their hearts. For this the speaker must, above all, be possessed by the things which he comes to discourse of, impressed with a sense of their reality and importance. *Pectus est enim* [1] (to quote again Quinctilian) *quod disertos facit, et vis mentis;* and hence, he justly adds, even among unlearned persons, if only they are stirred by some powerful affection, words are not wanting. The mind then, instead of turning its eye inward on itself, or fixing on a single point, pours itself forth on many things in succession, as when one glances along a straight path everything is embraced that is in and around it; not the further end merely, but the things also that lie between us and it. So that whatever any one may possess by nature, or may have acquired by learning and art, to fit him for the work of popular discourse, he must, if he has risen to any degree of perfection in it, have acquired the power of losing sight of these when actually engaged in its discharge; the energies of his mind must be wholly concentrated upon his theme. Here, as in other accomplishments, 'the skill of the artist and the perfection of his art are never proved till both are forgotten. The artist has done nothing till he has concealed himself; the art is imperfect which is invisible; the feelings are but feebly touched, if they permit us to reason on the methods of their excitement. In the reading of a great poem, in the hearing of a noble oration, it is the subject of the writer and not his skill, his passion not his power, on which our minds are fixed. We see as he sees, but we see not him. We become part of him, feel with

[1] L. x. 7.

him, judge, behold with him ; but we think *of him* as little as *of ourselves*. The harp of the minstrel is untruly touched if his own glory is all that it records. The power of the masters is shown by their self-annihilation.'[1]

Such are some of the more vital and important considerations which require to be attended to in connection with the art of public speaking generally ; which, therefore, can no more be neglected with impunity by the preachers of the gospel, than by any others who seek to influence their fellow-men by their capacity of speech in public. No talent or even genius in the speaker, and no peculiarity in the subject he handles, can compensate for such neglect, or render palpable defects in regard to the qualifications mentioned otherwise than an occasion of comparative failure. It would not be easy, perhaps, to find in a brief compass a description which might seem more thoroughly aimed at exemplifying this than the account transmitted to us, mainly by Isaak Walton and Fuller, of the justly-renowned Richard Hooker. The delineation presents him to our view as a man ' of mean stature, and stooping, of humble or low voice, his face full of heat pimples, gesture none at all, standing stock-still, his eyes always fixed on one place to prevent his imagination from wandering, insomuch that he seemed to study as he spoke.' Add to which, what is said by Fuller : ' his style was long and pithy, driving on a whole flock of several clauses before he came to the close of a sentence ; so, when the copiousness of his style met not with proportionable capacity in his auditors, it was unjustly censured for perplexed, tedious, and obscure.' In short, so defective was he in all the more noticeable qualifications of an orator, that one might almost suppose the trial to have been formally made in Hooker, how the most profound intellect, the most varied learning, the most fertile and lofty imagination, conjoined with a winning simplicity of manners and a spirit of

[1] Ruskin, *Modern Painters*, i. p. 22.

I

sincere fervent piety might all be possessed, and yet leave
the possessor at the remotest distance from the position of
an attractive and powerful speaker. It was impossible,
indeed, that such a man could fail to produce at times deep
impressions in spite of all disadvantages, and be listened to
generally by a certain number with respectful and loving
affection. Even with the commonest audience, there were
passages so finely conceived and expressed, that they could
scarcely fail to fall upon the ear like the sound of sacred
melody, such as the following : [1] 'The light would never be
so acceptable were it not for the usual intercourse of darkness. Too much honey doth turn to gall, and too much
joy even spiritually would turn us to wantons. Happier a
great deal is that man's case, whose soul by inward desola-
tion is humbled, than he whose heart is through abundance
of spiritual delight lifted up and exalted above measure.
Better it is sometimes to go down into the pit with him who,
beholding darkness, and bewailing the loss of inward joy
and consolation, crieth from the lowest hell, " My God,
my God, why hast Thou forsaken me ? " than continually to
walk arm in arm with angels, to sit, as it were, in Abraham's
bosom, and to have no thought, no cogitation but " I thank
my God it is not with me as with other men."' But whatever effect occasional passages of this kind might have had,
they could not tell enough upon the general aggregate to
render Hooker, with all his gifts and excellences, I shall not
say a popular, but even what may be called an ordinarily
attractive and effective preacher.

It is time, however, to quit this more general part of the
subject, on which it was not my intention to do more than
indicate a few leading principles, or points demanding careful consideration. We must now turn to those things which
have a more direct and special reference to that kind of
public speaking with which we are here more immediately

[1] Sermon on the Certainty and Perpetuity of Faith.

concerned : the preparation and delivery of discourses on things pertaining to the kingdom of God and the salvation of men.

II. *The fitting subjects of discourse for the pulpit, and the solution of appropriate texts.*—It has been the all but universal practice in the Christian Church, since she possessed in any measure of completeness the canon of Sacred Scripture, to take some portion of its contents as the ground of the discourses which are addressed to congregations when they meet for purposes of worship. And the practice is in itself highly commendable, and carries with it obvious advantages. It is, first of all, an important as well as a becoming testimony to the supreme authority of Scripture as the revelation of God ; and as such, the Church's sole warrant and guide in regard to all that concerns spiritual and divine things. It virtually proclaims to all whom we address, ' To the law and to the testimony ;' here is the certain ground and warrant of whatever as Christians we believe, and do, and hope for.   Then, this practice of preaching from a text serves in a very natural and fitting manner to bring people acquainted with the matter of Scripture, and to give them both a more intelligent and more comprehensive knowledge of the things which it presents to their faith and obedience. Finally, it tends to impart a distinctive character both of sacredness and unity to what is spoken, whereby the preacher himself is benefited in having a channel, as it were, provided by the hand of God for the orderly presentation of his thoughts on particular themes ; and the hearer also has his recollections aided by a passage in the written word which he can keep before him, or fall back upon as he may need.

A certain choice, however, is necessary in regard to the subjects of discourse.   One is, not to set out with the idea that any passage, or portion of a passage, in Scripture, simply because it is an integral part of what is collectively the word of God, may on that account be fixed upon as the proper foundation of a discourse to an assemblage of Christian people. The whole of Scripture, when rightly interpreted and viewed in connection with its leading purport and design, is certainly profitable for religious instruction and pious uses ; but not always profitable to such ends in the way of public discourse. Its aim in some portions may be best accomplished by private meditation, while others require to be looked at complexly as parts of a general whole, and do not so readily admit of being isolated, and made the ground or occasion of a somewhat lengthened discourse.   Containing, as the Bible does, historical records of the human family during many successive generations, touching incidentally on an immense variety of circumstances and objects, current events and settled institutions, in its didactic parts referring to numberless productions of nature and works of art, as well as to the things which most deeply concern the present and eternal interests of mankind,—it were quite easy to find in the Bible texts from which discourses could be delivered perfectly textual in their character, and yet in their tenor entirely alien to the great interests of Christianity. The Rationalists of Germany, and the Unitarians of our own country and America, when turning the pulpit, as they have so often done, into an arena of philosophical, or simply moral and political discussion, never needed to be at any loss for texts to start with, and on which to hang their ideas. Volumes of sermons have issued from the press, each with their appropriate text, which as to subject and matter might have suited the taste of an audience in ancient Rome or Alexandria.   And it is probable that there was no want of texts, or occasional Scriptural quotations, in those continental discourses mentioned by Dr. Ammon, one series of which treated of subjects connected with rural economy and fallow-grounds ; another, of the cultivation of the silkworm ; while

a third unfolded the duties of Christians on the approach of
a contagious disease among cattle.   The pastors of evangelical congregations are in little danger of falling into such
senseless extravagances ; their very position is a safeguard
against it.   But they may still be liable to go to some extent
astray, unless they are careful to keep steadily in view the
great end of preaching, which, like that of the Bible itself,
is the glory of God in the salvation of men.   Where this is
rightly understood and appreciated, the preacher will feel that
he has something else to do than to search for texts and subjects which are out of accord with the spirit of the gospel.

At the same time, a certain latitude should undoubtedly
be allowed in this respect to the Christian pastor.   He may
not be always preaching directly on the great theme, and in
his range of subjects may imitate in a measure the variety
and fulness by which Scripture itself is distinguished.
Nothing may be altogether excluded from the pulpit which
has an influential bearing on the Christian life, or admits of
being handled in a Christian spirit.   But much of which
this can be said may still be unsuited to form the leading
topic of a sermon.   The pulpit has not been erected, as
justly remarked by Vinet,[1] ' in order that everything may
be there treated in a Christian manner ; it has a special
object, which is to introduce the Christian idea into life.
I should say, then,' he adds, ' that everything which does
not conduce directly to edification ; everything which an
ordinary hearer cannot of himself convert into the bread of
life, or at least which the preacher does not acknowledge to
be such, should not be made a subject of his preaching.'
Or, if a licence may at times be taken to go somewhat
beyond this precise line, it should be distinctly announced
as a kind of exceptional effort, called forth by the circumstances of the moment, and of such a nature as to carry, in
a manner, its own justification along with it.

[1] *Homiletics*, p. 51.

It is quite possible for a minister when going to preach on a subject in itself appropriate to connect it with an unsuitable text ; and here, perhaps, it is that preachers in evangelical communities are most in danger of being betrayed into an impropriety in the choice of their pulpit themes. There are several ways in which this may be done. It sometimes, perhaps, takes the form of choosing a text which, as the ground of a discourse on matters of grave moment, has an indelicate, but more commonly an odd and fantastic appearance, creating a sort of ludicrous bond of association in the minds of the hearers between the preacher's theme and the formal warrant or occasion found for it in Scripture. And anything of such a nature is as much out of place in connection with the text as with the discourse preached from it. 'Of all preaching,' says Baxter in his own emphatic style,—' of all preaching in the world that speaks not stark lies, I hate that preaching which tendeth to make the hearers laugh, or to move their minds with ticklish levity, and affect them as stage-players used to do, instead of affecting them with a holy reverence of the name of God.' What else could be the effect on a general audience when hearing texts like the following announced as the subject of discourse : ' The old shoes, and clouted upon their feet ;' 'The nine and twenty knives ;' 'The unturned cake ;' or ' The axe, alas ! Master, it was borrowed'? Such texts, or fragments of texts, have not unfrequently been preached from ; some of them are associated with the name of the eccentric Rowland Hill ; along with several others of a like kind, they are found in a series of sermons which appeared in this country not many years ago, with the designation, 'Sermons on unusual texts.' It is to be hoped such texts will ever remain *unusual*, and that if our ministers are going to address their congregations on the subject of violence and war, they will be able to connect it with a more suitable form of words than Ezra's nine and twenty knives, and will light upon something more becoming than the old and clouted shoes of the Gibeonites, from which to expose the various workings of hypocrisy and deceit, and man's vain attempts to mend himself. The object of choosing such texts is too palpable to escape the notice of even the humblest audience. They will readily perceive the tendency it exhibits to attract notoriety, and acquire a name for what is smart and peculiar. But precisely as this object is gained, the grand aim of preaching is lost, and the preacher himself sinks to the level of the man who indulges in a perverted ingenuity and a vicious taste.

Another and less offensive, though still decidedly objectionable form of the same inappropriateness consists in selecting texts, which only in a figurative, obscure, perhaps even fanciful manner, can be made to express the ideas which are to be deduced from them. Supposing the subject of discourse were to be the important theme of Christ's righteousness, as imputed or savingly applied to believers, it would scarcely be wise to connect its illustration and enforcement with such a text as Isa. xlv. 8, ' Drop down, ye heavens, from above, and let the skies pour down righteousness,' a text, if I mistake not, chosen for that purpose by the excellent Mr. Romaine, yet not fitly chosen, since it is at best too general a declaration for so specific a doctrine ; while a plentiful variety of passages might be found in the later Scriptures which unfold it in a much more distinct and categorical form. In like manner, if the subject were to be the connection between faith and works, it would surely be travelling out of the proper way for a fitting text to repair, as has sometimes been done, to Ex. xxxix. 26, ' A bell and a pomegranate, a bell and a pomegranate ;' the bell, as the symbol of an articulate call, being taken to represent the preaching of the gospel which demands faith from those who hear, and the pomegranate following in close connection, pointing, as is conceived, to the fruit of holiness, which ever springs from the belief of the truth. How many hearers would be disposed to accredit the doctrine, were this a fair sample of the texts that establish it? How many, after every possible explanation has been made of this particular text, would feel quite satisfied that the doctrine is really expressed there? And if so, how unwise is it to bring into the very foundations of the subject an element of uncertainty, and start as it were with a note of interrogation, an involuntary doubt in the minds of our audience! If a text *were* chosen which exhibits the doctrine under a typical or figurative aspect, it should still be one that admits of a clear and easily perceived application to the subject of discourse. For whatever the subject itself may be, and whatever the specific character of the text on which it is grounded, the latter should always possess two properties in relation to the former; it should be such as to present a solid, in contradistinction from a fanciful or questionable, basis of discourse, and it should be in its own nature ample enough to bear all that in doctrine or duty is raised on it.

In the Evangelical Church (so called) of Prussia, I may notice there exists a temptation which is almost unknown elsewhere, to hang sermons on texts with which they have a very slender connection. The temptation arises from the practice of having prescribed by public authority for every Sabbath and religious festival of the year a series of Bible lessons, from which the preacher is required to select the subject of discourse. Hence there must either be a considerable sameness in the pulpit ministrations, or some ingenuity must be exerted to deduce a variety of themes from a limited number of texts; preachers must turn over the passages submitted to them in every conceivable way, and extract from them not only what they more directly teach, but also what they incidentally suggest, or by some influential process can be made to imply. The sermons of Rheinhard

are striking specimens of this sort of ingenuity.   The miracle
of Christ, for example, in feeding the four thousand with a
few loaves and fishes (Mark viii. 1–9) furnishes a text for
discoursing on the duty of relying on oneself more than on
others. The narrative of the paralytic borne on a couch, and
let down in faith to the chamber where our Lord was teaching (Matt. ix. 1–8), is made the occasion for exhibiting the
kind of behaviour which ought to be maintained by Christians, on account of the confidence that is ready to be
reposed in them by those around them.   The word of our
Lord to Peter in Luke v. 10, 'From henceforth thou shalt
catch men,' gives rise to a lengthened exposition of the
principle, that the faithful discharge of the duties connected
with each one's particular calling forms a natural and fitting
qualification for the exercise of higher functions.

One cannot but feel that, in connecting such topics with the
texts mentioned, there is what carries an artificial and forced
appearance, the endeavour by a tortuous line of thought to
get at what should have been found accessible by a direct
approach. In a course of regular exposition through a book
of Scripture, it might be proper to introduce a few brief
remarks on the points thus incidentally raised in them ; but
it is another thing when the incidental in the text becomes
the one and all in the discourse.   This cannot but be felt
to be unnatural ; it wants simplicity and directness.   At the
same time, it may be perfectly legitimate and proper to single
out from a text some particular idea, which forms a subordinate rather than the principal part of its meaning ; and on
this, occasionally at least, to raise a discourse which may
be designed to serve some special purpose, or to meet some
peculiar phase of thought prevalent at the time.   Rheinhard
also furnishes a very suitable example of this description
in a sermon on Matt. ix. 24, where, when Jesus affirmed of
the daughter of Jairus that she was not dead but asleep, it
is observed of the people present that they laughed Him to

scorn ; and of Himself that, notwithstanding, He proceeded to raise her up again. On this Rheinhard takes occasion to discourse, not of the miracle, or of the attributes of character it manifested on the part of Christ, but of the truth that Christians will often find themselves called to do what shall appear foolish or ridiculous to the multitude ; that their principles may be, and often cannot but be, regarded as absurd, their faith in God illusory, their zeal for the divine glory extravagant, their magnanimity indiscreet. And so he urges on them the duty of looking above the superficial multitude, of even suspecting their own piety if it does not prove the occasion of a certain measure of opposition or wonder among worldly men, and of being cautious lest they should be led to join in casting ridicule or reproach on those who are only going farther than their neighbours in doing God service. A discourse of Dr. Chalmers on Acts xix. 27 may be pointed to as another and not less happy example of the same description. From the outcry of De- metrius and his workmen, that their craft was in danger by the spread of the gospel in Ephesus, he undertakes to show how perfectly compatible the growth and prevalence of Christianity is with the commercial prosperity of a people ; since, while it may operate to the discouragement or sup- pression of some forms of handicraft and modes of gain, it is sure to open the way to others, and these of a more healthful and satisfactory kind than those it has supplanted. Special applications of passages of Scripture after this fashion, if confined to particular occasions, or employed only at dis- tant intervals, may not only be free from any just exception, but productive of important benefits, serving as they do to exhibit the pregnancy of God's word and the manifold wisdom of the revelation it contains, in its adaptation even to the affairs of this life and the ever-varying evolutions of the world's history. But the practice should not be very often resorted to ; and as a general rule, the principle should be maintained, that the prominent ideas of the text should also form the chief burden of the discourse that is professedly based on it.

A still further form of misapplied taste or judgment in the choice of texts has sometimes been exhibited, by turning them into a cover for the display of wit, or for conveying sarcastically, perhaps also sincerely, a rebuke to certain persons in the congregation.   In the hands of some, this impropriety assumes the form only of an unbecoming levity, or ludicrous employment of Scripture, which has already been adverted to, and which, even when most cleverly done, is still to be condemned, because unsuited to the dignity and sacredness of the pulpit.   It is still more objectionable when, under the phraseology or connection of the text, a hit is made at individuals ; for the levity in such a case is aggravated by the indulgence of a personal pique, the gratification of a testy humour, in a manner that must always carry an ungenerous aspect, taking advantage of one's position to shoot an arrow at those who have no power to defend themselves.   Such liberties are scarcely known in this northern part of the land ; but the greater tendency to the humorous which is characteristic of England, a tendency which sometimes appears even on the tombstones disporting itself with the dead, has also been wont to give rather strange exhibitions of itself, after the fashion adverted to, from the pulpit. I remember being told, when residing in an English parish, that the minister had some time before been presented at an episcopal visitation of the district as negligent of some parts of parochial duty by a respectable solicitor, and that on the following Sabbath he had chosen for his text, 'And a certain lawyer stood up, tempting him.'   In a story very commonly reported of Dr. Paley (in the little volume, for example, by Mr. Christmas, on *Preachers and Preaching*), there is certainly what must be regarded as a much better specimen of humour in this line.   On the occasion of Pitt, when still a comparatively young man, but already in the proud position of Premier, revisiting Cambridge, where he had studied, and receiving marked attention there from many old associates, who were known to be eagerly looking to him for preferments, Paley, it is said, gave forth for his text the passage in St. John's Gospel, 'There is a lad here which hath five barley loaves and two small fishes ; but what are they among so many?'[1] But the best in such a case is bad ; the preacher of Christ's salvation necessarily stoops from his proper elevation, when in the very discharge of his office he makes himself known as a humorist. And to display this character in the selection of his text, is virtually to release his audience from concern about higher things, and let the thought of amusement prevail over a regard to edification.

In the choice of a text, however, something more is needed than to consider how far it may itself be fitted to serve as the foundation of a public discourse ; its *suitableness* also to the preacher's powers and present or prevailing tone of mind requires to be taken into account. That a striking or impressive sermon has been preached by one person from a particular text, is no reason why another, though perhaps of not inferior abilities as a man or character as a Christian, should expect to do the same. The theme, or the form in which the theme has been presented, while suited to the one, may somehow prove unsuitable to the other ; it may call for the exercise of sensibilities and gifts, a reach of thought or a kind of experience, which are far from being equally shared by both. This is a point which each individual must ascertain for himself. But let it be kept distinctly in mind, that there is a certain measure of adaptation

[1] The story is not quite correct. Paley did not actually preach before Pitt. He was not even at Cambridge when Pitt visited it ; but he remarked to some one, that if he had been the preacher on the occasion, such would have been his text. See Life by Wayland, *Paley's Works*.

needed in the text to the preacher, as well as in the text
to the theme and the audience.   Some can succeed well
enough with a general or comprehensive text, having power
to give it, by means of suggestive thought and varied illustration, the requisite individuality.   But more commonly
the preacher will require a text which has itself some kind
of individuality, presenting specific points in the history of
God's manifestations, or in the experience and character of
His people, for consideration.   Preachers of considerable
mark have confessed that they could never find themselves
properly at home, excepting with texts of this description.
And when respect is had to the very great diversity which
exists in men's natural as well as acquired characteristics,
the greater preponderance of intellect in one, of feeling in
another ; here the logical, there the imaginative, and there
again the emotional powers in greatest vigour; in some only
the simpler phases known of Christian experience, in others
the sounding of all its depths and heights ;—it is manifest
that there must be subjects and passages in the word of God
which, in order to a properly successful and effective treatment, will require minds of a particular kind of calibre and
religious susceptibility.   A well-educated and experienced
teacher of divine truth may have a *general fitness* for all
topics, and yet only for some a *special and peculiar* adaptation.

Whatever the particular subject may be on which the
pastor is going to discourse on the approaching Sabbath,
and whatever the text to be chosen for the purpose, there
is one rule which he should, as far as possible, regularly
observe ; he should have it sought out and fixed on in good
time, not left over to the latter part of the week.   The
advantage of such a method is, that the mind is not only
relieved from the flutter of uncertainty and doubt when the
moment of actual preparation arrives ; but has already so
far become prepared that it has had leisure to examine the

text itself, so as to get thoroughly conversant with its import and connection, and have the subject embraced in it turned over in various aspects and directions. The truth has thus had time to *steep*, as it were, in the mind, and enter *in succum et sanguinem;* so that when one comes to apply formally to the consideration of the subject, instead of hastily snatching at the first thoughts that present themselves, there is already obtained a general acquaintance with the main theme, and more or less of the specific matter suitable for its illustration called up. With the view also of facilitating this preliminary sort of preparation, the practice is not unworthy of notice, which has been followed with advantage by some, of noting in a memorandum-book such texts as have, in the course of one's reading or meditation, suggested themselves for themes of future discourse, indicating at the same time the lines of thought which it seemed advisable to pursue in connection with them. Topics and ideas occurring in this incidental way are often helpful in striking the proper key-note for more careful and prolonged consideration.

The suggestions now offered concerning the choice of subjects of discourse, it will be understood, have respect merely to the ordinary course of pastoral ministrations. There are peculiar and exceptional cases, sometimes perhaps furnished by the pastor himself, when he feels prompted to deliver his views publicly on subjects important in themselves, yet somewhat away from the beaten track of pastoral duty, as Dr. Chalmers in respect to his astronomical discourses ; sometimes, again, by the state of the congregation, when, to save it from prevailing error, or recover it from deep spiritual lethargy, a mode of preaching to some extent peculiar may be required, as in Mr. Cecil's congregation at St. John's, or Mr. Robert Hall's at Cambridge. Mr. Dale of Birmingham also, in a volume of *Week-Day Discourses*, has given a very good example of the treatment of a class of subjects far from unimportant, but which call for illustrations and details that might seem somewhat out of place in the regular ministrations of the pulpit. But for cases of such a nature no general instructions can be given ; each must be carefully weighed and considered by itself.

III. *The matter in pulpit discourses, with reference especially to fulness and variety.*—In discourses intended for stated congregations, it is undoubtedly of importance that there should be not only appropriate matter, but that also in considerable fulness and variety. *Usually* this ought to be the case, though not by any means *uniformly ;* for there may be occasions and subjects, in respect to which it is the part of wisdom to concentrate one's thoughts on merely one or two ideas, for the purpose of giving them a greater prominence or a deeper impression. This may sometimes be proper in addressing audiences which we have reason to believe are in a very ignorant or lethargic state of mind, when the one object, in a manner, is to rouse to spiritual thought and obtain a lodgment in men's minds for some grand principle of truth or duty. It may also be proper, in dealing with congregations which are partial and one-sided in their views on some point of Christian belief or morals, when again the great object of the preacher naturally is to drive them from their false position, and have the light of conviction let in upon them where precisely it is needed. It cannot be disputed that some of Dr. Chalmers' most powerful and effective discourses were of this description. They embody nothing more than one leading idea; but this is usually so diversified in the manner of statement, so varied in the illustration, presented in so many fresh and vivid colours, that the attention of the audience was never allowed to flag, and the impression produced in behalf of the engrossing theme was like that of successive and ever-deepening strokes of some mighty weapon. Such a style of preaching, however, requires intense energy and concentration in the preacher to be prac-

tised with success. Very rarely, indeed, would it be safe
for persons possessed of only average powers to attempt
it when preaching to congregations which are composed of
different classes and conditions of people. Even when
done with success as regards the quality of the discourse,
few congregations would feel quite satisfied with it as a rule,
because wanting in the variety which is requisite for the
health and nourishment of their spiritual life. Preachers
should bear in mind that, as congregations generally consist
of persons differing not a little in their intellectual and
spiritual states, as well as in their external circumstances
and relations, there is needed somewhat of a corresponding
variety in the thoughts and considerations which are presented to them at their regular meetings for worship. Nor
should it be forgotten that, with the larger portion of those
addressed, the discourses they hear on the Lord's Day constitute by much the greater part of the spiritual instruction
they are to receive, in all probability the only instruction
they are to get from a living voice during the entire week.
So that they will almost certainly feel like persons stinted in
their proper nourishment, unless matter for reflection, at
once solid in kind and considerably diversified in its manner
of administration, be imparted to them on the Sabbath.

The work of preaching is often considered with reference
to a specific standard of eloquence, according to which it is
either appreciated or condemned ; and when so considered,
the stirring of the emotions and the influencing of the moral
judgments and feelings, with the view of raising them to the
right spiritual tone, readily come to be contemplated as well-
nigh the one object to be aimed at. But this is never more
than a part of the proper aim and function of preaching. It
has to do as much with instruction as with persuasion ; and
the enlightenment of the understanding holds even a more
prominent, as it does also a prior, place in its formal design,
than the excitation of the feelings or the immediate exercise

of the will.   But, rightly viewed, the one aspect of the
matter might as well be included as the other ; for the
didactic or instructive element is not less essential than
the suasive in the notion of true eloquence.   The noblest
specimens of eloquence that have come down to us from
ancient times, or that have appeared in modern, are equally
remarkable for the measure of light they were fitted to impart in a brief compass to the audiences addressed, as by
their adaptation to rouse and interest their feelings.   If you
take of the former class the oration of Demosthenes for the
crown, or of the latter Hall's sermon on modern infidelity,
or his discourse on the death of the Princess Charlotte, you
will not readily find productions treating of like subjects
which in the same compass contain a larger amount of solid
thought, and presented in a form better fitted to give the
minds of the hearers a just and intelligent apprehension of
the leading points proper to the occasion.   Still, when in
ordinary language one speaks of eloquence or oratory, one
naturally thinks of what is chiefly addressed to the feelings,
what aims at rousing an apathetic indifference or overcoming a reluctant will by fervid argumentation or powerful
appeals.   In the popular understanding it has come to be
associated with a certain degree of impassioned pleading,
with the view of impressing and moving the heart.   This,
undoubtedly, has its place in the pulpit.   Yet there is much
also that belongs to a somewhat different category.   For
amid the general knowledge which may be said to prevail
in connection with divine things, there is still always room
for plain instruction, such as is fitted to lay open the
meaning of Scripture, to explain and illustrate the all-important matters contained in it, and to exhibit the nature and
extent of men's obligations in regard to them.   Hence the
reason for a good deal of variety in pulpit ministrations,
since they have so much ground to travel over, so many
phases both of truth and duty to make familiar to men's

K

minds. Especially is it important for preachers in Scotland to aim at such variety; for they have audiences to address which are constitutionally of a thoughtful and intelligent character, and which never can remain long satisfied with any kind of preaching which does not furnish considerable supplies of food for their intellectual and moral natures. Something of a less solid, though possibly of a more showy and sentimental kind, may be relished for a season; but, like a surface stream, it is sure to discover its own shallowness, and will soon be forsaken for what is really fitted to enlighten and edify. Even in connection with the same ministry there are probably not many congregations in Scotland that will not be able to distinguish between discourses which are deficient, as compared with those which are replete, in the respect under consideration, or that will fail to appreciate what has been maturely considered, if only delivered in a manner suited to their capacities and fitted to engage their attention.

There is here also, however, a certain middle course which is the best; for it is possible to err by excess as well as by defect. And if, in preparing to address a congregation on any passage of Scripture, one should set out with the intention of saying everything of any moment that could be advanced on the subject, the discourse might no doubt contain a rich collection of material, but it would almost certainly fail of its proper effect with a general audience; they would feel fatigued and oppressed by it. Some of our older sermon writers fell into this mistake; Barrow may be named as a notable example. On some of the subjects discussed in his sermons it is scarcely possible to suggest any relevant consideration which had not already presented itself to his own fertile mind. But then a sort of repletion is created. The mind feels dissatisfied that nothing is left for itself to supply; and a sense of weariness is experienced even in reading so much upon the one theme, which would be

greatly increased if listening to it as a spoken discourse.
Barrow's age, however, was one of patience and leisure, and
fondness for detail; ours, on the contrary, is one of business and despatch; and people might at least bear with
and even admire then what they would not tolerate now.
It is indispensable for the great ends in view that there be
selection; and in the discrimination necessary to select
what is most fitting and appropriate, lies a main part of the
skill of an interesting and effective preacher. He has to
leave as much unsaid as what he actually says; and by the
judicious choice and excellent arrangement of his matter,
still more than by its quantity, he has to make his impression. The ancient apothegm ascribed to Hesiod has here
a quite legitimate application, 'The half is more than the
whole,' more, that is, with reference to the proper aim and
purpose of the speaker. By what he chooses out of the
whole materials before him he will be able to convey, in
the time allotted him, a far clearer idea of the leading
features of his subject, and impress it more vividly upon
the minds of his audience, than if he attempted to fill up the
picture by crowding into it every point of inferior moment
that might suggest itself to his mind.

There is, however, a possibility of another kind, a danger
of allowing the variety and fulness of which we have been
speaking to overshadow in a measure what should ever be
the grand theme of pulpit ministrations, a danger which the
very intelligence and generally diffused Christianity of the
age tends to increase. The fundamental truths of the gospel
are familiar to the bulk of his audience, as well as to the
preacher himself; and the cardinal doctrines of the Bible
having a recognised place in their creed, it seems no longer
needful to enter into any elaborate explanations concerning
them, or even to give them, perhaps, a very frequent and
prominent place in his subjects of discourse. The consequence comes to be, that the greater is to some extent

sacrificed to the less ; not formally displaced, indeed, yet practically allowed to lose the position of peerless value and importance to which it is entitled. The preacher endeavours to meet the desire of his hearers for instruction of a diversified kind ; he strives to give interest to his pulpit ministrations by introducing a multiplicity of topics, which by their number, if not by their freshness or importance, may serve to keep alive attention. And thus the pulpit is apt to be turned into an instrument of general religious culture and moral improvement, instead of being employed as the chosen means for awakening souls to a concern for salvation, and bringing them under the powers of the world to come.

Mr. Isaac Taylor, in one of his most thoughtful productions, *Saturday Evening*, a considerable time ago adverted to the tendency of things in the direction now indicated. He stated that, in the case of many an evangelical minister, ' the prime truth of the Scriptures scarcely occupies more than the proportion of one to ten in the gross amount of his public labours. The glory of Christ as the Saviour of men, which should be always as the sun in the heavens, shines only with an astral lustre ; or as one light among others. It is a natural, though not very obvious consequence of the intellectual progress which the religious community has made.' In regard also to what is called *intellectual preaching*, he says that it can hardly be made to consist with a bold, simple, and cordial proclamation of the message of mercy. Its fruit, he thinks, will commonly be an obtuse indifference in regard to the most affecting objects of the Christian faith. And he adds, ' The tendency at the present moment of the better informed portions of the religious body towards intelligent frigidity is a grave matter, and one especially which should lead to a reconsideration of our several systems of clerical initiation. The cause of so fatal a practical error should be made known, if the fact

be so, that numbers of those who come forth upon the
Church as candidates of the Christian ministry are fraught
with all qualifications and all acquirements, rather than
fervour and simplicity of spirit in proclaiming the glad
tidings of life.'

The state of things here described, it will readily be
understood, had respect to England rather than to Scotland,
and to England mainly as represented by the Established
Church.   It has prevailed to a considerable extent there for
many generations, and is largely owing to that almost exclusive regard which in the more highly educated classes, and
especially in those who pass through the universities to the
Church, is paid to the cultivation of science and classical
learning, or to the general refinement of the taste and
manners, while special preparation and fitness for official
duty are comparatively neglected.   It cannot, however, be
doubted that, since the remarks just quoted were penned,
the tendencies complained of have undergone abatement.
In most things, not an insipid frigidity, but life, warmth,
activity, have become the order of the day.   Even as regards
ministerial agency, it has seldom, perhaps, exhibited more of
lively and energetic working in England than at the present
time ; however much room there may still be in many
quarters for improvement, and particularly in regard to the
free and earnest proclamation of the gospel.   In *our* corner
of the land the change, so far as change can be marked,
has manifestly been in the right direction ; in the revival of
a more earnest Christianity, and a demand for that kind of
preaching which gives its proper prominence to the person
and the work of Christ.   Still, there are causes in operation
which constitute an element of danger.   The desire already
noticed, the necessity, in a sense, of diversifying the ministrations of the pulpit, is perhaps the chief one ; but this
again is increased by the growing literary character of the
age, and the tendency thence arising to assimilate prepara-

tions for the pulpit too closely in form and style to those of the press ; so that what they gain in elaboration, in correctness, in vigour of thought or variety of illustration, they are apt, in the same proportion, to lose in Scriptural simplicity and spiritual power. The grand safeguard here, as in so many other things connected with the ministry of the gospel, lies in the personal faith and devotedness of the pastor. If matters are but right there, they cannot be far wrong in what may be called the very heart and blood of his ministerial life. And as in the gospel itself everything is found linked on one side or another to the mediation of Christ, so in his public ministrations he will never want opportunities, whatever may be the particular theme or passage handled, to point the attention of his audience to the central object, and press on *their* regard what is uppermost in *his own*, namely, the surpassing love and beauty and preciousness of the Crucified One, and the alone sufficiency of His great salvation. The occasions, indeed, will be very few, if they occur at all ; they will be exceptions to the general tenor of his ministerial labours, in which the people are allowed to depart from the house of God without having had presented to them the essentials of saving doctrine. The Apostle to the Gentiles, in this respect pre-eminently the model of a Christian teacher, amid manifold diversities of subject and object, things present and things to come, never lost sight of his calling to preach the unsearchable riches of Christ, and made the crucified Redeemer the Alpha and the Omega of his testimony to men.

IV. *The principles to be observed in pulpit discourses as to order and arrangement.*—Next to the substance of pulpit discourses, or the matter contained in them, comes the consideration of its order and arrangement. No absolute and unvarying rule can, of course, be laid down here ; for different subjects necessarily call for different modes of treatment as to form or method ; and sometimes what might be best adapted to the mental capacities or acquired habitudes of one person, would prove quite unsuitable to another. At the same time, as there must be an order, so one may say in general, it should be *natural* and, as far as possible, *textual,* which will be found to contribute very materially to the securing of freshness and variety. For it is one of the characteristics of Scripture, that it exhibits great diversity, not merely in respect to the topics contained in it, but also to the very form and manner in which they are presented. And if the text is made the foundation, as well for the particular aspect and relations of the subjects handled as for the leading ideas involved in them, it will be comparatively easy to avoid falling into the same track ; diversities of many kinds will, as a matter of course, come into play. It will be quite otherwise if texts are taken merely as mottoes to head a discourse on some topic connected with Christian faith or practice ; for as often as the same subject returns for consideration, being dissociated from any individual traits or special circumstances, it will naturally present itself in much the same aspect that it did before, and be discoursed of much after the same manner. Nor does the result come to be materially different when texts are split, as it were, into fragments, and each part taken as the ground of a separate discourse. For, though this seems in one sense to be making much of the text, in reality it is making little ; since the text, by such a process, necessarily loses its proper individuality, and the several clauses or words of which it is composed are turned into so many mottoes or hints, whereon to raise a discussion on some point of Christian doctrine, or if of a practical nature, on some particular course of duty. The Puritan divines were fond of this method. A single text very commonly became in their hands the introduction to a whole body of divinity, or gave occasion to an entire series of discourses on some branch of Christian life or experience. Baxter's *Saint's Rest* is a specimen, certainly one of the best specimens, of this kind of sermon writing ; and so also are the more important of Howe's works, his *Blessedness of the Righteous, Delighting in God, Living Temple*, etc. They all started from an appropriate text, and by successive discourses from this they grew into considerable treatises. Howe was possessed of a singularly rich and elevated cast of mind ; so that he could infuse a measure of freshness and variety into a system that was essentially monotonous, and throw out new thoughts and illustrations even when travelling anew the same paths which had been trodden before. Yet with such a system even he could not avoid frequently repeating himself, as any one may see who will be at the trouble of comparing some of the treatises with each other. He will find not the same subjects merely recurring, but the same line of thought pursued regarding them, sometimes also the same figures and images used in illustration of them. To a congregation, also, it must have been wearisome to hear always the same text announced for consideration, not on one or two consecutive Sabbaths merely, but for months. The simplicity and freshness of gospel preaching was to a considerable extent lost by such a method ; there was too much seen in it of the hand of man, systematizing and arranging the materials of Scriptural truth and duty.[1]

In the present day there is comparatively little danger of a return to the Puritan method. But the same method in a sort of reduced form was much followed in Scotland at a greatly later period, and is not yet, perhaps, altogether disused. I have myself known persons, much beloved as men, and highly esteemed as preachers, who followed it, though never without a manifest disadvantage, arising from the

[1] It may be added that the preachers in question endeavoured to compensate for the defect mentioned by often introducing texts incidentally, and dwelling on them. Traill was particularly good at that.

comparatively little scope it afforded for the introduction of
the expository element, and the difficulty it presented of
avoiding an ever-recurring sameness.   According to this
plan of discourse, a text is taken embracing two or three
principal words or ideas ; and, instead of these being viewed
in their mutual connection, and discussed with reference to
the leading object in the eye of the sacred penman at the
time, they are taken apart, and made each the subject of a
separate discourse.   For example, such a text as Eph. ii. 8,
' By grace are ye saved through faith,' would not be treated
in its obvious unity as a declaration of the fact that the
salvation of the gospel has its origin in the free grace of
God, and in consequence must be received by men in faith
as a gift from above.   It would be divided into three distinct parts : the first comprising what is meant by the term
salvation, the second what is to be understood by the word
grace, and the third the relation between faith and salvation
that is by grace.   No doubt, by such a piecemeal treatment
everything that is in the verse might be fully brought out ;
but a great deal also that is not even incidentally found in
it would almost certainly be brought into consideration ;
and a vein of thought would inevitably be pursued, which
as a matter of course would be resumed when other texts
were chosen in which the same terms occurred.   Thus, if
Heb. ii. 3, ' How shall we escape, if we neglect so great salvation ?' were selected, and treated after the like fashion,
we should necessarily again have the import of *salvation*
discussed ; this would form, as before, the subject of one
discourse, and the thoughts presented in connection with
it could not deviate much from the previous track.   Of this
style of preaching Dr. Campbell, with some justice, though
not without a measure of exaggeration, said that those who
followed it, a good many undoubtedly in *his* day, had in a
manner but one sermon.   ' The form, the mould, into which
it was cast was different according to the different texts,

but the matter was altogether the same. You had invariably the preacher's whole system—original sin, the incarnation, the satisfaction, election, imputed righteousness, justification, and so forth.' He adds, that the preachers after this plan very slightly touched upon the duties which the Christian religion requires ; evidently intending by the remark to convey a censure on the evangelical preaching of his day, as improperly negligent of the practical bearing of Christianity ; for there can be no doubt that it was the more evangelical portion of the ministers in Scotland who in Campbell's time preached in the manner indicated by him. But it never was true of that party as a class that they were remiss in enforcing the moral obligations of the gospel, and it was true beyond contradiction that the parishes in which they ministered contained much more both of religion and morality than those where a different sort of preaching prevailed. With so cumbrous and formal a style of discourse, however, it may readily be supposed that the space for practical instruction would often be unduly limited ; and they would also probably be influenced to a considerable extent by the conviction, that the truth itself had only to be received aright to bring forth the fruits of righteousness.

But to revert to the subject itself, with the view of ensuring a natural and interesting variety in the exhibition of gospel truth, and also of connecting that exhibition in the minds of the people with the very terms of its announcement in Scripture, it is of importance that the text be really taken as the guide, in some way, to the order and method of treatment, as well as to the subject itself which it suggests for consideration. In order to this, it will, of course, be necessary to view the matter contained in it, not so much in its general and absolute character, as in its relative bearing and connection of parts ; and to regard some as primary, and others as subordinate, not with respect to what they may be in themselves, but in respect to the statement made concerning them in the particular text, and with an eye to its more definite scope. Thus in the text just referred to, ' By grace are ye saved through faith,' it is not salvation generally, or in its entire compass, that we are called to consider, nor faith in all its acts and operations. The more special object of the declaration is the *gratuitous character* of salvation, as being of grace on the part of God, in contradistinction to all that can be called works or merit on the part of man ; and as the necessary counterpart of this, its connection with the recipiency of faith in them who actually experience it. A discourse founded on such a text, after some preliminary statements, including perhaps, in order to prevent all ambiguity, a brief explanation of the terms *grace* and *salvation*, should manifestly have for its leading theme the gratuitous nature of salvation ; which might be exhibited, first, in regard to the provision of salvation through the mission and work of Christ, the *objective* aspect of it ; then, secondly, in regard to its appropriation by the soul through the effectual agency of the Holy Spirit, the *subjective* aspect; and from this may be shown, thirdly, the correspondence between a salvation so provided and so administered on the part of God, and the exercise of faith on ours, so as to bring out clearly the principle, if by grace, then of necessity by faith. And so in general, respect should commonly be had to the particular aspect in which the facts or ideas are presented in the text, and to the relation of greater or less prominence in which they stand one to another.

It is to be understood that these are only general directions, not by any means to be converted into rules of stringent uniformity. The Christian minister is under no imperative obligation to take the precise aspect and order of the subject presented in the text as his own. He may chalk out in this respect a path for himself, if some particular mode of treatment has commended itself to his mind. Especially he may do so when he is dealing with matters of a somewhat general nature, and on which the testimony of a specific text is less peculiarly needed; in such a case, if a particular line of reflection has suggested itself to him as the best for his purpose, it were undoubtedly wise to follow it. Yet I would rather that this formed the exception than the rule; that for the most part discourses were thrown into a textual form, the more so, as such a method tends to preserve a habitual and reverent regard to Scripture, as the fountain of all spiritual truth and instruction, while it cherishes the feeling that the preacher is not so properly declaring his own mind, as expounding and setting forth the mind of God. He will thus be able to work into men's thoughts, not the truth of God merely, but the very word in which that truth is embalmed. And it is this word of the living God which in all the more anxious and stirring movements of the soul is the great thing, the true germinating seed; as was well noticed by the acute and pious Halyburton in one of his later sayings, ' It is remarkable,' said he, 'that though God may make use of the words of man in letting into the meaning of Scripture, yet it is the very word of Scripture whereby He ordinarily conveys the comfort, or advantage of whatever sort; it is the tool of God's own framing that works the effect.' The history of genuine revivals, and indeed the private records of every ministry which has been much blessed for good, afford constant illustrations of this. And as it is the peculiar advantage of preaching above all other kinds of public speaking, and the main secret of its strength, that as it has the word of God to handle and apply, so it should be the aim of every preacher—the very method he employs should show it to be his aim—to do honour to this word, and secure for its utterances an enduring place in the minds of his auditors.

The whole, however, is by no means settled as to the order and arrangement of discourses when it is admitted, that as far as possible there should be an adherence to the course of thought indicated in the text itself.   For, with this general understanding, different persons might still pursue very different paths ; by one the ideas proper to the subject might be exhibited in a clear, exact, and logical method ; while, in the hands of another, the same ideas might be so exhibited as to embarrass rather than assist the memory, and disturb the natural sequence and connection of thought. There are preachers who seem always to be speaking to the text, and yet make no satisfactory progress in its elucidation ; often, it may be, uttering suitable or even profound thoughts, but in so loose or discursive a manner, that it is scarcely possible to retain any very distinct recollection of what has been said.   And there are others who have a method, and a method, too, based upon the text, who yet fail to present their thoughts in that natural progression, that dependence of part upon part, which is necessary to sustain attention, and leave a definite impression of the course of inquiry or reflection on the memory.   It was, no doubt, the differences observable in this respect, and the great importance of having the train of thought rightly adjusted, that led Herder to say, ' I easily pardon all defects except those of arrangement.'   He meant, that defects of this kind were more fatal, because they were like an organic disorder in the system ; they struck the whole discourse with feebleness, or involved it in confusion ; while others belonging to the execution would affect it only in particular parts, and might admit to some extent of compensation.

It is very justly said also by Vinet[1] upon this point, that a proper arrangement ' not only throws aside that which wanders from the unity of the subject, but assists also in finding everything which is included in the subject.   Many things which we had not previously seen are then discovered ; many lines of thought are finished, many intervals are filled

[1] *Homiletics*, p. 234.

up. It is the same with order in the arrangement of a subject as with economy in that of a fortune ; it enriches. Besides, arrangement gives or restores to each of the elements of which the subject is composed its real importance. Sometimes in separating ideas which were at first view confounded together ; sometimes in grouping what appeared separate, in managing contrasts, relations, subjects, or comparison, and luminous reflections of one idea upon another, we give to each of these ideas a new and unforeseen value.'

But when we have said this, we have said nearly all that can be done in a general way. Subjects of discourse differ so much, and so many diversities also exist in men's individual tendencies and habits of thought, that minute and stereotyped prescriptions would be entirely out of place. It is wiser to follow the discretion and judgment of Quinctilian, who, at the commencement of his Book vii., when he comes to speak of the arrangement that ought to be adopted in forensic discourses, abstains from laying down specific directions for every orator and every subject. He merely states that there ought always to be a *divisio*, a breaking up of the whole matter into distinct portions ; a *partitio*, that is, a fitting and orderly collocation of those portions, so as to connect properly together those that precede and those that follow ; and a *dispositio*, or a right distribution of topics and ideas to their several heads. But he immediately adds, that it may be expedient often to take different modes in carrying one's plan into execution, and points in proof to the two great speeches of Æschines and Demosthenes, in which, while both treating of one subject, and both admirable in their respective kinds, a precisely reverse order was followed. The accuser, Æschines, began with the question of right or law, where his strength lay ; the defender, Demosthenes, on the other hand, skilfully introduced all other things which seemed to favour his position first, and left the question of law to the last, when he had already won the favourable opinion of his judges. In reference to discourses for the pulpit, I would say first, that there should always be some clear and definite arrangement of the subject in the mind of the preacher, such as to admit of its being handled in so many distinct and regularly distributed portions. No matter whether it be an arrangement which has been adopted or might suggest itself to others or not, let it only be one that commends itself to the preacher's own mind as fit and proper. Secondly, it ought to be of such a nature that he can present it to the view of his hearers in a way they can readily apprehend ; therefore an order that does not turn upon minute and shadowy distinctions, and is neither very meagre on the one side nor very prolix and complicated on the other. And, finally, it should be an order which exhibits some principle, not merely of connection, but also of progression ; so that there may be room for the preacher's own mind growing, as it proceeds, in some quality of thought or feeling, and room also for the minds of the audience enjoying the interest of a conscious advancement. The interest will inevitably flag on the part both of speaker and of hearer if there is no sensible progress in some definite line ; or if, in a later division of the subject, there is a coming back again upon ground which has been already traversed in an earlier. Whatever the precise line thus marked out may be, whether it proceed from the more general to the more particular, or from the particular to the general; from cause to effect, or from effect to cause ; from doctrine to duty, or from duty to doctrine ; whatever it be, there should, if possible, be some easily recognised progression, such as may enable speaker and hearer alike to feel that they are not standing still or moving in a circle, but proceeding from one stage to another, in a course of spiritual contemplation or rational inquiry.

These plain directions may suffice for ordinary cases.

But it should be ever borne in mind that nothing here can be done, as it should be done, exactly to order; that no rules or prescriptions as to method can save the preacher who would succeed in the proper treatment of his subjects from thinking out his own plan, and adjusting the materials of discourse for himself. He may fitly enough take hints; occasionally, may even adopt an order which he knows to have been struck out by another; but even then he must by personal effort make it his own. And if to save himself from such labour he should make a practice of resorting to skeletons and outlines, he may rest assured that his discourses will also retain not a little of the skeleton character; they will not have much about them of the warmth of flesh and blood.[1]

I only add further, that while an order and a division also should commonly be adopted, it does not follow that this should always be formally announced. Usually, I think, it should be so, as people naturally desire to know, when going to be addressed at some length, what is the series of topics likely to be brought under consideration. But a tame, mechanical uniformity is to be avoided. Sometimes the interest may be best sustained, and the sense of novelty

[1] I have mentioned only one objection to the general use of such helps; but undoubtedly it is also objectionable, as Dr. Shedd urges, on the score of morality; not quite to the same extent that abstracting whole sermons is, yet in a measure. 'A preacher ought to be an honest man throughout. Sincerity, godly sincerity, should characterize him intellectually as well as morally. His plans ought to be the genuine work of his own brain. Not that he may not, at times, present a plan and train of thought similar to those of other minds; but he ought not to know of it at the time. Such coincidences ought to be undesigned, the result of two minds working upon a similar or the same subject, each in an independent way, and with no intercommunication. Then the product belongs to both alike; and the coincidence results from the common nature of truth and the common structure of the human mind, and not from a servile copying of one mind by another.'—*Homiletics*, p. 105.

gratified, by simply announcing as they arise the successive heads of discourse ; while the memory of the hearers may be assisted by a brief recapitulation of the particulars near the close.[1]

V. *The scope that may justly be allowed in preaching to the individual traits and characteristics of the preacher.*—It is a question of some moment, especially as regards the structure and composition of discourses, what scope should be allowed to the preacher in the indulgence of any tastes, tendencies, or habitudes of thought that may more peculiarly distinguish him ?   Should he, as a preacher of the gospel, endeavour to

[1] Sensible and good directions, though somewhat brief, and, as far as they go, coinciding with what has been said above on the structure and method of discourses, may be seen in the *Directory for Public Worship.* For example, ' In analyzing and dividing his text, he is to regard more the order of matter than of words ; and neither to burden the memory of the hearers in the beginning with too many members of division, nor to trouble their minds with obscure terms of art.   In raising doctrines from the text, his care ought to be, *first*, that the matter be the truth of God ; *secondly*, that it be a truth contained in or grounded on that text, that the hearers may discern how God teacheth it from thence ; *thirdly*, that he chiefly insist on those doctrines which are principally intended, and make most for the edification of his hearers.   The doctrine is to be expressed in plain terms ; or if anything in it need explanation, it is to be opened, and the consequence also from the text cleared.   The parallel places of Scripture confirming the doctrine are rather to be plain and pertinent than many, and, if need be, somewhat insisted upon and applied to the purpose in hand.   The arguments or reasons are to be solid, and, as much as may be, convincing.   The illustrations of what kind soever ought to be full of light, and such as may convey the truth into the hearer's heart with spiritual delight.   If any doubt, obvious from Scripture, reason, or prejudice of the hearers seem to arise, it is very requisite to remove it, by reconciling the seeming differences, answering the reasons, and discovering and taking away the causes of prejudice and mistake.   Otherwise, it is not fit to detain the hearers with propounding or answering vain or wicked cavils, which, as they are endless, so the propounding and answering of them doth more hinder than promote edification.'

L

suppress these? Or, should he here also give them free scope, and let them impart their full impress to the form in which he presents the great theme of salvation to his fellow-men? It is much more easy to put such questions than to answer them. But, in the general, I would say, that within certain limits, in the exercise of what may be called a decent and regulated freedom, it is perfectly allowable to give play to individual powers and susceptibilities, to the qualities which distinguish one man's mind from another; and that it may even be for the advantage of the work in hand, may tend to the more effective ministration of the word, if that measure of freedom is exercised by the preacher.

There is a general principle here which is of wide application to the relations and interests of the gospel; and it may not be out of place to make a few remarks on its more extended bearing, before considering how it applies to the specific subject of pulpit ministrations. We may the rather do so, as it is the natural tendency of the prelections and training of an academical course to aim at the production of attainments which lie within the reach of all who are possessed of respectable parts, rather than at the cultivation of peculiar powers, and the exhibition of distinctive excellences. A common education in theology, as well as other branches of learning and study, necessarily makes account of powers and attainments which the subjects of it have, or may have, in common with each other, not of those in which they mutually differ; it aims at establishing, as far as possible, a sort of community of acquirement and fitness for work. This is manifestly unavoidable; no theological training could succeed in its objects without looking thus at the general agreements more than at the specific and divergent tendencies of the minds subjected to its influence. And, indeed, it is requisite for the safe and profitable development, in due time, of what *is* special and peculiar to each.

For it is a great principle, pervading all the departments of nature, and needful to be borne in mind by those who would attain to eminence in anything for which they may have even a particular aptitude, that as there is nothing general which does not also possess something individual, so there is nothing individual but what springs from, or has its points of contact with, the general.   Whatever may distinguish one mind from another in its powers and tendencies, its veins of thought or emotional actings,—if it be simply an exercise or development of what nature has given, not a diseased and morbid affection, it will always find a measure of correspondence in other minds, something, however inferior in strength, to sympathize with it and respond to it.

It is well that this should be fully known and considered by those who are called by their position and aims in life not only to acquire a certain distinction for literary gifts and attainments, but also to possess the power of influencing the judgments and moving the hearts of others.   As such, they must stand above, and yet be on a footing with, those they have to deal with ; they must have certain things peculiarly their own, and yet through these find access to the common understandings and bosoms of their fellow-men ; and this they can only do by abstaining from all vicious excess, or by so cultivating the particular and distinctive elements in their mental constitution, as to prevent them from running into discordance with what is general.   'One touch of nature,' one great poet has said, 'makes the whole world kin;' it does so even though the touch be in itself of a peculiar kind, though it carry a very distinctive impress from the hand that gives it ; yet, being a touch of *nature*, conveying a genuine throb of feeling from one human bosom to another, it cannot but awaken a hearty response.   On this ground a great German authority, the greatest, indeed, in matters of this description (Goethe), said to a youthful disciple (Eckermann), 'You need not fear lest what is peculiar should want sympathy.

Each character, however peculiar it may be, and each object which you represent, from the stone up to man, has generality; for there is repetition everywhere, and there is nothing to be found once in the world.' Nothing, we must understand him to mean, in its fundamental elements; *these* are not found once merely anywhere, but are repeated in all objects of the same kind, while still in every particular object they have their specific combination and their characteristic development. So that if there should be in any writer or public speaker some preponderating talent or bias which is allowed to grow into a marked characteristic, it may be done, not only without the risk of his thereby losing hold of the sympathies of his fellow-men, but even with the effect of securing for him a firmer and deeper hold of them than might otherwise have been possible. For such is the constitution of the human mind, that so long as the individual characteristics of thought and feeling root themselves in the general, their very individuality gives them a freshness and power, it wins for them a sway over our hearts which an undistinguished flatness and generality never can command. We are touched by the greater strength and prominence of that of which we are ourselves not altogether unconscious; touched the more, as we see it working with a buoyant force and energy, far beyond anything of which we know ourselves to be capable.

The most eminent example of this in the religious sphere is Christ, viewed simply as the great teacher of the world; since, appearing as He did in an age and generation remarkable for their commonplace, one might almost say their effete character, there yet is in His manner of teaching, alike in respect to meaning and form, the expression of an individuality so marked, that nothing similar to it has ever again appeared among men. Yet nowhere can we find words that are in such general accord with the heart of humanity, words that reach so far and pierce so deep; the power of which is felt equally among high and low, by the man of profound culture as by the unlettered peasant.   What a depth was there in *His* look into nature !   In *His* revelations, what a disclosure of the mind and purposes of Heaven! Yet, withal, what a transparent simplicity in the one !   And in the other, what profound agreement with the better cravings and convictions of the enlightened reason !   Among the leading apostles, also, you see a measure of the same striking but genuine idiosyncrasies ; each giving indication, in his own particular way, of characteristic peculiarities of thought and feeling ; but along with these combining so much of simplicity and naturalness, that all who read their productions in a right spirit feel in unison with them, as if there were the answering of heart to heart ; and this even in regard to the more peculiar parts of their writings.   I should never, perhaps, myself have thought, if discoursing of the propriety of that retired demeanour which becomes the modesty of women, of connecting it with their lengthened tresses and overshadowing veils ; and these again with their original formation out of man, and the place they were from the first destined to hold in society.   I might have wanted the spiritual insight and delicacy of perception to see in such things nature's signs and witnesses to the fit position and proper bearing of woman.   But when presented as they are by the Apostle Paul in his First Epistle to the Corinthians, I am quite ready to enter into their spirit, and recognise their suitableness.   I am sensible that they have a foundation in nature ; and he who acts for me as nature's interpreter in the matter, applies in doing so a touch that makes me kin to him.

When speaking thus of nature, I am not to be understood as meaning that all here is simply of nature, as in the case of the poet, the artist, or the orator.   In the sacred writers primarily, and then also in those who at any period have to discourse of divine things, a higher element comes into play ; one by which nature is raised above itself, and sanctified to do service to God. Yet nature, let it be remembered, is not dissolved by this higher element; and no more dissolved in its separate individuality than in its general powers and properties. Every distinctive bent or original impulse of nature may still have its free and genial exercise, only elevated in its aim, hallowed in its forms of manifestation, by the baptism it has received into the spirit of truth and holiness. When so baptized, it is not lost, but renovated, and made capable of loftier aspirations and more energetic movements.

One has only to reflect how it is with the common run of believers. Of those who become, through the reception of the truth, sincere and earnest followers of the Lord Jesus Christ, a very large proportion are, no doubt, persons of quite ordinary minds, without any remarkable natural characteristic, either as to capacity for thought, sensibility of heart, or strength of will ; bearing, indeed, no very marked individuality in any respect. But from the moment they come under the power of divine truth, and are made partakers of the gift of God, this itself stamps them with an individuality ; it quickens into action powers and motions which were latent before ; in one prominent direction their mind acquires a determined bent ; and instead of the original tameness and insipidity which was wont to appear in their general tone of thought and feeling, there is now an intelligence, a discernment, an application of the right and good, sometimes even an elevation of spirit and strength of devotedness, which throw around their state and character a well-defined and estimable personality. Still more will such an effect of vital Christianity be perceptible in any one if he should be distinguished by any of the larger gifts of nature, whatever may be its precise character ; whether it may hold more directly of the reason, the imagination, the emotions, or the will, the more thoroughly it becomes imbued with the spirit of the gospel, and is directed into the channels of Christian worth and usefulness, the more will it acquire, so to speak, its proper set, and work to the production of important results.

Now it is the same thing, only in a higher degree and more conspicuously displayed, which often discovers itself with the more eminent preachers of the gospel, in their more impressive and memorable utterances. In listening to these, nothing perhaps strikes us more than the seeming naturalness of what is spoken, and its fitness and force for the occasion, although it may be such as would probably never have occurred to ourselves, or if in substance it had occurred, would not have been thrown into the touching or impressive form that it has assumed in the speaker's hands. Take the following, for example, from F. Robertson, as illustrative of the unexpectedness coupled with the certainty of the Second Advent:[1] 'Every judgment coming of Christ is as the springing of a mine. There is a moment of deep suspense after the match has been applied to the fuse which is to fire the train. Men stand at a distance and hold their breath. There is nothing seen but a thin, small column of white smoke, rising fainter and fainter, till it seems to die away. Then men breathe again . . . [but presently] the low, deep thunder sends up the column of earth majestically to heaven, and all that was on it comes crashing down again in its far circle, shattered and blackened with the blast. It is so with this world. By God's word the world is doomed. The moment the suspense is past. . . . We have fallen upon days of scepticism. There are no signs of ruin yet. We tread upon it like a solid thing fortified by its adamantine hills for ever. There is nothing against that but a few words in a printed book. But the world is ruined ; and the spark has fallen ; and just at the moment when serenity is at its height, "the heavens shall

[1] *First Series of Ser.* p. 177.

pass away with a great noise, and the elements shall melt with fervent heat, and the feet of the Avenger shall stand on the earth." '

Or, to take an example which carries with it a still more marked individuality, what a service does imagination render to the moral energy and fervid reasoning of Dr. Chalmers, not only in his astronomical discourses, but also when handling a much commoner theme, the utility of missions! He is combating the objections raised against them by the worldly-minded and unbelieving, and in doing so appeals to the effects which had been accomplished by means of them on the moral and religious aspect of the Highlands of Scotland. 'What would they have been at this moment,' he asks, 'had schools, and Bibles, and ministers been kept back from them, and had the man of a century ago been deterred by the flippancies of the present age from the work of planting chapels and seminaries in that neglected land? The ferocity of their ancestors would have come down, unsoftened and unsubdued, to the existing generation. The darkening spirit of hostility would still have lowered upon us from the north, and these plains, now so peaceful and so happy, would have lain open to the fury of merciless invaders. O ye soft and sentimental travellers, who wander so securely over this romantic land, you are right to choose the season when the angry elements of nature are asleep. But what is it that has charmed to their long repose the more dreadful elements of human passion and of human injustice? What is it that has quelled the boisterous spirit of her natives? And while her torrents roar as fiercely, and her mountain brows look as grimly as ever, what is it that has thrown so softening an influence over the minds and manners of her living population?' Here a vivid imagination lends a most effectual aid to the reason, and, as by a sudden blaze let in from a higher region, flashes such conviction on the mind as might well shame to silence all further opposition.

But a still higher service was exacted of this faculty when Robert Hall, at the close of his wonderful sermon on 'The sentiments proper to the present crisis,' the crisis, namely, of 1803, when the country was preparing to plunge into a most formidable war with Bonaparte, after having wound up his hearers to the loftiest pitch of excitement in respect to the necessity and justice of the impending struggle, referred to the virtuous heroes, legislators, and patriots of every age and country, as bending from their elevated seats to witness the contest, as if they were incapable of enjoying their repose till they saw the matter brought to a favourable issue.   And then, apostrophizing those departed worthies as actually present, he exclaimed, ' Enjoy that repose, illustrious immortals !   Your mantle fell when you ascended ; and thousands, influenced with your spirit, and impatient to tread in your steps, are ready to swear by Him that sitteth upon the throne, and liveth for ever and ever, they will protect freedom in her last asylum, and never desert that cause which you sustained by your labours, and cemented with your blood.'

A personification and appeal like this reached the very borders of that licence which must be allowed to imagination in the pulpit, and could only have been conceived and executed with the least prospect of success by one in whom the imagining faculty itself was strong, and by him only if he had wrought up his audience by previous descriptions and appeals to somewhat of the same rapt fervour with himself.   He certainly had done so ; they were at the moment like persons carried out of themselves, borne along by an impetuous torrent to think as the preacher thought, and feel as he felt.   Such, too, is reported to have been the case in a closely similar example of Whitfield's preaching, one characterized by the boldest flight of imagination he is known to have attempted, when toward the conclusion of a fervid discourse, throughout which his soul had been, as it were, on fire with zeal and love for the conversion of sinners, he demanded of his audience what account attending angels should carry to heaven of the tidings and invitations he had been addressing to them ; and as if afraid that the account should be prematurely closed, nay, as if actually seeing the heavenly messenger already on the wing, suddenly broke out with an imploring cry to Gabriel to stop, that a few more sinners might have time to send on high the news of their blessed return to God, and then with increased fervour briefly reiterated his appeals to the hearts and consciences of his auditors.

By all accounts the effort in this case also was successful ; the impression upon the audience was in the highest degree powerful and solemn ; but it could only have been so by preacher and audience alike having risen, through what went before, to a kind of enchanted ground, so as to have lost sight, in a manner, of the distinction between the visible and the invisible, the angelic and the human. Such things defy all imitation ; and those who would attempt to reproduce them (as in respect to this flight of Whitfield I have known a very common-place preacher do in a village congregation), only succeed in making themselves ridiculous. Peculiarities of any kind, and peculiarities of a far less marked description than those just referred to in connection with the imagination, can only appear natural, and strike a sympathetic chord in the breasts of others when they spring forth as from their native soil, and seem to blossom in the proper time and place. They must proceed from the cultivation of a real talent, not from the artificial search after what is unusual, or the vain attempt to wield on an occasion a giant's weapons. This can produce nothing great or good, and is sure to run out into grotesque forms, or explode in fanciful conceits. Here, above all, simplicity, genuine and unaffected, is requisite, showing itself in a determination to use only what is properly one's own, to *appear* to have just what is actually possessed, and to feel what is really felt. In so far as this is done, even though the talent exercised may not be of the highest kind, yet being a reality, and not an affectation, having its foundation in nature, not assumed for a purpose, its manifestation will always meet with some response, and will succeed greatly better than any pretension could do in a higher line of things.   For not only does nothing grow by mere imitation (*nihil crescit sola imitatione—Quinct.*), but the mind that makes the attempt to grow after that fashion is perpetually in danger of shooting into wrong directions, forcing itself into forbidden paths, and betaking to appliances which only create a recoil.

It is therefore very justly said by Vinet,[1] 'that while art in a sense is *one*, it is not so in all senses ; it multiplies itself with individuals ; it individualizes itself in each.   The question which will one day place itself before you will not be, What ought *one* to do ? but, What ought *I* to do ?   In this preparatory period oratorical discourse may appear to you as the object ; in the active labours of the ministry, it will only be *one* means of attaining an actual object on occasions which will actually resemble no other.   The professor you hear, the rhetorician you read or listen to, cannot make that rhetoric individual to you.   Every one must do so for himself.   It is not meant by this that each must have all, as it were, within himself ; that he must be indebted for nothing to others, copying after nothing wherein others have excelled, lest he should be chargeable with a vicious or feeble imitation.   No ; he should indeed beware of imitating in others what could not come naturally to himself, and should not even be partially influenced by the thought or manner of another without being at pains to assimilate it to himself. For if the things which proceed from his lips are to become a power in the hearts of others, they must first have struck

[1] *Homiletics*, p. 25.

their roots into his own spiritual being; they must teem and germinate within him, and mingle with the essence of his spirit; and must shape themselves into a new original growth.'

But with this caution, on the one side, against a too close approximation to others, especially in regard to what is somewhat peculiar to themselves, there is undoubtedly a legitimate benefit, on the other, to be derived from the study of the best models in those particular gifts and attainments wherein each most notably excels. Those, for example, who have comparatively little imagination, may have that little stimulated and improved by familiarity with the productions of those who have been distinguished for the large possession and happy use of the faculty. The man of discursive tendencies, apt to ramble in his cogitations and string his ideas somewhat loosely together, may have his reasoning powers strengthened, and his capacity for discoursing profitably on divine things increased by making a special study of such works as are remarkable for the lucid order and the argumentative skill they exhibit in the treatment of their respective subjects. And, in like manner, the man of dry intellect, or plain solid sense, may catch some inspiration of a livelier kind by sitting at the feet of those who are masters in the popular modes of address by means of touching allusions to Bible story, appropriate illustrations from the field of nature, or the incidents of every-day life. Though not destined to excel in such arts, yet he may acquire a certain facility in the use of them.

In regard to the persons themselves who *are* possessed naturally of some marked mental characteristic, the chief caution to be exercised is to beware of running to excess, indulging the special and peculiar, till, from forming an attractive distinction, and being an element of power, it becomes a sort of excrescence, which by its undue preponderance hinders the proper action of other faculties of the mind, or by its eccentricities serves rather to tickle people's fancies than promote their edification.   A tendency to pathos, for example, may be developed to the hurtful neglect of the manly exercise of reason, and the nursing of a comparatively weak, mawkish, sentimental piety.   The simply intellectual and logical powers, on the other hand, may be allowed to carry it so completely over the sympathetic and emotional, that the discourse shall become little more than a fine speculation or a well-reasoned argument, with something, possibly, to instruct or convince, but nothing to quicken or arouse, nothing to satisfy the spiritual appetite with the food it naturally desires and longs for.   But more than either of these, or indeed than any other prominent characteristic, is the danger, in the present day, of letting loose the imagination, where this faculty exists in peculiar strength, by a profusion of images, or multiplying unduly pictorial representations. A power of this kind is undoubtedly a great advantage to a preacher.   It enables him to bring to his hand a ready supply of the imagery which charms by its beauty, or interests and instructs by its fresh combinations and striking analogies.   But on this very account it is extremely apt to assume an undue prominence in the structure of the discourse, and even to lose, in a measure, its proper character, to pass from a means to an end.   Whenever the preacher glides into this excess, he may be said to have drifted from his mooring, he is but dallying with his theme. ' For every one must recollect,' as is well said by Mr. H. Rogers,[1] ' that if a speaker is in earnest he never employs his imagination, as the poet does, merely to delight us ; nor, indeed, to delight us at all, except as appropriate imagery, though used for another object, necessarily imparts pleasure. For this reason illustrations are selected always with a reference to their force rather than their beauty, and are very

[1] *Essay on Sacred Eloquence.*

generally marked more by their homely propriety than by their grace and elegance. For the same reason, wherever it is possible, they are thrown into the brief form of metaphor; and here Aristotle, with his usual sagacity, observes, that the metaphor is the only trope in which the orator may freely indulge. Everything marks the man intent on serious business, whose sole anxiety is to convey his meaning with as much precision and energy as possible to the minds of his auditors.' Mr. Rogers therefore wisely cautions preachers, and especially young preachers of imaginative powers, against throwing in epithets and employing images merely because he thinks them beautiful. 'As regards real impression, there is no style which has so little practical effect, even when there is real genius in it. The admiration which it so commonly awakens, but shows that the minds of the auditors are fixed rather upon the man than upon the subject; less upon the truths inculcated than upon the genius which has embellished them. The speaker has but succeeded in attracting the eye upon himself and his power of discourse, but it is a success won at the expense of what is his *avowed*, and ever ought to be his *real* object.'

Here, again, the only effectual safeguard lies in the personal state of the preacher. If he has the true spirit of his office, the singleness of eye and deep practical aim which are proper to one whose soul is alive to the great realities of salvation, and who feels his very life bound up with the success of his mission as an ambassador of grace, he will subordinate his use of imagery, like everything else, to his one grand aim. He cannot allow himself to play freaks with his imagination, in order to garnish his speech with sweet flowers, or get up a succession of graphic pictures merely for the sake of gratifying the taste or gaining the applause of his hearers. He has higher objects in view, although in aiming at their accomplishment one person may, the bent of nature so inclining him, infuse more of the graphic and pictorial into his representations than can be done by others. He may do so even more freely in the present age than he could well have done in the last ; for there is now, through all departments of literature, a strong current running in this direction ; and the eloquence of the pulpit, like popular speech generally, must to some extent bear ' the form and pressure of the time.' Desiring to speak to men's bosoms, it must adapt itself to existing habits of thought, and take advantage of prevailing tendencies. But still only within definite limits, never so as to do violence to the fundamental laws of human discourse ; therefore, as regards the point now more immediately before us, never forgetting that for purposes of persuasion the imaginative faculty has but a subordinate part to perform, should be used only as an occasional handmaid, not obeyed as an imperious mistress ; and that where the success of the speaker is greatest, the materials it furnishes are never more than sparingly introduced.

Indeed, one may say, in regard to the highest species of pulpit eloquence,—that in which the theme of discourse is so thoroughly transfused into the minds of the audience that the speaker himself is forgotten, speaker and hearer being alike absorbed in thought concerning the interests of an eternal world,—it never almost is the preponderance of any one faculty that has to do with the effect, but rather the happy combination of various faculties, only these quickened and ennobled, intensified to the highest degree of spiritual action by the powerful working of God's Spirit and the felt apprehension of divine things. The discourses which have produced the most profound impressions at the time, and which have been found afterwards to have yielded the richest harvest of spiritual good, have been of this character. Such, for example, appears to have been the discourse of Livingstone at the Kirk of Shotts, which scattered the seeds of a living faith through hundreds of bosoms in the Vale of Clyde. Such, also, was the extraordinary discourse on missions by Dr. Mason of New York, which made even experienced ministers of the gospel feel as if they scarcely knew till then what preaching should be, and gave a fresh impulse to their minds. Such was the character of one of Mr. Toller's sermons, a sermon every way impressive in itself, but rendered still more so by the pale, emaciated appearance of the preacher, as we learn from the striking account given of it by Mr. Hall. 'All other emotions,' he says, 'were absorbed in devotional feeling; it seemed to us as though we were permitted for a short space to look into eternity, and every sublunary object vanished before the powers of the world to come. Yet there was no considerable exertion, no vehemence, no splendid imagery, no magnificent description; it was the simple declaration of truth; of truth, indeed, of infinite moment, borne in upon the heart by a mind intensely alive to its reality and grandeur. Criticism was disarmed; the hearer felt himself elevated to a region which it could not penetrate; all was powerless submission to the master-spirit of the scene.' Such, undoubtedly, when viewed with reference to the great end of the ministry, is the highest style of preaching; and it is reserved, not for the man distinguished merely for powerful intellect or lofty imagination, but for the man whose conversation is in heaven, and whose soul lives and breathes amid the realities of salvation.[1]

[1] It is quite possible to find what have the appearance at least, perhaps also the reality, of exceptions to some of the statements made in this section. The maxim of Pope here also has its application—

'Great wits sometimes may gloriously offend,
And rise to faults true critics dare not mend.'

Men of genius, or of power so varied and attractive as to have nearly all the charm of genius, may in their vocation as preachers attain to great and deserved eminence, even though in some respects violating the rules which have approved themselves to the most matured critical judgment. By means of their peculiar resources they are able to bear,

This ought to be the more thought of and the more earnestly coveted, that it springs so much from those spiritual qualities which must ever constitute the more essential elements of the Church's power for good in all her departments of action and duty. It is that the Church is a society, holding not of earth, but of heaven ; connected by a living bond with the realities of an eternal world; connected by such a bond with Christ, the glorified Redeemer, so that the higher life that is in Him may be continually manifesting itself in the spirit and behaviour of her members. It is this which most of all enables the Church to act with reforming and blissful energy upon the world. And the ministers of the Church, those who are her more peculiar agents and representatives, both for keeping the flame alive in her own bosom and bringing it to act with quickening and attractive force upon the masses lying near and around her, while they may justly prize, and should diligently cultivate, such gifts of nature or resources of learning as they may have at command, still should feel that the main secret of their strength lies in the measure in which they themselves possess that higher endowment, that spirit of life in Christ Jesus, and by word and deed can transfuse it into their ministerial agency. God grant that there may be this feeling in all of us, and a fixed desire, through divine grace, to have it brought forth into practical manifestation !

VI. *The style proper to the pulpit, and the degree of attention*

and even to wield with effect, armour which in the hands of other men would only lead to misdirected effort or palpable failure, as in the employment, for example, of extended pictorial representations, which the late Dr. Guthrie certainly used sometimes with wonderful skill and success, but which many others have tried with no result but that of entertaining the fancy of the hearer, or begetting admiration of the artistic power of the preacher. Men should be well assured of their special aptitudes and gifts before they venture upon marked deviations from established principles.

M

that should be paid to it.—Some of the remarks made under
the last division had nearly as much respect to the style as
to the matter of discourses ; for in certain of its aspects the
one readily runs into the other. But the subject of style
demands a separate consideration, since not a little depends
on it for the efficient ministration of the gospel. At the
same time *negatively*, and with respect to its proper place, I
would say, that it should not be much taken apart, as a
thing to be considered or cultivated by itself. Some men
of note, seeing how much practically turns on style, viewed
as the right *setting* of the thought, have expressed themselves somewhat incautiously on the subject. They have
spoken so as to convey the impression that style, in a manner, is everything, and that the chief pains must be bestowed
upon this by those who would attain to a high place as
preachers of the gospel. To speak after such a fashion
gives, I believe, an exaggerated idea of the matter for effective oratory of all descriptions, and in particular of that
description of it which should be aimed at by preachers of
the gospel. Style is but the mirror of the thought, and the
one may be said to be perfect if it is in due correspondence
with, or gives a just reflection of, the other ; but if the cast
of thought be feeble or confused, so naturally will be the
style ; and then it is not so much the mirror as the thing
mirrored which calls for rectification. It is justly, therefore,
remarked by Vinet,[1] that 'the ambition merely to speak
well, in proportion as it obtains an ascendancy over the
minister, degrades the ministry. . . . A good style is
necessary, but a good style does not come by itself. The
style is not superadded to all the rest ; it is a labour of the
mind and of the soul which has only to be carried out.'
Precisely here, indeed, lies the distinction between the true
orator and the mere rhetorician, who may charm by his
language, and delight the ear as by the music of sweet

[1] *Homiletics*, p. 320.

sounds, but leaves no abiding impression, accomplishes no practical result. His mind, in short, is greatly too much occupied with the adjustment of words and sentences, while the real orator has his soul stirred with important ideas, and has no further concern about the form of expression given to them than that it should fitly represent the thoughts and feelings of which he seeks to be delivered.

Hence the saying of Montaigne, 'When I see these excellent ways of speaking, I do not say that they are well written, but that they are well thought.' The meaning is, that in the happier efforts of mind there is such a connection between thoughts rightly conceived in the mind and the proper mode of expressing them, that the one by a kind of moral necessity draws the other along with it ; or, as he again expresses it, 'Whoever has in his mind a vivid and clear idea will express it well enough in one way or other.' Hence, also, the happy distinction drawn by Augustine, in the case of the Apostle Paul, between following the rules of eloquence and eloquence following the excellent thought embodied in the discourse : 'Sicut apostolum præcepta eloquentiæ secutum fuisse non dicimus, ita quod ejus sapientiam secuta sit eloquentia, non negamus.'[1]

It were therefore a piece of folly in *any* public speaker, but pre-eminently in a preacher of the gospel, to address himself to the task of elaborating fine periods, and constructing sentences according to rule. By such a course he could, at the most, only draw attention upon himself, and win the petty distinction of being a man of superficial polish or rhetorical skill ; a distinction not to be coveted as a prize, but rather to be shunned as a misfortune, by any one who aspires to the possession of a real power in carrying the convictions and swaying the judgments of his fellow-men. All this, however, is merely negative ; it touches only on what is not to be sought after or done. But what, on the

[1] Verbaque prævisam rem non invita sequentur.—*Hor.*

other side, are some of the leading qualities which ought to appear in the style of those who can so think and so express themselves, as to exercise a salutary and powerful influence on a popular audience ?

(1.) Simplicity, perhaps, ought to have the first place ; for this is but another name, in most cases, for clearness and perspicuity ; and without the latter, as formerly noticed, success is impossible. Whatever else may be requisite in spoken or written productions which are adapted to the popular mind, simplicity must not be wanting. This has been well noted by Hume in his essay on *Simplicity and Refinement in Writing.* He says : ' A greater degree of simplicity is required in all compositions where men and actions and passions are painted, than in such as consist of reflections and observations. And as the former species of writing is the more engaging and beautiful, one may safely, upon this account, give the preference to the extreme of simplicity above that of refinement.' Yet, of this last he justly states, that it is ' the extreme which men are most apt to fall into, after learning has made some progress, and after writers have appeared in every species of composition. The endeavour to please by novelty leads men wide of simplicity and nature, and fills their writings with affectation and conceit.' I need not say, that everything which savours of this is peculiarly unsuited to a preacher of the gospel. If generally ' the language which is dedicated to truth should be plain and unaffected,'[1] most especially should it be so when applied in connection with that kind of truth which it is the business of the preacher to set forth,—truth which lies so near to the glory of God and the highest interests of mankind. But there are other reasons for it. In the great majority of cases any other kind must be unsuited to the audience addressed, as well as to the nature of the theme.

[1] Quæ veritati operam dat oratio, incomposita sit et simplex.— *Seneca*, Ep. 40.

Christian congregations, with comparatively few exceptions, are not only mixed assemblages, but assemblages containing a preponderance of but moderately educated or even unlettered persons, very few of whom, therefore, can be qualified intelligently to follow, far less to relish, a discourse which deals in unusual terms and artificial sentences—the ordinary marks of polish and refinement. And if some of the greater masters of English composition have of set purpose endeavoured to avoid such things ; have even, to be sure of their ground in this respect, at times tried the effect of their productions on men of common understanding, before committing them to the press, how anxious should the ministers of the gospel be to use great plainness of speech, that the simple in heart may understand, and nothing which it is important for sinners to know may lie hidden from their view under the folds of a learned phraseology.

Augustine, in the last book of his treatise, *De Doctrina Christiana*, presses very strongly this view of the matter, and commends this quality of plainness or simplicity of speech to all ministers of the word, as deserving of their greatest attention :[1] 'He, therefore, who teaches will shun all words that do not teach ; and if in place of them he can employ others which are pure, and which are better understood, he will rather choose these ; but if he cannot do so, either because there are none such, or because he cannot for the moment get hold of them, he will then resort to others which are less pure, provided only they serve to make the thing itself distinctly understood.' And returning to the subject again, he asks, 'What signifies a *golden* key, if we cannot open with it what we wish ? But if a *wooden* one will serve the purpose, what matters its inferior quality ?' And referring to Cicero's threefold distinction, *docere necessitatis est, delectare suavitatis, flectere victoriæ,* he urges on

[1] L. iv. 26.

preachers of the gospel that, while they should not, indeed, neglect the two latter, while they should endeavour so to speak as to please and to persuade, they should yet regard the teaching element as the prime and essential one, and for that end should make choice of such words as are fitted to convey clear notions of the truth.

This is, undoubtedly, what should be aimed at ; but even when honestly aimed at, it is not always quite easily accomplished. A long course of academical training, whatever advantages it brings in other respects, is apt here to throw a certain hindrance in the way. For it familiarizes those who are subjected to it to a style of thought and speech philosophical or literary rather than popular ; and modes of representation, forms of expression even, which have become perfectly natural to them, will be strange to the ears, and but imperfectly grasped by the understandings of a common audience. The progress of education, and the more general diffusion of intelligence through the community, have, no doubt, been tending to lessen the distance in this respect between the more and the less learned classes, but it is very far from having removed it. There may be little danger in the present day of introducing into the pulpit the kind of academical style of discourse which was by no means unusual with a certain class of ministers in the last century, when, as Dr. Campbell tells us, preachers were often found ' haranguing the people on the moral sense and universal benevolence, speaking of the symmetry of the universe, and the moral harmony and dissonance of the affections.' Such a style of pulpit ministrations may now be regarded as gone into deserved oblivion ; but there may still, and, unless special care is taken to prevent it, there will remain a tendency with those who have been trained to habits of study, and are more conversant with books than with men, to fall into methods of discussion and modes of speech which are not level to the capacities of the people, at least do not

properly reach their bosoms. And if there is any considerable tincture of fancy in the preacher's constitution, or
prompting of literary ambition, there will be the additional
danger of his overshooting the mark by using similitudes too
remote from common life, and displaying a fondness for what
will only be regarded as playful sallies or pretty conceits.

This false tendency, more especially in the latter form of
it, is so admirably exposed by South in his sermon on Luke
xxi. 15, and the proper style for an earnest preacher to
employ is so strikingly set forth, that I cannot forbear quoting the passage, although the tone of sarcasm so natural to
the author is not wanting in it, and in the present case is
venting itself against no less a victim than his celebrated
contemporary Jeremy Taylor : ' *I speak the words of soberness*, said St. Paul, *and I preach the gospel not with enticing
words of man's wisdom.* This was the way,' says South, ' of
the apostle's discoursing of things sacred. Nothing here
of " the fringes of the northern star ;" nothing of " nature's
becoming unnatural ;" nothing of the " down of angels'
wings," or " the beautiful locks of cherubims ;" no starched
similitudes introduced with a " thus have I seen a cloud
rolling in its airy mansion," and the like. No, these were
sublimities above the rise of the apostolic spirit. For
the apostles, poor mortals, were content to take lower
steps, and to tell the world in plain terms that he who
believed should be saved, and that he who believed not
should be damned. And this was the dialect which pierced
the conscience, and made the hearers cry out, " Men and
brethren, what shall we do ?" It tickled not the ear, but
sank into the heart ; and when men came from such
sermons, they never commended the preacher for his taking
voice or gesture, for the fineness of such a simile, or the
quaintness of such a sentence ; but they spake like men
conquered by the overpowering force and evidence of the
most concerning truths ; much in the words of the two

disciples going to Emmaus : *Did not our hearts burn within us while He opened to us the Scriptures ?* In a word, the apostles' preaching was therefore mighty and successful, because plain, natural, and familiar, and by no means above the capacity of their hearers ; nothing being more preposterous than for those who were professedly aiming at men's hearts, to miss the mark by shooting over their heads.'

If somewhat peculiarly, this is not too forcibly put ; and in order to avoid the errors pointed at, there is undoubtedly, first of all, needed on the part of the preacher a sincere spirit of self-denial, a determination to shun whatever might look like a needless display of learning, or a laying of traps for popular applause. Like a humble but earnest workman, he must seek the instruments, the plain and intelligible words, which seem best fitted to forward his Master's business. In order to this he must, as was said in another connection, by familiar intercourse with the people get well acquainted with the manner of thought and speech which is best adapted to their taste or capacities, especially must accustom himself to the use of the more common, chiefly Saxon, elements in our language, as contradistinguished from those which are of Latin origin. And in so far as recourse may be had to figures or similitudes to aid the imperfection of direct language, and give a more vivid representation of the truth, let them not be of a recondite nature, or far-fetched, but such as will really illustrate the subject, and make it better understood by the common understanding. Finer examples could scarcely be anywhere found of what is here indicated than in the sermons of Augustus Hare, the brother of the Archdeacon. They are the productions of a man of high intellect, fine taste, and varied accomplishments, yet subordinated all to the blessed work of endeavouring to bring down the great truths and obligations of the gospel to the level of a plain, rural congregation ; a work which, when perfectly done, and with respect to

things which are not trite, but of grave importance or difficulty, is, as Whately has remarked, 'one of the most admirable feats of genius.'[1]   I refer, in illustration, to his sermon
on the superiority of principles to rules ; and hence the far
greater importance of having the mind indoctrinated with
the one, than the conduct drilled into conformity with the
other;[2] a subject certainly far from being trite, or even such
as can quite easily be made patent to a common audience ;
yet see how distinct it becomes through Mr. Hare's lucid
exposition and homely speaking !   'A rule which has been
drawn up for any particular purpose, may be likened to a
loaf of bread ; a principle, on the other hand, is like a handful of wheat.   Every rule that is worth anything must be
taken from a principle, just as a loaf of bread is made of
wheat.   For the wants and uses of the moment a rule is
more serviceable than a principle, just as, when a man is
hungry, bread is more welcome than wheat.   For bread is
wheat ready prepared for the sake of satisfying hunger.
We have only to take it and eat it.   Hence, for a hungry
man a crust of bread is better and handier than so much
unground wheat.   Yet will anybody say on this account
that bread is a better thing than wheat?   Suppose a man
were going to some far country where no corn grows, which
would he take with him, bread or wheat?'   He illustrates
this a little, and then proceeds: 'This is the great advantage
which wheat has over bread.   Bread may feed us for the
moment ; but when once eaten it is gone for ever.   Wheat,
on the contrary, will bear seed ; it will increase and multiply ; after one crop has had its day, and been reaped, and
stored in the barn, and consumed, another crop, provided
seed be preserved, will spring up ; and so long as the earth
itself lasts, so long will corn last also.   Thus, too, is it with
rules and principles.   A rule is like a loaf of bread ; it is a
ready handy application of a principle, a principle made

[1] *Rhetoric*, p. 256.   [2] On Col. ii. 28.

up for immediate use. By rules we govern and rule our children. We say to them, " Do this," or " Don't do that," because it is easy for them to understand a plain order ; but it is not always easy to make them understand the principle or reason of it. When the child, however, comes to be a man, he puts away childish things. He wants a new set of rules adapted to his new state, for the rules of childhood he has outgrown, so that they no longer fit him. The rules which belong to one stage of life are many of them ill-suited to other stages of life.' And so with different classes of men, and different nations of the world. 'Therefore God, when He was graciously pleased to give us a law, which was to serve not for one country and one people, but for the whole world, did not give us an endless string of rules to be followed according to the letter in each particular case ; but gave us the principles which are the ground and sources of all rules, and from which the rules are to be drawn,' etc. He applies it to circumcision and other Jewish ordinances, which in *form* are dropt, in *principle* retained. 'Christ skimmed off the cream, as it were, of the law of Moses;' 'in the room of burdensome rites and formal rules He gave us the law of faith and love, and thereby made His doctrine a doctrine of principles, living, active, pure, universal and eternal.' [1]

It is quite true that a style like this, so remarkable for its simplicity both in the choice of words and the structure of sentences, is adapted for instruction rather than impression. True also, that it has been seldom attained in anything like the same perfection by excellent preachers of the gospel ; and some even of those who reached the highest distinction have rather been noted for the elaboration than for the plainness and simplicity of their style. Such, certainly, are the printed sermons of Dr. Chalmers ; they bear throughout

[1] Compare another fine specimen of Hare's method, in Ser. on John vii. 17—greatly superior to Archer Butler's on the same text.

the marks of elaborate preparation, in respect not merely to the thought embodied in them, but also to the structure of the sentences and the mode of expression, which were in a great measure peculiar to the man himself; nor was there ever probably an orator who, with no sinister object in view, with the simple desire of communicating his thoughts distinctly and forcibly to the minds of others, has formed for himself a diction so broadly marked by the impress of his own individuality. Yet, with all that is peculiar in his language and remote from the speech of common life, there is in it also a singular breadth and power, a living freshness and palpability, which, however unintelligible in particular phrases to unlettered hearers, could not fail to arrest their attention and find its way to their understandings and hearts. It was still, however, far from being a model style for the pulpit, especially in its relation to the general mass of congregations; and now that it is unaccompanied by the striking aspect and attractive presence of the man, it rests as a heavy drawback on the remains of his pulpit ministrations; it is the element which more than anything besides has impaired their permanent value, and rendered them comparatively strange in the homes of our Christian people.

Indeed, Chalmers may here be appealed to as an authority against himself. In a review of the sermons of Dr. Charters of Wilton, he dwells upon the appropriateness of a direct and homely style for the pulpit, in so far as regards the audiences which have most commonly to be addressed from it. 'In the language of Paul,' says he, 'it is right that we should be all things to all men, that we may gain some; and if a simple proselyte can be gained to the cause of righteousness by the embellishments of elegant literature, let every attraction be given to the subject which taste and elegance can throw round it. But let it be remembered that these attractions have no influence over the vast majority of the species, and that the only impression of which they are susceptible is that wholesome and direct impression which a clear and simple exposition of duty makes upon the audience. Let it further be remembered, that even among the cultivated orders of society, the appetite for mere gracefulness of expression is sure, in time, to give way to the more substantial accomplishment of good sense and judicious observation ; and that in every rightly-constituted mind the importance of what is true must carry it over what is pretty, and elegant, and fashionable.'

The case of Robert Hall admits of a similar explanation. In his grander efforts he was a preacher for a select class rather than for the body of the people. His more famous sermons (at least as printed), though perfectly clear and perspicuous for cultivated readers, could only have been imperfectly understood and appreciated by common audiences, and are, indeed, in point of composition, among the most classical productions in the English language. They are not, however, exactly specimens of his ordinary and especially of his more effective preaching. Speaking of this in his sketch of Hall's character as a preacher, Foster says, ' His language in preaching, as in conversation, was in one considerable point better than in his well-known and elaborately-composed sermons, in being more natural and flexible. When he set in reluctantly upon that operose employment, his style was apt to assume a certain processional stateliness of march, a rhetorical rounding of periods, a too frequent inversion of the natural order of the sentence, with a morbid dread of degrading it to end in a particle, or rather small-looking word ; a structure in which I doubt whether the augmented appearance of strength and dignity be a compensation for the sacrifice of a natural, living, and variable freedom of composition.' He adds : ' a remarkable difference will be perceived between the highly-wrought sermons long since published, and the short ones now printed, which were prepared without a thought of the press ; a difference

to the advantage of the latter in the grace of simplicity.'
Hall himself was perfectly aware of this difference, and
notes it very strikingly in a letter to Mr. Philips (16th April
1812), as connected with his greater success in the proper
end of preaching: ' Blessed be the Lord, my strain of
preaching is considerably altered ; much less elegant, but
more intended for conviction, for awakening the conscience,
and carrying divine truth with power into the heart !'   It is
worthy of notice, too, that even in the earlier period of his
ministerial life, his judgment pronounced in favour of a style
for the pulpit different from his own at the time in his
review, for example, of Foster's Essays, also of Gisborne's
Sermons. He admired the simple force and expressiveness
of the Saxon element in our language, as far superior to the
Latin for emphasis and impression, and sometimes expressed in a very marked manner his dissatisfaction with
the employment of the one class of words when the others
might, as he thought, have been with advantage preferred.
Thus, in a conversation with Dr. O. Gregory, having
observed that the latter had more than once spoken of
felicity, Mr. Hall sharply inquired, ' Why do you say *felicity*,
sir ?   Happiness is a better word, more musical, and better
English, coming from the Saxon.'   Hall, therefore, as well
as Foster and Chalmers, may be cited as a witness to this
style, as what may be termed the normal or usually appropriate one for the pulpit ; and if the bent of native genius,
or a regard to the peculiar circumstances of their own
position, rendered their example somewhat at variance with
their precept, this should rather tend to enhance the value
of their deliberate judgment.

On the whole, it is of importance to bear in mind that,
amid all the diversities in this respect which are inevitable
and even proper, the press and the pulpit have their distinctive requirements ; and that what may be comparatively
perfect as regards the one, may be obviously defective or

misplaced as regards the other. In particular, the pulpit demands plainness and simplicity beyond the written page, while the latter is greatly less tolerant of careless and slovenly forms of expression.

'There are preachers who, being deficient in the intellectual and moral attributes which are essential to those higher forms of popular eloquence which fascinate and impress all classes of the community, are resolved to grasp by illegitimate means at the same visible success. Unenriched with that bearing and intellectual vigour which enable a man to become the master of difficult and unfamiliar provinces of truth; unendowed with the rare genius which can create a heaven and earth of its own, and lift the thoughts of common men into a world whose paths they have never travelled, and whose atmosphere they have never breathed before; destitute of fancy, destitute of imagination, impatient of the labour and painstaking by which alone the power can be acquired of clothing our conceptions in the nervous and beautiful language which the great writers and orators of our country have been accustomed to employ, they utter paradoxes as though they were wonderful revelations of hitherto unknown truth; they distort and disguise thoughts which have been familiar to all mankind for centuries, and try to pass them off as brilliant originalities; they mistake spasmodic vehemence for strength, gaudy decoration for beauty, words of uncouth shape and sound, sentences of grotesque and unnatural structure, for freshness and force of style. Foolish men wonder, wise men are disgusted; but neither the foolish nor the wise will love God better, resist sin more resolutely, understand the Bible more profoundly, serve Christ more zealously, if they listen to preaching of this kind for half a century' (Dale's *Discourses*, p. 333).

(2.) Another characteristic that should more or less distinguish the style of pulpit discourses is strength or energy.

It is, indeed, a quality which every preacher may be said almost necessarily to aim at, if he has success in his work really at heart ; for in seeking that he seeks to persuade ; and this again implies the forthputting of such a power in the things spoken as may serve to beget the expectation of prevailing over the indifference or opposition of those who are addressed. The capacity, of course, to effect this will always depend to a large extent on the relative vigour of the preacher's mind, or what it is as to concentration of thought and depth of feeling ; and where these qualities are greatly deficient, it is not possible by mere outward expression to compensate for the want. A striving after what may be called an artificial energy, energy of style or action out of proportion to the elements of strength existing within, is sure to manifest itself in something forced, extravagant, or coarse ; and consequently must tend rather to defeat than further the object of the speaker. It is in this respect with mental action as with bodily ; the swoop of the arm must be in proportion to the vital force that moves it ; and, in like manner, the energy that a preacher can throw into his diction will be determined by the fire which glows within.

This is not, however, to be understood as disparaging the necessity for proper care and application ; for here, as in other things, even where the native talent exists, it may miss its aim by misdirected efforts, while, by being rightly improved and guided, it may gain immensely both in force and precision. No cultivation can enable a feeble or commonplace mind to clothe its thoughts in a nervous and stirring diction ; but where some degree of mental vigour exists, it may serve to give additional point to its expression, and recall the speaker from trying to reach his aim by a less, to a more effective mode of gaining it. A few leading points is all we can at present indicate on the subject.

As regards the choice of words, there can be no doubt that much depends on the skill to select the more specific and individualizing, instead of the more general and abstract terms. For it is the invariable tendency of a vivid realization or powerful emotion, to give a concrete form to its objects ; to clothe them, as it were, with flesh and blood, and consequently to deal in the language of impersonation and metaphor. 'The more general the terms are,' as Dr. Campbell remarks, 'the picture is the fainter ; the more special they are, the brighter. The same sentiment may be expressed with equal justness, and even equal perspicuity, in the former way as in the latter ; but as the colouring will in that case be more languid, it cannot give equal pleasure to the fancy, and by consequence will not contribute so much either to fix the attention or to impress the memory.' A better example could scarcely be given of this than one selected by Dr. Campbell from the Sermon on the Mount, comparing the specific form which it assumed in our Lord's hand, with what it would become if the specific were changed into the general. 'Consider the lilies, how they grow ; they toil not, they spin not ; and yet I say unto you, that Solomon in all his glory was not arrayed like one of these. If, then, God so clothe the grass, which to-day is in the field and to-morrow is cast into the oven, how much more will He clothe you ?' 'Let us here,' says Campbell, 'adopt a little of the tasteless manner of modern paraphrasts, by the substitution of more general terms, one of their many expedients of infrigidating, and let us observe the effect produced by this change. "Consider the flowers, how they gradually increase in their size ; they do no manner of work, and yet I declare to you that no king whatever, in his most splendid habit, is dressed up like them. If, then, God in His providence doth so adorn the vegetable productions, which continue but a little time on the land, and are afterwards put into the fire, how much more will He provide

clothing for you ? "   How spiritless,' Dr. C. justly adds,
' is the same sentiment rendered by these small variations !
The very particularizing of *to-day* and *to-morrow* is infinitely
more expressive of transitoriness than any description wherein
the terms are general, that can be substituted in its room.'

The Scriptures are full of passages to which the same
mode of criticism might be applied, passages which derive
much of their graphic and touching power from the use
made in them of what is specific and individual, and which
would in a great measure be lost by a more indefinite form
of expression.   Thus St. Paul's commission as an apostle to
' turn men from darkness to light, and from the power of
Satan unto God,' is much more vivid and expressive than if
we had been told of his being sent to instruct the ignorant,
and bring them from the love and practice of sin to the
ways of righteousness ! [1]   A telling effect is often produced
by turning, when it can be done without violence to the
idiom of the language, a noun into a verb, expressing an
action by what properly indicates a personality ; as when,
with reference to the bloody spectacles of the Roman
amphitheatres, the poet speaks through one of his characters of the unhappy creatures who were '*butchered* to
make a Roman holiday ;' or when St. Paul speaks of
' *crucifying* the flesh with its affections and lusts ;' or we
may say of the world, when unduly cared for, that it *dwarfs*
the life of religion in the soul.   But it is quite possible in
such things to go to excess, and in the search for greater
strength so to overdo it as to beget a sense of the strained
or the ludicrous.   The boundary line here between the

[1] Yet the individualizing may fail, if it goes to things too low or
minute for the occasion, as in Parr's Spittal Sermon : ' Within a few
days mute was the tongue that uttered these celestial words, and the
hand which *signed your indenture* lay cold and motionless in the
dark and dreamy chambers of death.' In such an effort at the solemn
and pathetic it looks too small to speak of signing an indenture for
boys.

true and the false, the allowable and the forbidden, is often a delicate one, and writers that may justly be pronounced classical in other respects will sometimes miss it. As for example, Archdeacon Hare, who usually exhibits a fine taste in the use of language, but whose mind was more remarkable for acuteness, sensibility, and polish than for strength, when, in his discourses on the *Mission of the Comforter*, he speaks of the soul which has yielded itself to earthly influences as 'having its feelings tarred and feathered with the dust and dirt of the earth,' and of Christ's righteousness as being perfectly pure, 'not covered with scratches and rents like a sheet of old blotting paper.' The images involved in such expressions are evidently too low for the subjects discoursed of, and the language rather jars on one's sense of propriety than adds to the vividness of one's perceptions. It is therefore to be remembered that *all* individualizing in descriptions does not confer strength, nor *all* energizings in the choice of words. The nature of the subject, the idioms of language, the very place and occasion, must each be taken into account. Especially must it be so in pulpit discourses, in which a becoming sense of solemnity should be apparent; and modes of speech, which might without impropriety be employed elsewhere, would then readily be felt to be out of place. Thus there is room for the exercise of taste, discretion, and sanctified feeling.

The same substantially may be said in regard to the other means requiring to be attended to, in order to the attainment of a nervous diction, such, for example, as the number and arrangement of words in sentences. It is a matter on which preachers should bestow *some* pains, yet without being finical or elaborate. Any one at all conversant with what constitutes power of expression, knows that a needless multiplication of words always enfeebles the sense, as does also a looseness of structure between one part of a sentence and another; and that the more tersely and pointedly a sentiment can be expressed, the more forcible will it be. Sometimes the effect will be found to depend as much upon the relative adjustment of the words, so as to give the prominent place to those on which the main stress should be laid, as on the kind and number of the words themselves. I should express quite an appropriate and wholesome sentiment, if I should say, 'It may now and then be our duty to others to suppress the truth, but duty to ourselves always requires us not to utter a falsehood.' Change the arrangement, however, and see how much more emphatically it becomes as given by Hare:[1] 'To suppress the truth may now and then be our duty to others; not to utter a falsehood must always be our duty to ourselves.' Whately gives the following from Burke as a good example of the same description:[2] 'Kings will be tyrants from policy, when subjects are rebels from principle.' And we may add this from Archer Butler:[3] 'There is no bond but his own love (namely, in the promises of God), yet that bond is stronger than iron; and He, whom the universe cannot compel, commands Himself.' In such sentences everything appears in the place it should occupy, to bring out distinctly the idea meant to be expressed.

But here also there is a measure to be observed in any kind of public discourse, but especially in preaching. For if brevity and arrangement were constantly pursued, it would make too great a strain on people's attention; they would come to feel like persons breathing in too dense an atmosphere; or, as Whately puts it,[4] like animal natures that are confined to food too simply nutritious, requiring more bulk and distension to render it altogether wholesome. Constructions formed with a view to emphasis, if too frequently indulged in, defeat their own object; what is always emphasized becomes monotonous, or loses effect by too palpable

---

[1] *Guesses at Truth*, ii. p. 319.   [2] *Rhetoric*, p. 209.
[3] i. p. 131.   [4] P. 260.

a straining after it. In such things, therefore, it is necessary to time oneself; and, indeed, to be little concerned about either special brevity or emphasis, except when particularly anxious to make impression.

(3.) Another characteristic, the only other I shall particularly mention, of the style proper to the pulpit, is that of a *Scriptural tincture or impress.* One can quite easily suppose that a discourse might be nearly all it should be for the pulpit as to simplicity, clearness, pith, and yet sensibly want something which one naturally expects in the discussion of a scriptural theme. There might be, whether from policy or from a regard to the supposed demands of taste, a studied avoidance of the more peculiar phraseology of Scripture, an employment of terms or a structure of sentences that bespoke no sympathy of tone or community of speech with the sacred writers. Mr. Foster, in one of his well-known essays, went so far as to recommend this as a wise accommodation to persons of cultivated taste, that is, to audiences composed chiefly of such, with the view principally of meeting the aversion such persons cherish to the subjects embraced in evangelical Christianity. In his judgment, a nearer approach to the simply literary style would have the advantage of presenting the ideas of the gospel, without in any way offending, but rather gratifying, their literary predilections. But it would be impossible to adopt such a style of discourse without not only refraining from the use of expressions which are the best our language supplies for the ideas they are intended to convey, but also losing that hallowed air which it is important to have thrown around religious topics for refined as well as ordinary hearers of the gospel. Mr. Hall therefore wisely took exception to the view of Foster in his review of the first edition of the Essays. In doing so he stated, that from the very nature of Christianity, which contains an exhibition of doctrine and requires the exercise of graces peculiar to itself, it necessarily

originated a phraseology of its own, for the purpose of conveying correct impressions of its great truths and principles;
and that this phraseology having been formed under the
immediate impulse and guidance of the Holy Spirit, it could
not be safely supplanted by another. While he could not
applaud the extent to which the use of Scripture language
was carried by some pious writers, he could still less throw
it so much into abeyance as it would be on the system
advocated by Foster. 'To say nothing,' he remarks, ' of
the inimitable beauties of the Bible, considered in a literary
point of view, which are universally acknowledged, it is the
book which every devout man is accustomed to consult as
the oracle of God; it is the companion of his best moments,
and the vehicle of his strongest consolations. Intimately
associated in his mind with everything dear and valuable,
its diction more powerfully excites devotional feelings than
any other; and when temperately and soberly used, it
imparts an unction to a religious discourse which nothing
else can supply.' He properly adds, that the avoidance of
Scripture phraseology in religious discourses might not
improbably lead to a neglect of the Scriptures themselves,
and the substitution of a flashy and superficial declamation
in the room of the saving truths of the gospel. Such an
apprehension, he also thought, was too much verified ' by
the most celebrated sermons of the French, and still more
by some modern compositions in our own language, which
usurp that title.' And he therefore held that ' for devotional
impression a very considerable tincture of the language of
Scripture, or at least such a colouring as shall discover an
intimate acquaintance with those inimitable models, will
generally succeed best.'

Such, undoubtedly, is the right view of the matter; and
there is the more reason for adhering to it, as in the
Authorized Version, whatever partial errors and minor imperfections belong to it, there is so fine an example of

general fidelity to the spirit and meaning of the original, embodied in a style which, for its object, may be said to approach very nearly to perfection. It puts a vocabulary and an idiom into our hand every way adapted to the purpose of its great mission as the revelation of God's mind and will to men, embalmed also in the pious recollections, endeared by the earliest and most rooted associations of those to whom we speak. We are not, however, to imagine, that in order to preserve this Scriptural tincture it is enough to crowd our discourses with quotations from the different books of Scripture. This may be done, often actually is done, with no other effect than to beget an impression of the preacher's want of independent thought, or such a sense of satiety as arises from listening to a continuous stream of commonplaces. Such, to a large extent, must be the effect of a kind of preaching which is sometimes practised, running out into a considerable variety of heads of discourse, and under each introducing so many passages of Scripture, that little space is left for more than a few connecting notes or illustrations. Preaching of this description can never tell with much quickening power, or produce lasting impressions. It is never to be forgotten, as one of the unalterable laws of mental agency, that if one is to beget thought and feeling in the bosom of others, there must first be the conscious possession and exercise thereof in one's own. Here, also, there must be a cause bearing some proportion to the effect; and even passages of Scripture, if they are to be employed as means of moral suasion, must first be identified in the experience of the preacher with his own spiritual life, and used, not to save thought and application, but because they form the most appropriate vehicle of the ideas he has conceived, the convictions, desires, and hopes which he wishes those whom he addresses to share with himself. When so used, it will usually be found that a comparatively small number of direct quotations will be sufficient; their appropriateness rather than their multiplicity will be the more noticeable thing about them; but the Scriptural impress will pervade the discourse and appear in the general tone and character it presents as well as in specific portions of its contents.

Very closely allied to this Scriptural tone of thought and expression, though not absolutely identical with it, is the quality in the higher style of ministrations called *unction*, a quality more easily felt than described. It is, undoubtedly, when existing in any proper degree, not as an assumed pietism, but as a real quality, a soft penetrating influence mingling with the tone and manner of the preacher, and shedding a kind of sweet and heavenly savour over the sentiments he utters. When existing thus, it must, indeed, root itself deeply in the spiritual characteristics of the man, and be in a peculiar manner the reflection of his own inner life. It implies, prior to any manifestation of it in discourse, a certain sensibility of soul, an emotional nature acting under a sense of divine realities, and elevated by close communion with God, and so naturally appearing when coming forth to act upon others with a mingled solemnity and tenderness of spirit, with a freshness of holy life and yearning solicitude of love, which seems allied to heaven rather than to earth, and is felt upon men's hearts as a sanctifying and subduing power. It will belong to any one very much in proportion as he has not simply acquired the language, but drunk into the spirit of the Bible, and has become penetrated with a sense of its all-important revelations. But it is not to be identified with a soft or mawkish sentimentality; for it has not rarely found its strongest development in men in whom the intellectual or imaginative faculties have held as prominent a place as the emotional, such as Howe, Edwards, Brainerd, Leighton, Thomas à Kempis, Pascal. But with whatever characteristics of mind more peculiarly combined, never can there be either a proper foundation for the quality or a healthful development of its power, except in connection with the intimate knowledge and habitual meditation of the word of God.

Enough, perhaps, has been said on the subject of style in pulpit discourses, as it is only the more essential points that can be noticed here. Impression, if not always the immediate, is assuredly the ultimate object to be aimed at, and everything should be considered and done with a special regard to this. The preacher should *prepare* for his work, and *go through* his work with the feeling, that if the truths he unfolds are not made to sink into the hearts of his auditors, let the effect otherwise be what it may, he has substantially laboured in vain. So that if he only can combine with the clear enunciation of gospel truth such nervous strength and spiritual unction as shall tend to win an attentive regard to what he says, and make it live in the remembrance of those who hear, the great object is gained to which his efforts should be directed. Such things, however, cannot be expected to come of themselves. They must be sought and striven for if they are to be found. The men who deem themselves superior to this, or who grudge the labour it exacts of them, must be content to remain deficient in the better and more effective qualities of discourse. But it does not follow that they should always work under the felt trammels of the preceding directions, and carefully elaborate every sentence in their discourses with a specific view to the attainment of the different kinds of excellence which have been mentioned. Composing or speaking well undoubtedly goes before composing or speaking quickly, as was justly said long ago by Quinctilian, '*Bene* scribendo fit, ut cito scribatur, non *cito* scribendo ut bene;' but when practice has enabled us to get some freedom and skill in the work, the most correct and powerful in form may also be the portions which have actually passed with the greatest promptitude from our hands. But this can only be if the mind has been well seasoned and prepared by previous application for the effort. 'Shakespeare,' says Carlyle,[1] 'we may fancy wrote with rapidity, but not till he had thought with intensity. It was for him to write rapidly at fit intervals, being ready for it. And herein truly lies the secret of the matter ; such swiftness of mere writing after due energy of preparation is doubtless the right method ; the hot furnace having long worked and simmered, let the pure gold flow out at one gush.' Yes, but comparatively few can either write or speak under the glow of such a well-formed and regulating impulse, and for the most part there will need to be a certain degree of conscious effort or toil in the actual bodying forth of one's thoughts, as well as in the earlier attempts made toward a distinct conception and disposition of them. But on this particular point something more will be said in another connection.

VII. *Elocution, or the delivery of discourses.*—This is the last point of a general kind, common alike to all discourses, to which it is necessary to direct attention. And in some respects it is the most difficult of all ; the most difficult to be discussed to any good purpose, and not unfrequently also the most difficult for the preacher to study, so as to reach in it some degree of perfection. The difficulty in both cases chiefly arises from the almost infinite diversity of the qualities to which an effective delivery may be ascribed, or which, at least, are capable of entering into it : the same qualities to which we feel disposed to ascribe it in some being precisely those in which others are markedly deficient, who yet attain to the power of an impressive or pleasing delivery. Fine expressive features, a majestic or heavenly aspect, such as partly from nature partly from grace belongs to some men, whose very appearance is a kind of sermon, an appropriate or graceful action, a voice of much compass and energy, capable of expressing by turns the most tender

[1] *Review of Sir W. Scott's Works.*

and melting, and the most lively or powerful tones; these are what may be called the leading elements of a constitutional kind in a good delivery; and when they meet in any individual, they seem quite adequate to account for his success, so far as that can be associated with exterior qualifications. They do, undoubtedly, constitute great natural advantages, for which those who possess them may well be thankful; for such a natural dowry is to the public speaker like what being born to a considerable fortune is for the man of business. Yet how many of those who have risen as speakers to the highest eminence, whether in the civil or the sacred arena, have been more remarkable for the want than for the possession of some of those qualities! Demosthenes, whose name has come down to us as the most consummate orator of antiquity, with respect to the delivery as well as to the composition of his speeches, of whom, when observing the burst of admiration which came from a company of persons who simply heard his oration for the Crown read, his rival Æschines is reported to have said, 'What would you have felt if you had heard *him* speak it?'—this same Demosthenes is known to have had a rather feeble constitution, and was so defective naturally in the organ of speech, that the nickname $\beta\acute{a}\tau a\lambda os$ (stammerer) was applied to him in his youth. It is worthy of notice, too, that the modern British orator, who is commonly regarded as approaching nearest to Demosthenes in some of the higher qualities of excellence, had very marked natural deficiencies of a somewhat similar kind. 'In most of the external qualities of oratory,' says Lord Brougham of Mr. Fox, 'he was certainly deficient, being of an unwieldy person, without any grace of action, with a voice of little compass, and which, when pressed in the vehemence of his speech, became shrill almost to a cry or a squeak; yet all this was absolutely forgotten in the moment when the torrent began to pour.'

Pitt, it is well known, had most of the qualities in this

respect which Fox wanted ; he had, at least, a dignified bearing and manner, such as commanded the deference and regard of others, though it sometimes wounded their pride ; and his voice is said to have been in a high degree sonorous, and capable of giving full effect to all the varieties of style in which he excelled ; clearness of statement, close argumentation, cutting sarcasm, and vehement invective. And another person, a contemporary of these great rivals, himself also a man of rare excellence in some departments of oratory, stood much superior even to Pitt in the exterior qualities of an orator ; he had them in a sort of ideal perfection.   I refer to Erskine, who was possessed of such a noble figure as struck every one with admiration : an expressive countenance, a brilliant and piercing eye, a most graceful and appropriate manner; altogether such, that juries felt it impossible to withdraw their looks from him when once he had secured their attention ; and the whole coupled with a voice peculiarly sweet, clear, flexible, adapted alike to earnest pleading, playful humour, and strains of melting pathos.   What an accumulation of advantages ! Yet great as they were, and great also as was his success in public speaking, neither he nor Pitt come up to that kind of action which was exemplified in Fox, and which, with all his disadvantages of form and gesture and voice, sufficed to render him the most effective speaker of his time in Parliament.

In turning from the senate to the pulpit we meet with precisely similar anomalies.   The qualities which seem to have commanded for some great distinction, scarcely, if at all, appear in others, who yet have been able to throw into their manner the most powerful attraction.   By all accounts, Whitfield, who perhaps more nearly realized than any other in this country the true ideal of a preacher of the gospel, had most of the natural elements that contribute to a good delivery : a prepossessing appearance, a quick, glancing eye, an elastic and powerful voice, and an action full of grace and propriety. The young Spencer of Liverpool, who for the short period of his career made a singular impression, and to whose wonderful power as a preacher Hall has given in one of his notes a very emphatic testimony, appears to have been equally favoured by nature; as he is represented to have been of a most engaging countenance and form; to have had a fine eye and voice, a natural and impressive elocution, which, combined with much devotional fervour and simple earnestness of spirit, threw a quite unusual charm over his preaching; the more remarkable as his sermons, when published after his decease, proved to be rather tame compositions. But when we turn to others, even to some of the most eminent of recent preachers, we find a very scanty distribution of these exterior qualities. Hall had, no doubt, an expressive countenance and a commanding appearance, but he had a weak voice, and next to no action in the pulpit. Contrasting himself with Robinson of Cambridge, whom he succeeded, and at first unfortunately fell into imitating, he said, 'Mr. Robinson had a musical voice, and was master of all its intonations; he had wonderful self-possession, and could say *what* he pleased, *when* he pleased, and *how* he pleased; while my voice and manner were naturally bad; and far from having self-command, I never entered the pulpit without omitting to say something that I wished to say, and saying something that I wished unsaid.' Yet, while the natural qualities which tend to secure a pleasing and effective delivery were so imperfectly possessed by Hall, as compared with his predecessor, there can be no doubt that the delivery which was actually the most perfect, the one which most completely riveted the attention of the hearers, and served to impress the sentiments of the speaker most deeply upon their minds, belonged to Hall in a far higher degree than it ever did to Robinson.

In like manner, Chalmers, whose manner for earnestness and force was probably never surpassed in the pulpit, owed wondrously little to the merely external gifts of nature. He had a voice firm indeed, and moderately strong, but utterly devoid of music, flexibility, or softness, singularly hard and uniform in its intonations; an eye that expressed nothing but the utter absorption of the speaker in his own theme ; and a manner without grace or polish, rarely serving more than to embody the one idea of tremendous energy and vital force. Yet the effect, not merely with the general public, but with the most severe and keen-eyed critics, was of the most impressive kind. One of the latter class, John Lockhart,[1] after pointing to what was defective, and mentioning that 'his voice was neither strong nor melodious, his gestures neither easy nor graceful, his pronunciation not only broadly national, but broadly provincial, distorting almost every word he uttered into some barbarous novelty,' proceeds to say : ' But, in truth, these are things which no listener can attend to while this great preacher stands before him armed with all the weapons of the most commanding eloquence, and swaying all around him with its imperial rule. . . . I have heard many men,' he adds, 'deliver sermons far better arranged in regard to argument, and have heard very many deliver sermons far more uniform in elegance both of conception and style; but most unquestionably I have never heard, either in England or Scotland, or in any other country, any preacher whose eloquence is capable of producing an effect so strong and irresistible as his.'

Were we to multiply examples, it would only be to produce fresh diversities in respect to the degrees in which things naturally conducive to a good delivery have been found in preachers of eminence ; and even that which might seem the most indispensable of all qualities for the purpose

[1] In Peter's Letters.

of impression, the power of a sustained pitch of voice, has sometimes failed so much in preachers of great excellence and power, that their most impassioned and solemn passages have had to be delivered in a kind of undertone, little more than an audible breathing. The conclusion, I think, to be drawn from the existence of such diversities is, that an effective delivery depends upon a considerable variety of things; upon qualities partly corporal, partly mental; and that though all or nearly all of them *may* be united in a single individual, yet in reality they very seldom are so; nor is it at all necessary that they should be so united in order to the attainment of the highest success as to power and impressiveness of action. It would even seem, from the facts connected with the subject, that there is here also a law of compensation which very commonly comes into play; and that it is rarely indeed those who are most fully endowed with the exterior gifts of nature, but those rather who have some marked defects in this respect to encounter and overcome, for whom the highest place is reserved: the very effort in overcoming the difficulty, or triumphing in the face of an obvious disqualification, being thereby made to turn to the account of the speaker, and imparting to his utterances a charm they could not otherwise have possessed.

All this must, of course, be understood with certain limitations. A measure even of the more superficial endowments of nature must be held indispensable to even a moderate degree of success. There are voices not only naturally defective, but so inherently bad, so grating, so harsh, or so impotent, that it is not conceivable they could by any application of art or labour be rendered subservient to a good delivery. There are also constitutional temperaments so nervously shy or timid, and features so uncouth in their appearance or grotesque in their movements, that they present difficulties too great to be surmounted by any ordinary amount of industry, although, it may be admitted,

such cases are not of very frequent occurrence.   They form
but a fragmentary portion of the number who pass through
the preparatory education and training which in every
well-regulated church precede admission into the rank of
preachers of the gospel.   So that one can hardly say it is
from absolute deficiency in the simply natural and physical
qualities, if more than a very small proportion of them
should fail in the attributes essential to a becoming manner
for the pulpit.   Yet *comparative* failures, there can be no
doubt, are far from being uncommon.   In numberless instances the remark is extorted from Christian congregations,
that the discourse they had listened to was Scriptural, well-
digested, in substance excellent, and only wanted to be
otherwise delivered ; but the defect there spoiled all.   I
have known not a few men of superior talents and learning, apparently of a right spirit, and perfectly capable of
thinking out their ideas clearly and giving them adequate
expression, lost in a great measure from mere defects of
manner.   They seemed to have almost everything necessary
to make them able ministers of the New Testament, but the
somewhat superficial accomplishment of a proper address.
This defect will, no doubt, be found in a number of cases
to have its root in the mental constitution of the individual—
in an imperfect possession of the qualities which form points
of sympathy and contact with the popular mind ; so that
while there may be a considerable dowry of natural and
acquired gifts, these somehow, in their mode of application,
acquire a *set*, which wants adaptation to the popular mind,
and one which it may become extremely difficult, if not impossible, to rectify.   Indeed, the cases generally of a defective or vicious delivery are of a kind that, when once
acquired, are not likely to be much improved by such
directions and precepts as can be delivered in a class-room
or set forth on the printed page.   They are so various in
themselves, and stand connected with such diversified ten-

dencies or imperfections, that, to be dealt with effectually, they would require to be dealt with individually. Somewhat possibly may be done in the way of prevention, or in guiding beforehand into the right track ; and it is mainly with that view that I am going to offer a few suggestions on the subject.

Before doing so, however, I would have it to be distinctly understood, that the things to be noticed should not be deemed as in themselves of more than secondary rank. The primary and more essential attributes belong to the state and temper of the soul. They consist in its enlightened views of divine truth, its firm grasp of the principles of a living piety, and its earnest desire to promote the great ends of the Christian ministry. Nothing can possibly compensate for the want of these, as the possession of them is the great spur to excellence. The very spring and heart of all effective preaching may be said to stand in this, feeling with all the soul, and then speaking with all the soul.

1. With this precaution as to the relative importance of things, and omitting all that is of a subordinate and merely circumstantial kind,[1] I notice, in the first place, that great care should be taken to acquire *a distinct and proper enunciation.* If there is any obvious defect here, every effort should be made by a resolute and continued application to get rid of it. For, whatever may be the peculiar style of the preacher, whether it may naturally assume a calm and dignified or a lively and impassioned form, it will always be a great advantage to possess, and a corresponding disadvantage to want, a clear and articulate enunciation. Should the words be uttered in too rapid or mumbling a fashion to be distinctly caught by the audience, should there be any broad or

[1] There are things of this sort, however, which are well deserving the attention of preachers, such as their mode of entering the pulpit, their bearing in it, their treatment of the congregation : all should be serious, without levity or undue familiarity.

obvious provincialism in the mode of expression, or should the tone of voice have got anything of a monotonous or sing-song manner, there is necessarily so far a grave impediment in the way of success ; and if not earnestly grappled with and overcome, it will be almost sure to grow into a confirmed habit.

But one of the main difficulties, when such a defect really exists, lies in the unconsciousness of the individual : it is a chance if he ever becomes duly sensible of it. Every one readily gets accustomed to his own manner of speech and action ; and nothing is more common than for those who have some marked peculiarities of utterance or gesture to fall into a sort of unconsciousness about them. It is here that the lessons of an elocution teacher may lend important service, not so much by imparting any positive element of success, as by awakening a full consciousness of the evil that exists, showing it to its owner as it appears when transferred to the person of another. In this way a too quick utterance, a bad intonation, a misplacing or neglect of emphasis, a tendency to strike upon some disagreeable key, or to use certain kinds of provincial mannerisms, may be detected before they have settled down into permanent habits, and brought under correction. Even with some pains and help of this description before the work of preaching has been actually commenced, it will rarely happen that nothing more in the way of correction needs to be effected ; and young preachers, if they are wise, will keep their ears open to any hints or suggestions that may be tendered them on the subject. It is a point of some delicacy how far *settled pastors* should encourage animadversions upon their manner in the pulpit, any more than upon the substance of their discourses, though even *they* should beware of drawing too tight a cordon around themselves ; but *preachers*, who are only, as it were, feeling their way to the right manner of speech and action, should be less scrupulous about being spoken to. And, I repeat, if they are wise, they will for a time keep their ears open. It requires a good deal of wisdom to do so; wisdom grounded in deep humility of spirit, godly simplicity of purpose, unfeigned desire to know the real truth of the case in order to turn it to profitable account; for it is apt to come like a chilling blast upon one's spirits, after having plied every effort to deliver the divine message according to the best of one's ability, to be told of some unhappy blemish or imperfection that considerably interferes with the impression. Yet remember, if there *be* such a hindrance to your proper success, it exists whether you are told of it or not; and in such a case ignorance is emphatically *not* bliss; nay, 'open rebuke is better than secret love.' It is much better to be made acquainted with the evil, when it may still be remedied, though the discovery may haply come as a stroke on the cheek, than that it should be allowed without a struggle to root itself in your being. Preachers should hold it for certain, that for the first four or five years, at least, they are in the position of learners, with not a few things about them that require to be improved and rectified; and that they can attain to the relative perfection of which they may be capable no otherwise than by becoming alive to the evil as well as the good in their characteristics, and striving with manly resolution to make the best of it. Perfection here, as in other things, comes not so much from being originally destitute of faults, as from knowing well what faults exist, and then aiming at their rectification.[1]

2. A second point to be attended to, is to endeavour to obtain *naturalness* in voice and manner. Nothing in this respect can be quite good which is not natural, or which attempts to put nature to an undue strain, doing some sort of violence to it. In all departments nature must be the

[1] See Miller's *Clerical Manners*, p. 99. There are also some good remarks on the subject in Beecher's *Lectures on Preaching*, Lect. vi.

foundation of art, in a great degree also the *measure* of art ; and not what, abstractedly considered, may be the best, but what is best relatively to the powers and situation of each individual, *that* is for him the point especially to be aimed at. Very commonly it is some time before this can be quite surely ascertained. The man must be regarded as unusually skilful and fortunate who gets all at once into the kind of voice and manner which it is most becoming in him to cultivate as a public speaker. In the majority of cases there will probably be found an ideal excellence set up in the mind's eye, derived more or less from the known characteristics of some particular individual. And from that imitative principle in our nature which has so many important functions to fulfil, we are extremely apt to fancy that what seems natural to others must be the same with ourselves. Hence it so often happens that artificial mannerisms, strained and unnatural modes of speech, which are utterly unknown in youth, spring up in after life, and become all the more inveterate that they are acquired. And if in higher things the way to the right has many times to be sought by returning whence one has set out ; if, as has been said, 'Childhood often holds a truth with its feeble fingers which the grasp of manhood cannot retain, which it is the pride of utmost age to recover' (Ruskin) ; so with the earnest student, in regard to what is for him the proper style of manner and speech, his chief endeavour will often need to be directed to the getting rid of the false set he has acquired, and resuming the simple tones, the natural cadences, and unforced gesticulations of childhood. Let every one try to bear in mind, that so far as in these respects he departs from the simplicity of nature, his manner inevitably loses in power and attractiveness ; while, by taking nature for his basis, he may make almost incredible advances.

On this point the question was asked by one who was

himself a distinguished and most useful preacher,[1] 'When will preachers learn that preaching is but talking in a louder tone, and with a little more emphasis of manner? Why affect a preaching or a praying tone, a manner of speaking peculiar to the pulpit? The conversational manner, occasionally elevated, animated, and energetic as impassioned passages and feelings may require, is what we want. There are some men who are good talkers out of the pulpit, yet bad speakers in it. How much more acceptable would they be, if they would carry their easy, natural manner of conversation with them into the sacred desk!' Yet it is possible to go to excess also in this direction; and there is truth in what Adolph Monod says,[2] that 'too great familiarity is almost as great a fault as declamation. It is the tone of *good* conversation, but this tone ennobled and exalted, which seems to me to be the ideal of oratorical delivery.' Very much to the same effect is said by Whately:[3] 'It would not be by any means natural to an educated and sober-minded man to speak like an illiterate enthusiast, or to discourse on the most important matters in the tone of familiar conversation respecting the trifling occurrences of the day. Any one who does but notice the style in which a man of ability, and of good choice of words and utterance, delivers his sentiments *in private*, when he is, for instance, earnestly and seriously admonishing a friend, defending the truths of religion, or speaking on any other grave subject on which he is intent, may easily observe how different his tone is from that of light and familiar conversation, how far from deficient in the dignified seriousness which befits the case! Even a stranger to the language might guess that he was not engaged on any frivolous topic. And yet, when an opportunity occurs of observing how he delivers a written discourse of his own composition, or perhaps the very same

[1] James, in *Earnest Ministry*, p. 118.
[2] Discourse on *Delivery of Sermons*.   [3] *Rhetoric*, p. 364.

on a similar subject, will it not often be perceived how comparatively stiff, languid, and unimpressive is the effect ?'

In short, there are two extremes here to be guarded against. On the one side a stiff, formal mouthing, or monotonous manner ; on the other, the quite free and easy, or simply conversational tone. The latter is so far better than the former, that it *is* natural, though wanting the proper force and elevation of tone. And he who can hit the happy medium between the two is the person who here lights upon the proper track.

3. Another thing of great importance, and materially conducive to the end just considered, is getting the mind well prepared on the subject of discourse, at home in it, and alive to it. Every one is sensible of the difference of manner in the person who, whatever be the matter in hand, shows himself to be well acquainted with the topics he discusses, and the same person, perhaps, when conversing about what he neither very well knows nor cares much about. In the former case there is sure to be a precision, a freedom, and a warmth in what is said, of which little or no trace is found in the other. There is no conceivable reason why it should be otherwise in the pulpit. The difference in the two cases may rather be expected to be more marked there, as the speaker is less at his ease, and he can less readily conceal any deficiency in knowledge or interest under which he may labour. If a preacher goes to the pulpit with his ideas imperfectly arranged or dimly apprehended ; or if, having all in that respect much as it should be, he has still not got his heart about the subject, so that the matter he has to bring forth may rather be said to lie before him than to be incorporated with his inner man, it is in the nature of things impossible that the mode of delivery can be engaging or impressive. It may well enough be distinct, correct, or possibly animated and vehement, but it can have nothing of true kindling warmth and stimulating power.

Undue familiarity with the subject of a discourse may produce substantially the same effect as comparative strangeness to it; everything by frequent repetition has lost its freshness to the preacher's mind, and become in a manner stale. Indeed, whatever has the effect of keeping the speaker himself at some distance from his theme, of rendering it either faint to his apprehension or dull to the feelings of his heart, cannot but in a like proportion affect the manner in which he discourses of it to others. And no one who has any experience in preaching can have failed to perceive how differently in point of naturalness, life, and energy he has spoken what was perhaps to a nearness the same discourse at one time, compared with the tone and spirit which characterized his delivery of it at another. It is necessary, therefore, to remember that no general propriety of manner, nor even this coupled with a clear and accurate knowledge of the whole matter of discourse, will be sufficient to ensure, regularly and unexceptionably, a mode of delivery that will meet either the expectations of the hearers or the desires of the preacher himself. Much will still depend upon his state of mind at the time; and only when, by previous meditation and prayer, this has been brought into suitable accordance with the message he has to deliver, will the words he speaks pass from him with due emphasis and power. No art in the mere modulation of speech, no straining or energy of action, can ever make up for the want of a heartfelt appreciation of the things discoursed of, or a rightly attempered frame of mind.

4. A further point which calls for some consideration and adjustment, is the adaptation of the mode of delivery to the precise character of the discourse, or particular portions of the discourse, delivered. Varieties in the one naturally call for corresponding varieties in the other. If the discourse were altogether of an explanatory or expository nature, it would not do to be spoken with the same tone

and tension of manner, which might be quite suitable and appropriate if one were endeavouring to illustrate and enforce a principle, or exhort to the performance of some arduous duty.   But a pulpit discourse will, in general, only in part belong to any specific kind ; in some portions it will aim more immediately at the enlightenment of the understanding ; in others, at the excitation of the feelings, or the guidance and direction of the will.   It should therefore differ materially in its structure from an essay, which, calling into play the intellect or taste merely, may preserve throughout an almost unchanging equability of tone.   The other requires a certain measure of variety ; variety, first, in the method and style of discourse, and then somewhat of a like variety in the manner, which is associated with the delivery of its several parts.   If the whole should be gone through in one strain, the attention of the audience will inevitably flag ; a sense of satiety or weariness will be produced, and the preacher may not improbably come to be viewed much in the light of a performer who has a certain taskwork of duty to overtake, rather than of one who has to play skilfully on an instrument, so as, if possible, to touch the various sensibilities, and work into proper harmony of thought and feeling with himself the minds of those he addresses.   There should therefore be an effort to vary the manner according to the nature of the discourse ; and to *time* oneself as to strength and energy, by interposing quieter and calmer passages between those requiring somewhat of sustained and vigorous action.   Sometimes even brief pauses are advisable, if the discourse is of such a nature as to demand continuous thought and sustained application ; it being no small part of practical wisdom to take one's breath at the right time, and thereby give seasonable relief both to speaker and hearer.

5. The remarks hitherto made have had reference to delivery in general, whether the discourse may be simply in the pastor's mind or lying in a written page before him.

Nothing further has been implied than that the matter he is going to address to his congregation has been made the subject of previous thought and consideration, so as to qualify him for speaking intelligently and feelingly about it; without which, directions as to manner will be of little moment. But it would be improper to quit this branch of the subject without paying some attention to the question as to the relative merits of preaching from or without manuscript; or as it is very commonly put, preaching, or simply reading sermons.

If one were to be guided by authorities on the art of public speaking, the question would be easily decided; for while I know of many writers on this art who have spoken very decidedly against reading discourses, I know of none worth mentioning who gives the preference to the opposite practice. Campbell says:[1] 'That a discourse well spoken has a stronger effect than one well read, will hardly bear a question. From this manifest truth I very early concluded, and was long of opinion, that the way of reading sermons should be absolutely banished from the pulpit. But from further experience I am now disposed to suspect that this conclusion was rather hasty.' He goes on to state that he found so very few attained to excellence in speaking their discourses, while a considerable number read tolerably, that he deemed it, upon the whole, preferable to have the plan, which in itself was inferior, and admitted only of a respectable mediocrity, generally adopted; not, therefore, because he thought it better, but because a certain degree of success in it was easier. Blair, with all his coldness and moderation, gives his decision in a tone still more decided. He says:[1] 'The practice of reading sermons is one of the greatest obstacles to the eloquence of the pulpit in Great Britain, where alone this practice prevails' (alone in Blair's time, though far from

[1] *Lectures on Pulpit Eloquence*, p. 159.
[2] *Lectures*, ii. p. 297.

being so now). 'No discourse which is designed to be persuasive can have the same force when read as when spoken. The common people all feel this, and their prejudice against this practice is not without foundation in nature. What is gained hereby in point of correctness is not equal, I apprehend, to what is lost in point of persuasion and force.'

In a former generation, Bishop Burnet spoke of the practice as one 'peculiar to the English nation, and endured by no other.' So distasteful was it on its first general introduction there, that Charles II. issued a proclamation forbidding it as 'a supine and superficial way of preaching,' as it was characterized, which had lately sprung up, and ought to be laid aside. Whately, in more recent times, refrains from pronouncing a judgment on the comparative advantages of the two methods with reference to the pulpit; for he will hardly allow himself to regard it as an open question, whether sermons should be read or not. He takes it for granted that they will be read, and contents himself with giving some directions which might help preachers to attain to a style of reading that would approximate preaching as to apparent naturalness and real power. But his very speech betrays how he felt as to the relative tendencies of the two modes, and which of them he thought best calculated in itself to produce effect. 'It has been already remarked,' he says, 'how easy it is for the hearers to keep up their attention when they are addressed by one who is *really speaking* to them in a natural and earnest manner, though the discourse, perhaps, may be encumbered with a good deal of repetition, awkwardness of expression, and other faults incident to extemporaneous language; and though it be prolonged for an hour or two, and yet contain no more matter than a good *writer* could have clearly expressed in a discourse of half an hour, which last, if read to them, would not, without some effort on their part, have so fully detained their attention.' Of course, therefore, other things being equal, the speaker has a great advantage over the reader for sustaining the interest of his auditors, and gaining the practical ends he aims at. Hare, who was more free, and less trammelled in his judgment on such matters by conventional arrangements, leaves no room to doubt how he thought upon the subject :[1] 'What do our clergy lose,' says he, 'by reading their sermons? They lose preaching ; the preaching of the voice in many cases, the preaching of the eye almost always.' And to name but another, the late excellent Mr. James very earnestly dissuades from the practice of reading :[2] 'Nothing,' he says, 'can be conceived of more likely to repress earnestness and to hinder our usefulness than this method becoming general. True it is, that some preachers may rise up, who, like a few living examples, may in despite of this practice attain to eminence, to honour, and to usefulness, such as rarely falls to the lot of ministers in any denomination ; but this will not be the case with the greater number, who, having no commanding talent to lift them above the disadvantage of this habit, will find few churches willing to accept their dulness for the sake of the accuracy with which it is expressed. And who can tell how much greater our greatest men would be if they delivered their sermons without their notes ?'[3]

Certainly, as regards the general feeling in congregations, at least in Scotland, there is a strong advantage on the side of the non-reading preacher. He takes the course which appears to them both natural and proper, so that the way is

---

[1] *Guesses at Truth*, vol. ii. p. 214.   [2] *Earnest Ministry*, p. 124.

[3] It is worthy of note also that the introduction of the practice among the English Nonconformists was not of very happy omen. 'In the course of the second period (that is, near the close of last century), it became the fashion among the Dissenting ministers to read their sermons. Brief outlines of the sermon had been made use of by some of the Nonconformists to assist the memory ; a few had the whole placed before them, which they looked at occasionally ; but the greater part made themselves masters of the subject, and preached without notes.

in a manner open for him to make such impression on their minds as the matter with which he is charged is calculated to produce.   With the person, however, who reads his discourses there is, first of all, a repugnance to be overcome ; he has to fight his way, in a manner, to a favourable hearing, to confront and triumph over an acknowledged prejudice. All must admit this to be so far a disadvantage were the feeling in question nothing but a prejudice without any valid grounds to rest on ; for there *are* prejudices which wise and prudent men will never fail to respect, which apostles even were obliged to humour in order that they might not preach in vain, or labour in vain.   But I doubt if, in the present case, the feeling should be treated simply and in all cases as a prejudice.   Even Blair says : ' It has its foundation in nature,' as, indeed, the general practice of mankind in regard to public speaking clearly evinces.   It springs from a prevailing and deep-rooted conviction, that when men thoroughly in earnest undertake to speak to their fellow-men on a subject of importance, they should be able to give expression to their views and feelings without the formal apparatus of a book, and with the freedom and elasticity of a spoken address.   It undoubtedly has also, in this country at least, the general testimony of results on its side ; for the preaching which has usually been most appreciated by the better portion of the community, and which has yielded by much the largest harvest of spiritual good, is undoubtedly preaching

By degrees reading slipt into general use with those who wrote their discourses at full length, not only among the Presbyterians, but the Independents too; and there were few of the London ministers in either of these denominations who did not pore very much over their notes. Towards the close of the period the practice was at its height.   Not to use notes was at that time accounted methodistical ; and in the metropolis, reading was the evidence of Dissenting regularity.' [1]

---

[1] Bogue and Bennett's *Hist. of Dissenters*, vol. ii. p. 263.

in the stricter sense, preaching as contradistinguished from reading ; the latter also, in many parts of the country, being associated with sad memories of cold and lifeless ministrations. And there is, I suspect, in the better class of our Scottish population, a deeper and more sacred feeling still at the bottom of their dislike to read sermons. They have elevated views of the ministry of the gospel when it appears to be prosecuted in an earnest and believing spirit. He who comes forth in such a spirit to discharge its duties, especially in the preaching of the gospel, is regarded by them as the bearer of a message from the Lord ; not as if he had any new tidings to divulge, or truths never heard before to communicate, but because he has on his spirit portions of the word of God to unfold in its proper meaning and various application, so that, relatively to their state and sense of obligation, it comes to them as a fresh exhibition of divine truth, a new opening to them of the counsel of Heaven. Impressed with such a conviction, and justly impressed with it, they cannot understand how that should possess anything like the character of a message to them from the upper sanctuary which they see the minister reading calmly from a paper before him. This presents to their view the aspect of an essay composed, or a line of argumentation pursued, by the reasoning faculties of the man ; a thing for the family or the closet rather than for the house of God, where the special presence of the Spirit is expected, and where living communications should be ever passing between heaven and earth. They judge, of course, from appearances. You cannot get them to throw themselves back upon the pastor's study, and consider whether there may not, for a well-spoken discourse, have been as much previous preparation going on there as for a read one, and whether the one kind of preparation may not have been as much made under the guidance of the Spirit as the other. They judge, as I have said, in great measure from the appearance ; the one mode of delivering the testimony of God has much more than the other the aspect of a real message, a direct dealing with their souls about divine things; nor can they easily persuade themselves that the pastor has the interests of salvation properly at heart if he cannot discourse to them with some freeness on the subject. And I fear, if the practice of reading should become altogether or nearly universal, it would go far to undermine the salutary feeling of which I speak. Sermons read from the pulpit will come to be regarded much in the light of a kind of book literature, and the idea cease to be entertained of its being one of the appointed channels through which the Spirit maintains living intercourse with the souls of men.

Taking all these things into account, considering also the difficulty, with all possible care and application, of acquiring a manner in reading which shall approximate speaking in naturalness and life, considering further the almost inevitable loss it involves of what Hare calls the preaching voice, and especially the preaching eye, I have no hesitation in giving my decided and earnest recommendation in favour of preaching without manuscript, as in itself, and apart from any peculiar circumstances of place or otherwise, the method that ought to be preferred. So clearly does this appear to me to be the right course, that there should always, I think, be strong and somewhat special reasons to warrant a departure from it. I am by no means disposed to say such reasons may not exist, and would deprecate any stringent regulation on the subject, absolutely proscribing the use of papers in the pulpit. Sometimes the character of the congregation may furnish an adequate reason, namely, when it is almost wholly composed of persons of much culture and polish, naturally disposing it to prize—to prize, perhaps, unduly— the correct or the beautiful in thought and expression above the emotional and impulsive; in such a case it may be usually the wisest course to adopt the practice of reading.

The great majority of preachers, even of such as are distinguished by their powers of speech, might find this the mode best adapted to render their ministrations most acceptable and useful to the class of minds they have to deal with. Sometimes, again, the occasion may furnish an adequate reason, as when the discourse to be delivered is on some topic on which it is desirable to bring forward a considerable amount of specific information, or to treat it with much precision of thought and language ; in that case few congregations would be so unreasonable as to object to the free use of written preparations, for it is rather the solidity of the matter, and the well-weighed, carefully-balanced expression that is given to one's views respecting it, by which the discourse is to succeed in its aim, than its power to interest and move the feelings. Still, again, there may be reasons in the mental constitution of the preacher himself rendering it every way probable, if not absolutely certain, that his manner of delivery, on the whole, would be rather injured than improved by the disuse of his notes. The case of Dr. Chalmers may be referred to as one of the most noticeable examples in this class. His cast of thought so deeply impressed itself on his style, and that style was so much more adapted for written composition than for extemporaneous address, that his discourses, in anything approaching their actual form, could scarcely have been delivered otherwise than by reading from the manuscript. Yet their vehement and persuasive oratory was so intimately connected with the very form in which they were produced, that one could hardly have advised the alteration of the form in order simply to get rid of the manuscript ; the more especially as in his case, more perhaps than that of any other great exemplar of eloquence, there was such an absorption of the man in the subject, that it seemed much a matter of indifference whether he read or not. The rapt enthusiasm of the speaker made everything external be forgotten ; and as it was clear that the eye moved too much in a region of its own to keep up the play of any direct interchange of feeling with the audience, the effect was not sensibly marred by its resting so much on the written page. His case, however, was altogether peculiar; it must be excepted from the common category; for as few could *read* like him in the pulpit as *write* like him at the desk.

Most commonly, when reasons are drawn from the personal idiosyncrasy of the preacher, they turn upon the felt difficulty, the practical impossibility, of getting the subject of discourse in the mind without writing the discourse in full, and then committing it to memory, so that it must be much the same thoughts and expressions which in either case are presented to the minds of the congregation; and as to the preacher's own consciousness, there is little difference between the discourse as spoken or as read. As, moreover, the preparation necessary to speak it costs much time and irksome labour, and the actual speaking is attended with manifold anxieties, not to say risks of failure, which are avoided by the smoother course of reading, he deems himself justified in resorting to this latter method, and thinks it reasonable that the grounds of his decision should prevail also with his audience. I have no doubt that there are persons of good natural abilities, and in many respects so qualified for the work of the ministry, that it were to be regretted if the Church should lose their services, who yet, from defect of memory or from nervous temperament, find the work of preaching without manuscript so beset with difficulties, that the other practice appears to them the only one properly within their reach. It is also possible, by due pains and well-directed effort, to get into a mode of reading so easy and graceful and impressive, that it resembles much a spoken address; for in this respect great diversities undoubtedly exist. It is possible, yet one cannot say frequent; and there are two considerations which should have much weight in disposing candidates for the ministry to be cautious in giving way to such a style of thinking. One is, that the practice of reading discourses ministers so readily to the love of ease, that it is almost sure to call forth by degrees less application, to grow less like speaking rather than the reverse; the manuscript, when once fairly trusted to, will be increasingly depended on, and at last, perhaps, slavishly adhered to. The other consideration is, that unless one sits resolutely to the work of studying his subject with the view of being prepared to preach without notes, he scarcely knows what he can do in the matter, or what, in the long run, would be the actual cost to him in time and labour. The greatest difficulties lie here at the threshold; they call for vigorous and persevering application at the outset; but if this is given they gradually diminish, till an amount of work is done, and done with comparative ease, which at one time would have appeared incredible to the person himself who succeeds in accomplishing it.

Take as an example the case of Thomas Scott the commentator. In a letter to a country clergyman, Mr. Coffin, published along with many others so late as 1845, Mr. Newton sought to stimulate and encourage his correspondent by the experience of Scott. 'Mr. Scott,' he says, 'is perhaps the most ready and fluent extempore preacher amongst us; yet when he agreed with me upon other points, he still insisted that he should never be able to preach without a book. For some time he read his prayer in his chamber with his wife, and had not confidence to let even her hear him without a form. . . . One day he was so taken up that he could not possibly write his homily. He was forced to speak; and was not a little surprised when some of the people told him they hoped he would read no more, for they had never heard him so well before. From that time he laid his notes aside.' Indeed, he went to the opposite extreme, of not only laying aside notes, but ceasing to write them; he simply premeditated his subject, and used what words and illustrations came to his hand at the moment of delivery, an extreme I by no means recommend. But in Mr. Scott's case its injurious tendencies would probably be in good measure counteracted by the vigour of his understanding, his uncommon acquaintance with Scripture, and the constant exercise of his pen in other departments of labour. I point to his example mainly in proof of the success which often attends the resolute endeavour to overcome the difficulties that seem to render progress in the line I recommend all but impracticable. For those, however, who resolve to make the attempt of preaching without manuscript, various methods may be adopted, according to their own peculiar gifts and predilections. In every case, where absolute necessity does not prevent, there should be careful preparation. But this, with some, may take the form of fully thinking out the subject in their mind, with comparatively little in the way of writing, which, by practice, may be carried to the extent of arranging almost every line of thought and illustration, many a paragraph also of the discourse, while still leaving the mind at some liberty to follow the impulse of the moment, and to speak as the Spirit may give them utterance. This is the plan that has been followed by some of the most eminent preachers, as well in former as in present times. Of Mr. Hall, for example, we are told by Dr. Leifchild in his memoirs : ' I learnt from him that most of his great sermons were first worked out in thought, and inwardly elaborated in the very words in which they were delivered. He ridiculed the delusion of those who supposed that the perorations of his sermons were delivered *impromptu*, observing that they were the most carefully studied parts of the whole discourse.' Or the method may be adopted of writing the introduction in full, one or more of the heads of discourse, with select portions of other parts ; and, for the rest, merely placing the thoughts in order, adjusting the materials, but leaving the language to the moment of delivery. This method has the advantage of obliging the mind to have its course of thought and illustration very distinctly marked out beforehand, and also of providing it with a certain amount of suitable matter for the occasion, while at ever-recurring intervals it gives scope to the free expression of thoughts and feelings as they arise. Only, as in the former case, it will certainly require, to be managed with success, a considerable degree of self-possession, with clearness of vision and readiness of utterance; otherwise there is sure to appear at particular parts a hesitancy, a confusion of thought, or perhaps a tendency to fall into repetitions. With the requisite amount of talent and adequate preparation such things may be prevented, but they will need to be well guarded against. Still another method has been adopted by some, that of writing the discourse throughout, then reading it carefully over once and again so as to get the entire train of thought on the memory, and many of the particular expressions also in which it is unfolded; yet without attempting to have it committed *verbatim*, which, from experience, they find to be irksome and embarrassing. When such a plan *can* be followed without material inconvenience, that is, when it suits the preacher's mental habits, it may be followed with advantage, combining, as it does, careful preparations with a rational freedom in the use of them. But the instances are not, perhaps, very numerous in which it will be found practically available. For, generally speaking, when one has been at the pains of writing all beforehand, the mind will not be satisfied with itself if it does not also present its thoughts in the same form to others; and a conscious departure from that form in the delivery will usually have the effect of disconcerting the preacher, and of rendering his manner hesitating and embarrassed. It will only succeed where there is such a want of faithfulness and precision in the memory as convinces the individual of his utter inability to adhere closely to what he has written, and at the same time a conscious need of the support it provides.

But, undoubtedly, the more common method, and the one that will probably be found in the great majority of cases to be most practicable, is to write, if not absolutely all the discourse, yet all that is of much moment, and so far to commit it to memory as to be able to deliver it with substantial correctness from the pulpit, with nothing more, perhaps, than a brief outline of the train of thought. At first, no doubt, this will usually be accompanied with a sense of irksomeness in the effort to get such a mass of preconceived matter upon the mind, and a feeling of restraint in uttering it. But by exercise these gradually give way; the manner of composition adapts itself more and more closely to the manner of delivery, and the memory both acquires more easily, and with more fidelity retains, what has been written, so that the preacher comes to write much as he would speak, and to speak much as if he was not adhering to any pre-arranged form of words. People who have not fairly tried this method can have no adequate idea of the extent to which it can be realized, and of the indefinite nearness to which the utterance of the speaker can be made to approach in style and spirit the habits of the writer.

The degree of preparation, however, which has now been recommended, is sometimes thought too much, has even been stigmatized by persons of some standing and experience as at variance with the apostolic idea of preaching, and incompatible with the true power of the pulpit. It is done particularly in the spirited treatise of Dr. Arthur, *The Tongue of Fire.* The treatise contains not a little that is excellent and deserving of serious consideration, but is somewhat one-sided, looking at the subject from what may be called more especially the Methodist point of view, as if the end of preaching were almost exclusively conversion, and the minister had only to aim at the bringing of souls to Christ. And this, as formerly stated, is so very fundamental and primary an object in the ministerial calling, that I regret having to say anything that may even seem to take off the mind from it, or to lessen its relative importance. It is immensely the greatest, but still it is not the whole ; and to contemplate it as the exclusive object of a minister's anxiety and labour, is not, I am convinced, the best way of securing even that, as it naturally leads to the undue elevation of some elements of power, and the comparative or total neglect of others. Contemplating the matter chiefly from the point of view now mentioned, the writer in question states it to be the right feeling for every one who goes to preach the gospel, after having been at some pains to think over and digest the truth : ' I am here to say just what God may enable me to say ; to be enlarged or to be straitened, according as He may be pleased to give utterance or not.'[1] And with this feeling, he says, 'all appearances ought to correspond. It ought to be manifest that, while he has done what in him lies to be thoroughly furnished, he is *trusting* for utterance to help from above, and not *ensuring* it by natural means, either a manuscript or memory. We put these together, because we do not see that any distinction really exists between them. The plea that the manuscript is more honest than *memoriter* preaching has some force, but certainly not much, for he that reads from his memory is to the feeling and instinct of his hearers as much reading as he who reads from his manuscript. In neither case are the thoughts and feelings gushing straight from the mind, and clothing themselves as they come. The mind is taking up words from paper or from memory, and doing its best to animate them with feeling. Even intellectually the operation is essentially different from speaking, and the difference

[1] P. 322.

is felt by all. For literary purposes, for intellectual gratification, both have a decided advantage over speaking; but
for the purposes of pleading, entreating, winning, and creating a sense of fellowship, for impelling and arousing, for
doing good, speaking is the natural, is the Creator's instrument.' He admits that other modes may be, and have
been, blessed for good; but still he says of reading, either
from the manuscript or from memory, that it is not Scriptural preaching. 'It is not ministering after the mode of
Pentecostal Christianity; it is a departure from Scriptural
precedent, an adoption of a lower order of public ministrations, and a solemn declaration that security of utterance
gained by natural supports is preferred over a liability to be
humiliated by trusting to the help of the Lord.'

With much esteem for the author of these sentiments, I
yet feel constrained to say, that the passage appears to me
to contain quite false assumptions, false alike in the psycho-
logy and in the Scriptural idea of the subject, and is much
fitted, if reduced to practice, to lead to disappointed hopes
and unsatisfying results. First of all, it is ridiculous to say
that to speak from memory what has been committed to it
beforehand is all one with reading, as in both cases alike
the mind can only take up the words which lie before it,
and do its best to animate them with feeling. Can a sentiment not be impregnated with the feelings of the heart
which is presented to it even in the most definite form
through the memory? What, in that case, would become
of the great Pentecostal address itself, one half of which and
more consists of Scripture quotations, and which, doubtless,
came into Peter's lips through his memory? Shall we say
of that portion of his address, that he was only reading from
memory, and doing what he could to animate it with feeling,
while the other portions alone were what he uttered from
the Spirit? But why may not the memory, as well as any
other part of the mental constitution, the reason, for ex-

ample, or the feelings, be used by the Spirit to bring
thoughts and words seasonably to the preacher's mind ? If
I study and digest my subject carefully beforehand, as Dr.
Arthur advises, I necessarily exercise my reasoning powers
and my memory too ; and in doing so I necessarily employ
natural means to ensure, so far as such means *can* ensure, a
suitable and appropriate command of thought and expression when I actually preach. But, on Dr. Arthur's principle,
this is to distrust the Spirit ; it is to resort to natural means
for what He alone is competent to give, so that to refrain
from *all* special preparation beforehand would be the
legitimate result of such a mode of contemplation ; the
whole should be left to the voluntary impulse of the
moment. This, however, is simply fanaticism ; it is to
confound the Spirit's ordinary influence with a supernatural
afflatus, given independently, and apart from the exercise of
the mind's own faculties. Even inspiration, the highest
form of spiritual influence, was not so arbitrary and independent in its action. It, too, gave free scope to the
memory and the reason, as well as the emotional faculties
of the soul; and on various occasions we find both prophets
and apostles, when speaking as they were moved by the
Holy Ghost, reiterating, not the thoughts merely, but the
precise words of entire sentences and paragraphs of former
messengers of God. If *they* could thus serve themselves of
other men's words and ideas—serve themselves, of course,
through memory—while not the less speaking under the
power of the Spirit, surely I, speaking under an inferior
action of the same power, may still more make a similar use
of my own.

But again, even if it were the case, which it is not, St.
Peter's preaching on the day of Pentecost proceeded, apart
from the natural use and exercise of the memory, in recalling previous trains of thought and forms of expression, we
should not have been warranted to conclude that the em-

ployment of memory, or of any other natural faculties, was thereby disparaged in the future preaching of the gospel. It is an essential and general characteristic of the Spirit's work, that He adapts Himself to the laws of mental action in those through whom He works, and to the circumstances in which for the time they happen to be placed. Beyond all question, the circumstances of the day of Pentecost were to a large extent peculiar, both as regards speakers and hearers. What mainly was needed on that memorable occasion was conviction, and for this, only the exhibition of a few simple facts respecting the person of Jesus, His death and resurrection, brought to bear with power on the hearts and consciences of men : this was all. And accordingly the speech of Peter on the occasion consisted mainly of a brief rehearsal of the great facts of the case, with the application of a few ancient prophecies referring to them, followed by a personal appeal to the individuals addressed. For a speech of that description, not only no previous writing, but not even any special forethought and meditation of the subject, could be required. But look to other apostolic speeches, to St. Paul's speech, for example, before the Areopagus, where not so much the feelings as the reason of the audience had to be won, do we not feel in reading it as if we had to do with a compactly arranged and most carefully thought out discourse ? Or look to the two accounts he gives of his own conversion, though traversing substantially the same ground, yet each of them admirably adapted to the different audiences he addressed, and the more immediate objects he had in view : all showing what varieties the Spirit can employ in the style and mode of address, and consequently in the faculties called into play for its conception and utterance. Dr. Arthur himself, in another part of his treatise, admits this, and apparently forgets at one place what he has written at another.[1] ' This fire,' he says, ' may be combined with

[1] P. 255.

any form of talent, and with any style of composition. Who has not seen a tranquil man, whose tones seldom rose to passion, and never went beyond the severest taste ; whose thought, demeanour, phrases, all breathed a gentle and quiet spirit ; and yet, with the placid flow of instruction or exposition, a heavenly influence stole silently along ; stole into the veins of the heart, diffusing a sacred glow, a desire to be holier, a sense of nearness to God, a refreshing of all the good principles within you, a check and a restraint on all the evil ? Again, you have seen a man, who begins with some calm argument, passes to another point, closely reasoned, which again leads him to another well-pointed stroke at some error or prejudice ; no by-play of imagination, no home-thrust to your heart, but one steady grapple with your intellect, a discourse which would be pronounced dry were it not for a mysterious power which accompanies it,' and so on with several other varieties of mental action and well-constructed discourse. But I wonder how many such discourses one might reasonably expect to hear on the author's view of the Spirit's influence and the preacher's duty. Depend on it they will seldom be met with, except in connection with the sedulous employment of natural means, as well as humble trust in spiritual agencies ; and memory will have its full share in the matter, calling up the various forms of thought and modes of expression, which had previously been cogitated as best fitted to promote the end in view.

The more, too, that the world advances in knowledge and refinement, the higher that any particular congregation stands in intellectual culture, the greater always is the variety of talents that must be called into play, and the more may the Spirit be expected to make use of the treasures of memory, as well as other resources, to act upon the soul. For the classes that evangelistic agents or itinerant preachers have chiefly to deal with, a comparatively small range of topics may be sufficient ; and the power to be put forth has only to rouse insensibility and impress the heart. Very commonly in such cases, the bluff, off-hand, earnest, but coarse and rambling speaker is the instrument best adapted to the purpose. But the same speaker might produce only disgust elsewhere ; and hence it is that the most eminently useful of that class of preachers, within a limited circle, very rarely succeed as pastors of regular congregations.

Still further, the view against which we argue is not borne out, but, on the contrary, opposed to established facts. No doubt there *are* facts in abundance to support the view in question *so far*. If the case had been put conditionally, if it were said that preaching *memoriter* may be, and often is, only a sort of reading, the mind being chiefly taken up with its effort to remember what was written, and able to do nothing more than utter with formal correctness its prepared sentences, one could not have questioned the fact, and as little commended the practice in that form of it as a proper specimen of apostolic preaching. But if properly cultivated, it both may and will exist in a very different form, and also be productive of far other results. When the method is followed as it ought to be, that is, when the discourse has been prepared with a suitable adaptation to the preacher's own manner, as well as to the audience he has to address, and has been thoroughly got upon the mind and heart of the preacher, there will usually be a marked difference in his mode of delivering it from what would have been the case if it had been simply read from his notes ; a difference such that the auditors cannot with any certainty infer how much is due to previous preparation, how much to the feeling and impulse of the moment. Did not He who spake as never man spake Himself repeat over again on several occasions the very words He had uttered before ? But if so, wherein did this differ from preaching *memoriter ?* It is notorious, also, that some of the most gifted preachers, not excepting those who were not in the habit of writing out their discourses, Whitfield for example, have been known usually to preach with most effect when for the second or third time they spoke from the same text. The reason is that they had then come to obtain a more thorough command of the subject, so that the thoughts and words came more promptly to the call of memory. Were I to refer to my own observation and experience, I should have no hesitation in saying, that the discourses which I have listened to with most profit, which have raised the deepest spiritual feeling, and which manifestly bore with them the largest unction from the Holy One, were discourses which came from the preacher, indeed, with the greatest apparent freedom, but which I knew to have been carefully prepared beforehand ; yet surely, operating as they did, they were in the strictest sense the Creator's instrument of working. I have seen whole audiences moved by such discourses as I have never seen them moved by any others. And in the course of my own ministry, I have noted that the occasions on which the most distinct benefit was reaped, have with few exceptions been those in which my own preparations had been most careful and complete.

But in saying this, is anything indicated at variance with the idea, that only when the Spirit accompanies the efforts of the preacher does the word go forth with power ? Would I, or any one who has experience in the work of God, ever dream of making human preparations independent of the Spirit? No, assuredly; it is still that Spirit alone which quickeneth, quickeneth the soul of the preacher to utter aright the things of God, as well as the souls of the people to hear them aright. Without the Spirit breathing as a divine power through his heart, and giving life to his words, let those words be ever so correct in themselves, and ever so fitly remembered and spoken, they will be found at most as a pleasant sound to the ear, or a gratification to the intellect ; but with no saving or permanent results. Yes, the Spirit is the one effective agent ; and only in so far as we are in communion with His fulness of life and blessing can our pulpit ministrations proceed either with comfort to ourselves or with spiritual profit to those who wait on them.

My earnest counsel and advice, therefore, to those who are entering on the work of the ministry, is, Let no one dissuade you from the painstaking and careful preparation of your discourses. Your manner of delivery *need* not suffer by it, *will* not suffer, if you go rightly about the work ; and your matter will assuredly gain. The cases are few, indeed, of those who can adequately minister to stated congregations without such preparatory work, compared with those who indispensably require it. But beware of trusting unduly to it ; as if, when you have written well, and delivered accurately what you have written, nothing more were needed. Believe, rather, that nothing can be done to purpose unless the Spirit of God mingle with *your* spirit, and give effect to the words you speak. And even as regards the method, do not tie yourselves up to a specific line. In practical appeals especially, and the improvement of particular points, give yourself up occasionally to the impulse of the moment. And at what may be called extra services, and in district prayer meetings, cultivate a freer manner of speech, learn to speak from premeditation merely, not from written preparations. And thus, in this respect also, becoming all things to all men, disusing at one time what you feel you must use at another, you may the better hope to succeed in the great object of your calling.

See some good remarks and advices in Bautain's *Art of Extempore Speaking*, as to the details of manner, the management of bodily feelings, voice, etc. And on the matter of careful preparation, the following statements of Lord Brougham are deserving of consideration ; the more so, as he was himself regarded as one of the readiest as well as most effective speakers of his time in Parliament. It may be added, that Robert Hall, on hearing the sentiments read from the 'Inaugural Address,' said, 'Brougham is quite right, sir. Preparation is everything. If I were asked what is the chief requisite for eloquence, I should reply, *preparation ;* and what the second, *preparation ;* and what the third, *preparation.*' Then, with a sigh, 'If I had prepared more for the pulpit, I should have been a much better preacher.'[1]

After stating that generally the ancients showed even ' excessive care in the preparation of their speeches ;' that Cicero kept a ' book of passages, to be used on occasions ;' that Demosthenes probably had the same: 'At all events,' he says, ' one thing is certain, that he, Demosthenes, was very averse to extempore speaking, and most reluctantly, as he expressed it, " trusted to his success in fortune ;" and his orations abound in passages, and even in parts of passages, again and again used by him with such improvements as their reception or delivery, or his own subsequent reflection, suggested. I have examined this subject very fully on different occasions, and I find the views taken are approved by Attic scholars both in England and France. But I dwell upon the subject at present in order to illustrate the necessity of full preparation and of written composition to those who would attain real excellence in the rhetorical art.' He admits that ' a certain proficiency in public speaking may be acquired by any one who chooses often to try it, and can harden himself against the pain of frequent failures.' But he denies that any one can ever in this way become truly eloquent : ' The loose, slovenly, and poor diction, the want of art in combining and disposing of his ideas, the inability to bring out many of his thoughts, and the incompetency to present any of them in the best and most efficient form, will reduce the speaker to the level of an ordinary talker. His diction is sure to be clumsy, incorrect, unlimited in quantity,

[1] Greene's *Reminiscences of Robert Hall*, p. 138.

and of no value.   It is the greatest of all mistakes,' he adds,
' to fancy that even a carefully prepared passage cannot be
delivered before a modern assembly.   I once contended on
this point with an accomplished classical scholar, and no in-
considerable speaker himself, Lord Melbourne, who immediately undertook to point out the passages which I had
prepared, and those which were given off-hand, and on the
inspiration of the moment.   He was wrong in almost every
guess he made.   Lord Denman, on a more remarkable occasion, at the bar of the House of Lords, in the Queen's case,
made the same mistake upon the passage delivered before
the adjournment in the middle of the first day of the defence.
The objection made,' he continues, ' that prepared passages
are artificial, and disclose the preparation, is groundless.   In
the first place, nothing can be more artificial than a speech
must in almost all cases necessarily be, which is anything
beyond mere conversation.   Next, it is the diction, not the
substance, which is prepared ; and, finally, if the art used is
shown, and not concealed, the artist alone is in fault.'[1]

Indeed, the same things substantially were said, though
with a little less of personal allusion, in his Inaugural Address at Glasgow in 1825.   ' I should lay it down as a rule,'
he then said, 'admitting of no exception, that a man will
speak well in proportion as he has written much ; and that
with equal talents he will be the finest extempore speaker,
when no time for preparing is allowed, who has prepared
himself the most sedulously when he had an opportunity
of delivering a premeditated speech.   All the exceptions
which I have ever heard cited to this principle are apparent
ones only, proving nothing more than that some few men,
of rare genius, have become great speakers without preparation ; in nowise showing, that with much preparation they
would not have reached a much higher pitch of excellence.'
He then refers to Cicero and Demosthenes as one of the

[1] Installation Address at Edinburgh, 18th May 1860.

best proofs of what he has said ; and afterwards remarks, 'We may rest assured, that the highest reaches of the art, and without any necessary sacrifice of natural effect, can only be attained by him who well considers, and maturely prepares, and oftentimes sedulously corrects and refines his oration. Such preparation is quite consistent with the introduction of passages prompted by the occasion ; nor will the transition from the one to the other be perceptible in the execution of a practised master.'

CHAPTER V.

DIFFERENT KINDS OF DISCOURSES.

THE observations hitherto made on the composition and delivery of discourses have had respect to discourses generally, with little or no reference to the distinctive properties which ought to characterize one species of discourse as compared with another. There *are* specific differences which it is not unimportant to note, as on the proper observance of them not a little depends for the attainment of success in the several kinds. Not to speak of minor shades of distinction, there are at least four pretty distinctly marked classes, although these may at times approach indefinitely near to each other, and the same discourse may occasionally admit of being assigned partly to one class and partly to another.

I. *Expository Discourses.*—Discourses of an expository character, *lectures*, as they are usually designated in Scotland, can never fail to be at least occasionally delivered, where there is an evangelical ministry, animated by a just desire to have the people brought to an intelligent acquaintance with the word of God. But nowhere, perhaps, has the practice been so generally followed as in Scotland, where the custom has long prevailed of having one, and commonly the first, of two discourses on the Lord's day of this description. As early as the times of the Commonwealth, this practice of expounding in order a few verses out of

some book of Scripture existed as a recognised and established part of the ordinary church service ; and some of the
best remains of the pulpit literature of the period consist of
the expository discourses so delivered.   It is enough to
name those of Leighton, Binning, Hutcheson, and Durham.
These expository preachers, however, were but followers of
other and in some respects still greater men, who preceded
them in the same line.   The more eminent Reformers were
masters in this species of discourse, Calvin in particular, a
large portion of whose published writings, bearing the name of
commentaries, first took shape as expositions delivered from
the pulpit ; and not a few also of the freshest and most valuable of Luther's works had the same origin.   Indeed, we may
ascend to a much earlier time still, even to the flourishing
period of Patristic literature, which, if not to the same extent,
yet in a very considerable degree, was distinguished for the
regard it paid to expository preaching.   The expositions of
Augustine on the Psalms and on the Gospel of John, as well
as the homilies, as they have been called, of Chrysostom on
many of the books of New Testament Scripture, all originally
addressed to congregations in the sanctuary, are, as a whole,
decidedly the best specimens which have come down to
us of the pulpit ministrations of those ancient times.   In
England the prevailing practice now, and for a long period,
has been quite different : discourses of this description can
scarcely be said to form a recognised and distinct class.
For the most part, they are given very occasionally ; so
much so that Alford[1] says, ' the general neglect of this kind
of preaching among them is lamentable,' worse even than in
Popish countries ; for ' any visitor,' he tells us, ' to Roman
churches abroad will be deeply sensible of the loss which
we thus incur in our influence from the pulpit.'   I confess I
did not know that the balance in this respect lay so much
on that side ; but, certainly, one seldom hears from English

[1] *Essays and Addresses*, p. 12.

pulpits discourses which take the form of an exposition of a particular passage of Scripture, still more seldom of an exposition in regular order of a particular book.   And hence the comparatively small proportion which such works form of English theological literature.

From the greater scope allowed in expository discourses, the broader Scriptural basis assumed for them, and the wider compass of doctrine or duty embraced in them, an impression not unnaturally prevails, that they are more easily constructed than discourses on single texts, that it is a simpler matter to *lecture* than to *preach*.   It, no doubt, may be so after a fashion.   A kind of tolerable exposition of a passage may be given, some useful explanations thrown out upon its meaning, and just observations raised on its contents, with less expenditure of thought than would be required for the production of a connected discourse on a single text.   But that very facility which is afforded by the nature of the discourse for making the necessary preparation too commonly proves a temptation to its being done in a much less effective and satisfactory manner than is both practicable and proper.   And hence, probably, it is, that the expository discourse is so often relatively inferior to the sermon : the one presenting a regularly constructed whole, with clear arrangement, judicious selection of matter, an order and progression of thought such as the mind can readily perceive and follow with interest ; while in the other, all is loose, rambling, undigested, no proportioning of part to part, no exercise of skill in bringing out the spirit and connection of the whole, much introduced that had better been omitted, and points of interest and importance overlooked which should have received careful consideration.   And it is not, perhaps, too much to say, that a considerable number of preachers of average abilities and resources, have never got a sufficiently definite conception of what an expository discourse should be, at least have failed in any competent degree to realize it.

(1.) In throwing out a few suggestions upon the subject, it will not be necessary to dwell on what, in certain discourses, is a matter of some importance, the choice of the passage or subject ; for, usually, the practice is to be preferred of proceeding in regular order through an entire book, or some considerable portion of a book of Scripture. There are obvious advantages connected with this method. In the first instance, it provides the preacher with a subject which he feels himself in a manner called in providence to handle ; and so not only saves him from much wasteful expenditure of time in doubt and hesitancy, but also obliges him to give himself to the orderly and systematic study of Scripture. It also accustoms the people of his charge to somewhat of the same careful, continuous search into the meaning of Scripture, as the Book which is throughout given by inspiration of God for the instruction and guidance of faith ; so that they come to know it, not in a few select and isolated fragments, but, in a measure, according to its variety and completeness. Besides, opportunities thus continually present themselves of directing attention to many things which call for correction or advice ; but which are either in themselves of so delicate a nature, or so apt to give occasion in some quarters to offence, that one would rather, if possible, avoid the appearance of expressly choosing a text for the purpose of bringing them into notice. These, taken together, will be found practically no slight advantages connected with the method of a regular course of exposition through some portion of the word of God. And, as a general rule, it will be best to adhere to this method, yet without binding oneself down to a rigid uniformity, and losing the benefit of a little variety by occasionally turning to other pastures.

Still, with the adoption of such a rule, there is room for

the exercise of prudence and discretion in the matter of
selection. For, while all Scripture is profitable for instruction, it cannot be all handled with equal adaptation and
advantage by the same individual. There are portions
which, partly from their own nature, and partly, perhaps, from
the relation in which they stand to his mental endowments
and Christian experience, may be said to lie, in a measure,
out of his beat for continuous treatment ; and it is well to
know that there are *books*, as well as *texts* in Scripture,
which may suit one, but not another. Even what portions
of Scripture the pastor does resolve at one period or another
to overtake, it may be of importance to take in one order
rather than another. Of New Testament Scripture, for
example, the Gospels will almost uniformly be found better
suited for a *first* course of exposition than any of the
Epistles ; and of the Gospels themselves, which ever may
be first chosen, it should certainly not be that of John,
which, with all its apparent, and also real simplicity, possesses a depth and fulness of meaning, a lofty grandeur and
spirituality of thought, which cannot be successfully grappled
with in a course of regular exposition without considerable
maturity of Christian knowledge and experience, as well as
exercised skill in the work of interpretation. The Epistles,
also, differ considerably from each other, in respect to the
comparative ease or difficulty which attends their successful
elucidation ; but no graduated scale can be applied to
them ; for a particular cast of mind, or a definite course of
preparatory study, may render one or other of them more
readily capable of fitting treatment by particular persons,
than might be judged likely from the nature alone of the
epistle. But in respect to the closing book of Scripture,
the Revelation of St. John, I am inclined to say, that except
in select portions, such as the three first chapters, and
several very precious and pregnant passages which occur at
intervals elsewhere, it is not adapted to a course of *ordinary*

exposition ; and if respect be had to the common mode of dealing with its prophetic symbols, I would say, not even for *extraordinary*. The manner in which some preachers rush into the popular arena with this book, and the readiness and confidence with which they apply its mysterious imagery to specific events in past and present times, is to me a source of unfeigned regret. The book undoubtedly has most important uses, important for the Church at large as well as for the retired student of Scripture ; but these are scarcely for exhibition in a series of popular discourses before a general audience ; and when so employed, the strain of exposition is extremely apt to run into what tends rather to gratify a love for the novel or the marvellous than to promote personal edification.

The Scriptures of the Old Testament are characterized by much the same kind of differences as those which are found in the New, only somewhat more variously and strongly marked. The portions best adapted, upon the whole, for a series of expository discourses are the historical books, the historical at least more than the prophetical ; for, in consequence of the imperfect nature of the dispensation under which the prophets lived, and the comparatively obscure medium through which the things of God's kingdom were presented to their view, passages are ever and anon occurring which are of difficult interpretation even to the most skilled interpreters, and which it is not quite easy to make perfectly intelligible to an ordinary congregation. Experience has brought me to the conviction that, in regard to most of the prophetical writings of the Old Testament, a course of exposition on select portions would be more satisfactory to the preacher, and more profitable to his hearers, than one that should aim at embracing every chapter and verse in each. But the book of Psalms, which contains prophetical as well as devotional and didactic elements, might be taken almost entire, and for the most part is well adapted to this species of discourse ; only, from the poetical colouring that pervades it, and the manifold variety of life and experience it embodies, very few preachers will find themselves equally at home in all the portions of it ; so that it may usually be most expedient to take it at intervals, and as much as possible in connection with the parts of Old Testament history on which it so often leans. It has been the practice also of some of our best expository preachers to alternate between the books of the Old and those of the New Testament, for the purpose of securing a greater variety to their ministrations, and getting an opportunity of explaining more fully the things pertaining to both covenants. But in such matters no one need bind himself to the method of another. Respect must be had to the circumstances of one's own position, and to what may seem, upon the whole, best calculated to promote the spiritual good of the people entrusted to his care.[1]

(2.) When the general subject for exposition has been fixed, the next thing demanding consideration is the proportion of text to be embraced in each particular discourse. This will very commonly, at least in the historical books, well-nigh determine itself; but it may also, both in these and other portions, call for some care and discrimination. It is easier, however, to say regarding it what should not be done than what should. A very lengthened portion should not usually be taken, as the topics in that case will be too numerous and varied to admit of that precision and individuality which are essential to the interest and usefulness of a discourse. On the other hand, a very limited portion, comprising not more, perhaps, than one or two verses,

[1] It is scarcely necessary to remark, that there are passages, both in the historical and prophetical books of Scripture, which, on the score of delicacy, are not suitable either for being read or expounded in a promiscuous assembly. All Scripture is profitable for instruction, but not necessarily as matter of public discourse.

would commonly narrow so much the field of discussion, that the discourse would possess the characteristics of a sermon rather than of an expository lecture. Passages will occasionally, however, be met with, especially in the doctrinal parts of Scripture, so pregnant in meaning, or calling for so much in the way of explanation, that a single verse or two may be all that can be adequately handled at a time. But for the most part it is desirable that a passage of some extent should be included, though it should, if possible, be a passage presenting some sort of unity, or having such threads of connection between one part and another as to admit of the discourse based on it being something else than a succession of remarks that bear no perceptible relation to each other, a series of scattered observations rather than parts of a continuous discourse. In expository as well as other discourses, it must always produce a measure of dissatisfaction if two or three subjects altogether distinct are brought together for discussion; the mind, in such a case, has to pass too rapidly from topic to topic, and without being able to retain that continuity or progression of thought and feeling which it instinctively craves.

So much depends for the sustained interest and impression of a discourse upon a due regard to this internal unity and connection, that the neglect of it may justly be reckoned among the chief causes of failure. Even when the verses taken contain a manifestly related whole, this is often in a great degree lost sight of in the actual treatment given to them; they are gone over in a kind of loose, desultory manner, without any proper plan formed beforehand, or distinct order followed; little more attempted than the raising of a few general remarks or observations upon it. The parables of Jesus also, which, from their very structure, seem to invite a different treatment, are sometimes subjected to the same mode of dealing. Plainly, each parable should first be contemplated in its entireness, with the view of obtaining a clear and distinct apprehension of its general scope, so that afterwards the course of thought and illustration may be arranged in such a manner as may seem best fitted to bring out the main theme, and exhibit the bearing which the several parts have in regard to it. In doing this, however, whether in respect to the parables or to other portions of Scripture, it should not be deemed necessary to adhere to the precise order in which the topics present themselves on the sacred record. Sometimes it may be advisable to depart more or less from this, in order to secure a more natural progression or a better adjustment in the different parts of the discourse. Nor should it be held as at all essential that a formal announcement be made of the plan and order intended to be pursued; less so here than in the case of sermons founded upon a single text, where the mind is shut up to a narrower field, and requires to have the lines of thought more definitely marked out before it. In expository discourses, though this method may at times be fitly enough adopted, yet it may also, and perhaps more commonly should be dispensed with, as the subject itself will often suggest an order to the preacher, and one that can quite readily be perceived by the mind of the hearer without the formality of a regular division.

(3.) To come now to the substance of the discourse; its distinctive aim and character, we should ever remember, is *exposition;* so that to explain the meaning of the words where any explanation is needed, to render clear and intelligible to all the mind of the Spirit conveyed in them, to explicate difficulties, and bring out with due prominence the principles of truth and duty involved, this must be taken as the more direct and primary object of the discourse. To do it properly will, of course, require some measure of exegetical talent, by which I mean, such a combination of taste and judgment as fits one for discerning the right in cases somewhat critical, weighing probabilities, tracing con-

nections, distinguishing between what is extraneous or incidental and what is essential to the train of thought which
forms the leading theme of discourse. Not the process
itself, by which all this is to be done, should be laid open
in the discourse, but the results of the process; the talent
should appear in the work it accomplishes, not in the
methods by which it operates. Anything like an exhibition
of skill or a parade of learning must be out of place in a
discourse which is professedly directed to the object of
expounding the will of God for the spiritual enlightenment
and comfort of men's souls. Even in the treatment of
passages which have some difficulty in them, on which a
certain diversity of opinion has prevailed in the past, and
may still perhaps be expected to prevail in the future, it is
hardly ever advisable to go much into the contending views
of interpreters, which is extremely apt to create bewilder-
ment in the minds of a general audience, and possibly also
to produce a painful sense of the darkness and uncertainty
of Scripture. It is an easy method of consuming time and
of giving an air of learning to a discourse, to tell what this
commentator has said, and how the conceit of that other
may be disposed of. But for the most part it is a far more
excellent way, and greatly more serviceable to the flock,
when the pastor takes time and pains in his own study to
examine and weigh all these competing authorities; and
though, perhaps, not concealing the fact that there are
certain difficulties or diversities of opinion hanging around
the subject, yet coming forth with a plain and intelligent
exhibition of what has commended itself to him as the
mind of the Spirit regarding it. If, after all his care and
application, he should still find reason for hesitation, let
him state candidly whence it arises; or if there should be
more than one view which may justly be considered as
somewhat probable, let this also be noticed. But such
double interpretations should obviously be presented as

rarely as possible ; and with due pains beforehand, supposing that there is some fitness for the work with a few of
the better exegetical helps at hand, and prayer continually
made for a blessing on their use, they cannot be of very
frequent occurrence.   It is a good rule to mention no view
from the pulpit which may not reasonably be supposed to
have occurred, in their own meditations or reading, to some
members of the congregation ; to mention none simply for
the sake of propounding and refuting it.   Should, however,
an incorrect view, however absurd, be understood to have
gained currency, or should it be not unlikely to have
occurred to some one on a superficial consideration of the
passage, then it may most justly be noticed.   At the same
time, the clear and satisfactory exhibition of the true sense
will commonly be found the best safeguard against false and
shallow interpretations, and when thoroughly done will save
the necessity of spending much time on what is only to be
rejected.

In a number of cases in which some difficulty has to be
encountered, the difficulty turns upon the precise meaning
of the original words, and raises the question, whether the
rendering of the Authorized Version gives a correct view of
their import.   If the matter is very clear as against this
version, and anything of importance depends on the difference; or if by some slight variation a fuller, clearer, or more
profound meaning could be elicited, in such cases there can
be no impropriety in indicating what is entitled to the preference.   Only, a certain prudence should be observed as
to the manner of doing it, avoiding the appearance of seeming anxious to obtrude a piece of learning somewhat out of
the way, but being concerned only about bringing out a just
representation of the truth of sacred Scripture.   The middle
way here also is the best; on the one hand, to guard against
the undue disparagement of the version, which to the great
body of the people is the only form in which they know the

word of God ; and, on the other, to keep them in mind that it is still but a version, and must not be allowed to overshadow the original.[1]

(4.) In regard, finally, to the hortatory, or more peculiarly practical matter of the discourse, this should nearly always form a pretty large portion of the whole, but it may be variously introduced. When the subject happens to be one that calls for a good deal of explanation, or consists of parts very closely related to each other, it may be best to reserve the chief application to be made of it for practical uses to the last. When the whole subject has been placed before the understandings of the people, then press home the lessons of duty it contains on their hearts and consciences. But usually it will be found both more natural and more profitable to interweave the practical throughout with the expository, and make the improvement of the subject keep pace with its elucidation. For in this way the hearers have the subject as it proceeds brought into contact with the moral as well as the intellectual parts of their natures, and are never allowed to forget the aim to which all should be subordinated. Not only so, but the awkwardness is thereby avoided of needing to return back upon topics which have been discussed at an earlier stage, and have not quite recently been engaging attention. When this has to be done, a certain amount of repetition is inevitable, and this is apt to induce satiety or languor in the audience. On every account, therefore, it is advisable to intermingle the word of exhortation with the word of knowledge, while still the most prolonged or urgent of the practical appeals may fitly be reserved to the close.

[1] There are certain renderings fitted to mislead which should certainly be noted, such as 'straining at a gnat;' 'eating and drinking damnation;' 'after Easter,' Acts xii. 4; 'called *to* glory and virtue,' 2 Pet. i. 6; also the changes undergone in the sense of certain words, such as 'earing,' *conversation, nephews, take no thought.*

II. *Doctrinal Discourses.*—By doctrinal discourses I mean such as have it for their more prominent and leading object to set forth some important truth or doctrine of the Bible, to commend it to men's intelligent convictions, and work it into their settled and conscientious belief. As Christianity owes its primary distinction to the doctrinal truths which it unfolds, and by the belief of those truths seeks to accomplish all the present and eternal results it aims at, a very prominent and essential part of the calling of a minister of the gospel necessarily consists in what he has to do for the manifestation and defence of the same. The exposition in one aspect or another of saving truth must form the staple of his ministrations. But the precise form under which this is to be done may be infinitely varied, and must to a certain extent be modified by the circumstances of time and place. Even in the cast and structure of discourses which may, in a somewhat peculiar sense, be designated doctrinal, there may be a considerable variety ; and, in particular, they may be made to assume sometimes more of a controversial and again more of a simply didactic character, according as the special object may be to vindicate and defend, or to explain and enforce the truth. It will rarely happen but that the faithful pastor will require to avail himself of the one mode as well as the other ; for in present times at least he will scarcely find it possible to obtain a field of labour where the prevalence of doctrinal error, or the danger of some being misled into it, will not occasionally call for a defence as well as exposition of the truth. At the same time, even in those situations where the danger in question exists, discourses avowedly and predominantly controversial should not be of frequent occurrence ; indeed, I would say, they should form rather an exceptional part of a pastor's public ministrations. For, as they necessarily present a polemical appearance, their tendency is to beget an intellectual sharpness and combative zeal for orthodoxy, much more than to awaken earnest convictions and hearty love of the truth. And it should ever be remembered, that it is this latter and not the former, it is the doctrines of salvation, not simply as reasoned out and grasped by the intellect, but as embraced and loved in the heart, which alone fulfils the design of the gospel, and is also the only sufficient bulwark against the assaults of error. For the things of this description which prove real sources of danger are always such as fall in with some corrupt tendency of human nature, flatter its pride of reason, or allow freer scope to its fleshly inclinations and desires. Hence the faithful pastor must aim at something more than a mere speculative knowledge of the truth. He must seek to have the truth itself effectually lodged in the understandings and hearts of his audience ; since, in proportion as this is done, the antagonistic forms of error will of themselves fall away or meet with a stout resistance. Keeping in view what has been said as to the general character and object of this species of discourses, I proceed to offer a few plain hints respecting them.

(1.) Whatever the particular doctrine may be which is to form the theme of discourse, care should be taken to have a text that is sufficiently clear and broad to bear the superstructure which is going to be reared on it. There should be no appearance of constraint or violence in the effort to adapt the one to the other, as this would inevitably raise distrust or suspicion at the very outset. The doctrine, it is true, may not be treated as if it rested for proof exclusively or even mainly upon the particular text from which the sermon is preached. There both may and should be a judicious use of other passages bearing on the subject introduced in the course of the discussion. But this will not lessen the propriety of having an appropriate text for the groundwork of the whole ; for whatever afterwards may be brought forward by way of supplementing it in the minds of the audience, it will almost certainly be with the text itself that the doctrine will be chiefly associated.

(2.) Some discrimination also should be made between doctrines, not for the purpose of exempting any from discussion in the pulpit which have a place in the revelation of God, for it is the part of a minister to declare the whole counsel of God ; but so as to give the chief prominence to those which are most vitally connected with the work of salvation and men's spiritual progress.   There are doctrines which may at particular times be brought formally into discussion, but which usually should be taken for granted rather than systematically and at length treated in the pulpit; such, for example, as the doctrine of the Trinity, the doctrine of angels, or the doctrine of divine predestination.   Many opportunities will present themselves in the regular course of exposition or preaching for referring to such topics, and bringing forth proofs in illustration of them, in a kind of informal and incidental manner.   But it is scarcely possible to take them for the theme of an entire discourse without giving to the discourse somewhat more than is meet of a dry, theological, perhaps speculative turn. When such topics *are* handled, it should be as much as possible after the pattern of Scripture, that is, not abstractedly or metaphysically, but by means of known analogies, and in their bearing on the scheme of God and the spiritual well-being of men.   So contemplated, they will be presented in a sort of concrete form, associated with what has an objective existence in men's experience, and runs more or less into the lines of their present or future destiny.   Take, as an example, the doctrine of election as exhibited in Scripture, which is not as a thing swimming in the air, but intimately associated with the safety and blessedness of believers, tending on the one side to humble them, as showing that they are indebted for all they receive to the sovereign goodness and mercy of God ; and on the other to fill them with

peace and comfort, as presenting whatever belongs to them
of good in connection with the everlasting love and unchanging faithfulness of God. Thus exhibited, the doctrine will
be received by believers with a heavenly sweetness and
consolation ; while those who are still strangers to the grace
of God may have the salutary feeling awakened in them,
that it were a happy thing for them if they could but attain
to some comfortable assurance that they had personally to
do with the things which pertain to it. Until they get into
that better position, however, and with the view of helping
them to do so, such persons should be reminded that they
have primarily to address themselves to another class of
God's revelations, those, namely, which have respect to the
guilt of sin, and the necessity of fleeing to Christ in order to
escape from its deserved doom.

Indeed, both for the subjects of grace and for those who
are still strangers to its power, the great themes of doctrinal
preaching must be, not the darker, but the plainer things in
God's revelation, the reality, the deceitfulness, and the evil
of sin; the way of salvation by Christ, Christ Himself in His
adorable person, and perfect righteousness, and infinite
satisfaction ; His amazing condescension, His matchless
love, the inexhaustible riches of His grace, the comforts of
His Spirit, and the glory of His kingdom. Whatever
besides may at times be exhibited of Christian doctrine,
such topics ought ever to occupy the foreground ; for they
have the more fundamental place in the elements of the
Christian economy, and they serve to keep the soul ever
conversant with Christ, in connection with whom alone is
to be found true peace and blessing.

(3.) I remark again, that in setting forth such topics as
those now referred to, the utmost pains should be taken to
have the leading positions laid down regarding them, what
will usually be the heads of discourse enunciated in very
clear and intelligible statements, such as every person in

the congregation of ordinary intelligence can understand. The main part also of what is said in illustration should, if possible, be done in so lucid and orderly a manner, that only the wilfully ignorant and inattentive can fail to apprehend it.   This, when it is in some good measure done, will save a great deal of needless verbiage and prolonged argumentation on points of some difficulty ; for, as has been truly said, 'a question well stated is half solved.'   But it can be so stated only when one has been at pains to get the particular subject clearly apprehended in the mind, and in the exposition of it to confine oneself to what has thus been properly mastered.   Should the preacher attempt more than this, or be imperfectly prepared for what he does attempt, there will be sure to be found an indistinctness, a want of order or coherence, in his statements concerning it; his course will be, as it were, through a hazy atmosphere or with a halting and uncertain tread, in which comparatively few are likely to attempt following him.   To know well, and to know also what it is one does know well, is indispensable to being able to discourse on it to the interest and edification of others.

(4.) Along with this distinctness and precision of view, there will always be required, as a further element to success in this kind of discourse, a real heartfelt sense of the importance of the doctrine handled, and a corresponding desire to have the knowledge and belief of it wrought into the minds of others.   To a shortcoming in this respect, perhaps more than to an actual deficiency in the formal apprehension of the truth, is to be ascribed the defective interest that too frequently attaches to such discourses. For the complaint which has been uttered on the subject by an English prelate, has its application to other sections of the Church:[1] 'How many sermons,' says he, 'seem to be

[1] *Addresses to Candidates for Ordination*, by the Bishop of Oxford, p. 54.

composed with no better idea than that they must occupy a certain time prescribed by custom, and that they must be filled with the religious phrases current in this or that school of theological opinion ! Hence we find in them prefaces of inordinate length, porches larger than the buildings to which they lead, truisms repeated with a calm perseverance of dull repetition which is almost marvellous, vague generalities about the fall and redemption, as if these awful mysteries were empty words, and not living, burning realities. We hear the sermon, perhaps wandering languidly over the whole scheme of theology ; or we find the faintest and most general description of sinners, such as can reach no one in particular ; mere outlines of men in the abstract, not por-traits of individual men, amongst which each hearer shall find himself ; empty general exhortations not to sin, not revelations of sin in itself, or sin in its deceitful working ; cold, heartless, unreal words about Christ the healer, not the earnest, plain-spoken zeal of one to whom, because he believes, Christ is precious.' All this, so far as it exists, comes from the want of a realizing sense in the preacher of the vital importance of the truths about which he discourses. He must go through his task, but there is no living warmth and energy in his mode of executing it ; and the impression produced, faint at the first, soon vanishes away.

(5.) In regard, finally, to the practical improvement con-nected with the treatment of doctrinal subjects, this may, as in the case of expository discourses, be managed in two different ways. It may either be interspersed through the several parts of the discourse, or reserved mainly to the concluding portion. In Scripture itself we have examples of both these methods. The two largest doctrinal epistles or discourses in the New Testament are those addressed to the Romans and the Hebrews ; and they are constructed respectively upon the two methods just mentioned. In the Epistle to the Romans, the first part, reaching to the close

of chap. xi., is chiefly occupied with the discussion of the
great doctrines of sin and redemption ; and then, com-
mencing with chap. xii. onwards to the close, there is a
rich and varied application of the truth to the personal and
social state of believers ; a close and earnest dealing with
the conscience in respect to the obligations resting on believers, one toward another, and toward those around them,
in the different spheres and relations of life.   In the Epistle
to the Hebrews, on the other hand, each doctrinal topic,
as it comes into consideration, has its practical bearing
noticed and pressed home before it is dismissed ; so that,
throughout, the argumentative continually runs into the
hortatory, and successive phases of doctrine are no sooner
commended to the apprehension and faith of the readers,
than they are turned into matter of counsel, warning, or
encouragement to their hearts.   With such examples of
these diverse methods from the pen of inspiration itself, we
may certainly leave the question undecided, which is the
better of the two.   Rather, perhaps, we may say that both
are in themselves good ; and that it will be the part of
wisdom in the preacher to vary his plan, and make his
discourse assume now more of the one, and again more of
the other method.   For the most part, however, it will be
the more advisable, for the reasons already stated under
the preceding division, to approximate more nearly to the
second mode of distribution than to the first.   For, if all is
doctrinal in the earlier part of a discourse, and all practical
in the later, it will probably seem to a certain portion of
the audience allowable to relax their attention while the
one or the other portion of the discourse is in progress of
delivery.   But, indeed, the two elements admit of being in
a good degree combined together, as they are in the Epistle
to the Romans ; for, while the chief burden of the practical
matter is reserved to the concluding chapters of the epistle,
it is by no means wanting in the earlier portions.   Nay,

R

some of the most powerful and touching appeals are there ; and the whole of that part which is more especially doctrinal, so far from possessing the character of a dry discussion, is instinct with the living warmth and earnestness of a soul penetrated to its inmost depths with the reality and greatness of the truths unfolded in it. When such is the spirit that characterizes the treatment of any particular subject, it will be comparatively of little moment how the more distinctly practical matter is introduced and distributed.

III. *Experimental Discourses.*—Experimental preaching may justly enough be treated as a distinct class, although in the general run of pulpit discourses the experimental element should not be wanting, and should rather appear in the tone and spirit pervading the whole, than as something existing apart. The revelation of God generally, and that part of it in particular which relates to the life and resurrection of Christ, with the present and eternal issues depending on them, cannot but powerfully affect, when seriously apprehended by men, their emotional natures, and deeply impress their feelings. To its wonderful adaptation in this respect the gospel owes much of its quickening and im pulsive power. And the measure of the skill which any preacher possesses to awaken feeling along with believing thought in the minds of his audience, in connection with the great themes he handles, will also be, to a large extent, the measure of his success in getting into their bosoms, and winning them to the love and obedience of the truth.

There are subjects of discourse, however, which are in their very nature experimental, and which should from time to time be brought out for formal discussion. Such, for example, is the passage in Rom. vii. 9, ' I was alive without the law once ; but when the commandment came, sin revived, and I died,' which, in both its parts, relates to experience; in the first, to the soul's consciousness, its conceit, we should rather say, or *false* consciousness of life, while still ignorant of the spirituality and depth of the law's requirements; in the second, to its consciousness of death, its stricken and prostrate condition, with an overpowering sense of guilt and danger when the law enters in its true meaning and commanding power. Such also, but with special reference to the grace and truth of the gospel, are Rom. viii. 15, 'Ye have not received the spirit of bondage again to fear,' etc.; 2 Tim. i. 12, 'I know whom I have believed, and am persuaded that He is able to keep what I have committed to Him against that day;' 2 Cor. v. 14, 'The love of Christ constraineth me,' etc. Texts like these necessarily carry the thoughts inward to the state of the heart and the working of its affections, as wrought upon by the great truths and realities of the gospel. And if they are handled in a lively and earnest manner, the discourse must possess much of an experimental character; it will not simply describe how the things in question *should* operate on the feelings and affections of the soul, but so do it as to awaken and call forth somewhat of a corresponding frame of mind in the hearers. Can this be done unless the preacher himself has undergone what he describes? Can he preach experimentally without being a man of Christian experience? Or should his own experience be the measure and limit of what he attempts to work through Scripture into the convictions and feelings of his people?

Preachers require here to walk softly, and with a prudent step. It is one thing to set before a Christian audience a sort of picture, an ideal representation of the manner in which they should desire and feel on spiritual things, but another thing to make them properly sensible of the characteristics of a gracious work, to give them to know these as things which have been known in their real character, appreciated and felt. Yet there is nothing more common than for preachers, young preachers more especially, to mistake the one for the other, or to think that they are accomplishing the one when they are only doing the other. It were, perhaps, too much to say that no effect of a salutary and permanent kind is likely to be ever produced by a discourse in which the work of grace upon the soul and the actings of the soul as operated on by grace, have been drawn from the imagination merely of the speaker, or taken at second hand from the testimony of others; but assuredly very little of that description will usually be found to come of it. Grace, like nature, has its own look, its own tones, its own veins of thought and feeling; and discourses which, without any true or adequate participation of these, profess to lay open the secrets of the divine life in the soul, will be felt to be unsatisfactory by those who know the reality of that life, and will fail even to make much impression upon others. My advice, therefore, in regard to such subjects of discourse is, Let each one first try to ascertain what is his own spiritual state and temper in relation to them; let him, for the most part, be sure that he has at least the elements in himself of the gracious feelings and dispositions which he means to exhibit for the spiritual instruction and comfort of others; and if at times he should be led to go somewhat beyond what he has himself experienced, not, perhaps, having been placed in the circumstances which are needed to bring it into full operation, let it be done discreetly, and on the ground of results and testimonies which admit of no reasonable doubt. Where more than this is attempted, where at least the attempt is systematically made to strike a higher key, one of two results is almost sure to become manifest: either the preacher will fall into the style of some particular person or party, adopting a sanctimonious mannerism, which is always a defect and a misfortune; or his preaching will betray a false glow, a kind of pretentious unreality, will indeed be a preaching *about* the things of God rather than an actual and earnest grappling with the things themselves.

One point more may be noticed which has respect to the matter itself of such discourses, the subject, namely, of Christian experience. In so far as this is really the operation of divine grace, it must, as to all essential features, be the same in the true children of God; for it is the work of one and the same Spirit, and the work of that Spirit in applying the same great truths to the conscience, awakening the same convictions, desires, and hopes in the heart. But along with this general resemblance there may be individual characteristics; there certainly will be such in proportion as there are what the apostle calls 'diversities of operations' in the Spirit's work, as well as varieties of gifts. This arises primarily from the *natural* diversity which exists in people's physical and mental temperaments, since here also the supernatural bases itself on the natural; and the manifold diversities also of place, and circumstance, and position in life, amid which, in different individuals, the work of grace is begun and carried forward, cannot fail to exercise a moulding influence on the particular hue and aspect of the religious character. Thus, while it is true of all who have really been born again of the Spirit, that they have been brought to know for themselves the fearful burden of sin, and have seen somewhat of its exceeding sinfulness, with persons of deep sensibility or sombre feeling there may justly be expected a greater perturbation of spirit than in others during such convictions, and at times even a tendency to sink into the depths of wretchedness and despair. A similar difference in respect to natural temperament or intellectual acuteness will also give rise to a corresponding difference in the measure of distinctness with which the successive stages of thought and feeling are marked in the spiritual history of individuals, which in some will be found more vivid and perceptible than in others; in some, again, more rapid and violent, in others more gradual and progressive. Preachers should therefore beware of representing the experiences belonging to the Christian life in such a manner as to give rise to the impression that not only every feature, but every line, as it were, of that feature, every shade and aspect of life which has developed itself in one Christian, must have its parallel in another. Besides, it is to be borne in mind that a distinction has often to be drawn between the *experience of Christians* and *Christian experience.* Whatever may justly be designated Christian experience is of the working of God's word and Spirit upon the heart. But in the actual experience of Christians there is often found intermingling with that workings of the flesh, fears and hopes, joys and sorrows, and in these again heights and depths, which are either altogether the offspring of peculiarities in men's natural constitution, or receive their distinctive colour from these, together, it may be, with certain discomposing influences derived from the circumstances of their condition. The holiest men are not free from the action of such merely physical or local influences on the atmosphere of their soul; as may be seen, for example, in the case of Brainerd, whose memoirs exhibit a great deal of what may justly be called unhealthy experience; the experience, no doubt, of a profoundly earnest, spiritual man, and an experience conversant throughout with the things of the Spirit, but still by no means a uniformly Christian experience, in many respects morbid and introverted, and, as a whole, reflecting too much the shady aspect of the law, too little of the genial warmth and gladsome light of the gospel. It was the natural consequence of his consumptive frame and sequestered position, with which he had to maintain a perpetual conflict of feeling, and should therefore be carefully distinguished from that profound lowliness of spirit, that sure and stedfast faith, self-sacrificing zeal, unwearied patience, heavenly elevation of soul, and burning desire for the glory of God, which were his grand characteristics as a missionary of the cross, and which have been rarely surpassed, seldom even equalled. And so as regards the case of many others.

I may add, however, that even in those cases which exhibit something peculiar, and require to be considered apart from the general run of Christian experiences, there still is a certain affinity with what others are conscious of ; and if the descriptions given of such are drawn from real life, they will not be in vain even for those who are very partially cognisant of the things described. Hence the importance in this connection also of a minister's familiar intercourse with his people, so as to become properly acquainted with their actual state and character, their misgivings and fears, their trials and perils and difficulties. He will thus be able to speak more directly to their bosoms ; and even when, perhaps, speaking with a view to what may seem applicable to only one or two individuals, he will touch the hearts of a considerable number. For, as justly remarked by a German pastor,[1] and by him gathered as the result of ministerial experience, ' he who hits the case of one hits the case of a class ; and, besides, whatever has the impress of truth and reality will interest even those who are not directly concerned in it.'

IV. *Ethical Discourses.*—In mentioning ethical discourses, I am not to be understood as meaning what are simply or absolutely such ; but discourses which have for their chief object the exhibition of some one of the moral obligations binding on Christians, and the duties of every-day life. Every discourse, as already stated, should have more or less of a bearing in this direction ; it should be pervaded by a perceptible moral element, and at certain points should touch upon the things proper to be done, even though mainly occupied with those which are to be believed. But

[1] Büchsel's *Ministerial Experiences*, p. 37.

it will also be wise, occasionally at least, to discourse on particular branches of the dutiful behaviour and moral excellence which ought to distinguish the members of a Christian community, and to awaken a sense of shortcoming and guilt, where the good is not sought after or realized.

1. Now, in regard to such discourses, the first and most important direction which has to be given is, that while the moral or spiritual element must be made to predominate, it should never be allowed to stand alone. Precisely as doctrine should ever be set forth in its relation to practice, so when practice is the more immediate theme, its relation to doctrine should never be lost sight of; and that more especially for two reasons. First, because the moral precepts and obligations which believers are called to discharge, have much in their nature, and still more in their spirit, to do with the revelations of the gospel; and it is impossible to give, in connection with any department of Christian life and behaviour, a full representation of what believers should actually do, without bringing the subject into contact with the realities of the gospel. For, since the revelation of these has greatly elevated the position of those to whom the gospel has come, has placed them amid a clearer light, and invested them with other privileges and prospects than they could have known while living in a state of nature, so it has immensely increased their obligations to follow after righteousness, and provided them with means altogether peculiar for understanding the real nature and claims of righteousness. There is, however, another, and, if possible, a still stronger reason; for faith in the blessed truths of the gospel is the only vital root of the practical goodness which we would have people to exhibit in their walk and conduct; and one might as well expect to find fruitful trees growing where there has been planted no living germ, as to see a community adorned with the virtues of a pure, upright, and heavenly behaviour,

apart from the believing reception of the truth as it is in Jesus.

In the present day it is scarcely necessary to give any special illustrations of this, as with all who are in any measure acquainted with the history of religion in this country it has passed into a generally received maxim. It is well, however, that the pastors, or such as are preparing to become pastors, of Christian congregations should remember some of the more striking proofs of it, which are known to have taken place in the past, that they may be saved even from the *partial* misjudgments and misdirected efforts into which they might otherwise be led. In the particular sphere of a single ministerial life, none perhaps can be found more marked and instructive than that of the case of Dr. Chalmers, especially as he himself has depicted it. Shortly after his removal from Kilmany to Glasgow, he published an address to his former parishioners ; and in that address he referred to the change which had taken place on the character of his ministrations during the period of his residence in Kilmany, describing also the effect which this personal change produced on the results of his pastorate. ' I am not sensible,' he said, ' that all the vehemence with which I urged the proprieties and virtues of social life had the weight of a feather on the moral habits of my parishioners. And it was not till I got impressed by the utter alienation of the heart in all its desires and affections from God ; it was not till I got the Scriptural way of laying the method of reconciliation before them ; it was not till the free offer of forgiveness through the blood of Christ was urged upon their acceptance, and the Holy Spirit given through Christ's Mediatorship to all who ask Him, that I ever heard of any of those subordinate reformations, which I aforetime made the earnest and the zealous, but, I am afraid, at the same time the ultimate object of my earlier ministrations.' Then, appealing to those who had latterly undergone a change corresponding to his own, and in consequence of it, he says, 'You have at least taught me, that to preach Christ is the only effective way of preaching morality in all its branches; and out of your humble cottages have I gathered a lesson, which I pray God I may be enabled to carry with all its simplicity into a wider theatre, and to bring to bear with all the power of its subduing efficacy upon the vices of a more crowded population.'

Substantially the same contrast, but with reference to a much wider sphere, was drawn by Bishop Horsley in one of his charges, in which he gave a severe but faithful delineation of the kind of preaching which was prevalent among the clergy of the Church of England during the latter part of last century, contrasting it with the proper idea of gospel preaching. 'The clergy of those days,' he said, 'had lost sight of their proper office, to publish the word of reconciliation; and made no other use of the high commission they bore, than to come abroad on one day in seven dressed in solemn looks, and in the external garb of holiness, to be the apes of Epictetus. A general decay, not merely of piety, but of all the fruits and excellences of a Christian life, was the natural consequence;' and therefore he fitly concludes by indicating the right path: 'Practical holiness is the end, faith is the means. The practice of religion will always thrive in proportion as its doctrines are understood and firmly received; and the practice will degenerate and decay in proportion as the doctrine is misunderstood and neglected.'[1]

This, however, may quite readily be admitted by persons in the present day, who yet, perhaps, are in danger of giving

[1] On the negative side, practical illustrations of this may be found in the fruitlessness of Societies for the Reformation of Manners formed during last century (see Gillies' *Historical Collections*), as compared with the results of evangelical preaching by Whitfield, Wesley, and others.

DIFFERENT KINDS OF DISCOURSES. 267

way to the same tendency in a somewhat modified and subtler form. There is a kind of refined morality and spiritualism, which partakes to some extent of a Christian character, and is all that certain ministers either know or preach; but which, as a scheme of instruction, wants the living warmth and quickening influence of true evangelism. A more favourable and instructive example of it could not well be found, than in the amiable and very estimable Henry Woodward, an Irish clergyman, not long since deceased, who himself relates the phase of things connected with his ministerial position and agency to which I refer. He had gone through a very remarkable, one might almost say, singular experience, several years after he became an ordained minister, the chief characteristic of which was an intense realization of spiritual and eternal things, which changed the whole tone of his mind, and rendered ministerial work a very different thing from what it had been before, yet without any special prominence being given to the subjects of sin and salvation. Before long, he removed to a neighbourhood where were some men of distinguished parts and good character in the Church, 'whose agency tended to promote spiritual religion, with disconformity to the world; but upon the subject of the atonement there was somewhat of reserve. It was not denied, it was held as a part of Catholic truth; it was occasionally preached, but it was not prominently put forward.' Falling in with this system of thought and teaching, Mr. Woodward says of himself, 'My favourite topics from the pulpit, and from house to house, were such as, from my own experience, I could set my seal to: that sin is misery, and holiness is but another name for happiness; that the ways of religion are ways of pleasantness, and all her paths are peace; that God is Himself the shield and the exceeding great reward of them that love Him; that Christ is the living bread which alone can feed the hungry soul,' and so on. 'He did not absolutely omit,' he says, 'to preach forgiveness through the blood of Jesus, and justification by faith in His righteousness ; but this doctrine had not the prominence which is understood to characterize evangelical preaching ; and it was only when he came to perceive the far more marked and blessed effects which flowed from preaching more distinctively evangelical, that he began seriously to consider the defects of his own, and gave that prominence to the doctrines of sin and salvation which they unquestionably have in Scripture. I saw,' he states, 'that God was pleased to bless this mode of preaching ;' and He does so, we must remember, just because it thoroughly meets the case of sinners, and, with the knowledge of the good, supplies the only effectual means and motives for their actually attaining it.

2. But to proceed to another point : while the moralities of the gospel in discourses of this nature should ever be based upon its beliefs, in the mode of doing it some variety is advisable, so as to avoid a tame and mechanical uniformity. Suppose, for example, that humility were the subject of discourse, and the text 1 Pet. v. 5, 'Be subject one to another, and be clothed with humility,' it might be equally appropriate to begin with a delineation of the grace of humility, its thoughts and feelings with reference to self, its actings toward God, its outgoings of will and purpose towards others amid the intercourse and relations of life ; and then to point to the spiritual root out of which it springs, and the manifold considerations presented in the gospel which are fitted to nourish and stimulate it. Or, reversing the process, bring forward first what grounds or reasons there are in Scripture, as well as in the nature of things, for the cultivation of a spirit of humility, and then show how, when these are properly apprehended and felt, they will of necessity prompt to the exercise of humility, dispose the believer, as it were, to clothe himself with it, so that it shall

impart a distinctive tone and impress to whatever he does. In like manner, with regard to all the other graces of the Christian life, and the duties of moral obligation, it is immaterial whether the discussion of the duties or the exhibition of the truths and principles which should find their development in the duties have the precedence in the discourse ; and not stringent uniformity, but rather variety of order and method is to be cultivated.

3. A still further direction may be indicated, namely, that care should be taken so to exhibit the moralities, or practical duties of the gospel, that these shall appear really practicable to the body of sound Christians. Representations are sometimes given of these, and of the obligations generally of a Christian life, which look too much like ideal pictures, and which, from want of adaptation to people's circumstances, are fitted rather to discourage than prompt their zeal to the performance of what is required. ' Our system of preaching,' Mr. Cecil justly observes, ' must be such as to meet mankind. They must find it *possible* to live in the bustle of the world and yet serve God.' And this should lead, not only, as he suggests, to a prominent exhibition of Christian privileges, and the refreshing of men's harassed spirits with the cheering manifestation of Christ's truth and love, but also to such a statement of the way of holiness as shall not appear to overtax the energies of ordinary men, a truthful yet homely and reasonable view of the relative obligations and duties of life. This should especially be attended to when pressing duties of which the formal discharge must necessarily vary with the means and opportunities possessed, such as liberality to the poor, the expenditure of time and resources in the cause of Christ, the exercises of meditation and prayer. That the genuine Christian will always be characterized by a certain regard to such things, we must leave no room to doubt, and a regard that will always grow in proportion to the growth of

Christian principle in the heart. But let hearers at the same time be reminded, that they have to do with a God who knows their frame, and sets the bounds of their habitations; so that while the spirit which animates all true followers of Christ must be the same, there cannot be for each the same formal rule and measure; and they may be liberal even in the highest degree, not by giving *much*, but by giving *heartily* according to their means, and by doing kindly; they may be meditative, and yet go through their daily taskwork of bodily labour; may be prayerful and yet without a closet to retire to, or hours of repose which they can consecrate to devotion. In all such cases let it be clearly understood that the spirit of the work done or the service rendered is the main thing, and that if the spirit but exist in sufficient strength, it will not fail to obtain scope for itself in appropriate forms of manifestation.

CHAPTER VI.

SUPPLEMENTARY METHODS OF INSTRUCTION. PERSONAL IN-
TERCOURSE. DEALINGS WITH SPECIAL CASES. PASTORAL
VISITATIONS. CATECHETICAL INSTRUCTION. VISITATION
OF THE SICK, THE AFFLICTED, AND DYING.

WE have dwelt at some length upon the homiletical
department of pastoral duty, because it is that
through which, when properly discharged, the pastor exercises
his most extensive influence over the understandings and
hearts of his people. Other methods of instruction, however important as accessories, must still be regarded as of
secondary rank in relation to it. Should the regular ministrations of the pulpit be either undervalued, or from any
cause feebly performed, it will be impossible to compensate
for the defect by other appliances. For, even if we could thus
succeed in awakening some degree of spiritual concern, the
better tendencies would again be checked, or at least fail to
reach their proper consummation, not finding the requisite
impulse and supplies of nourishment ministered on the
Sabbath. But there is a danger also in the opposite direction, which the faithful and earnest pastor will do well to
guard against. Pulpit ministrations may be too exclusively
relied on, and may in turn fail to yield the spiritual harvest
expected to be reaped from them, being left too much alone.
The divine seed, it may be, has been sown on the Lord's
day by a wise and discriminating hand ; but being cast into
so many different soils, and exposed thereafter to such
diverse influences, more fitted in many cases to mar than to

cherish and foster its future growth, nothing of solid and permanent growth is produced. And the more gifted the preacher is, he may only be the more apt to neglect the minor solicitudes and agencies which are needed to secure a better result, under the impression that when his discourses appear to be so much appreciated, and to find such attentive and serious audiences, all is done that can well be expected of him, or is actually required for the success of his ministry. Practically, however, such a mode of reckoning will usually be found a great mistake; and whatever may be any one's qualifications for public discourse, there are certain things by which his efforts in that respect should be followed up, otherwise they may prove comparatively unavailing.

I. *Personal Intercourse.*—First of all, it is of importance that, as far as possible, a pastor should cultivate personal intercourse with the people of his charge. By this is not meant such intercourse as arises from the exchange of social visits, or giving and receiving friendly entertainments. Things of that description, within certain limits, are both allowable and proper. They indicate a disposition in the pastor to be on neighbourly terms with his flock, and to partake with them in the common bounties of Providence and the innocent refreshments of life. But they need to be very jealously guarded, and restrained within narrow limits, otherwise they are sure to occasion a serious waste of time, and tend also to bring the minister in his feelings and conversation too much down to the level of ordinary society, or to give him too much the air and tone of a man of the world.

Different from this is the kind of personal intercourse which is now under consideration as a department of pastoral duty. In seeking to cultivate it, the pastor must make himself accessible to his people, and be ready to avail himself of such opportunities as occur to draw forth their hearts toward him, and induce an interchange of thoughts. These, no doubt, will very materially differ according to the nature of the sphere he occupies, and the worldly circumstances of his people. A good deal may often be done even in his casual meetings with them through the week, especially if he is himself gifted with somewhat of a natural frankness of manner, and, along with this, has his heart so much in the work of his sacred calling that every one knows what are the themes most congenial to his spirit. But he may also, and should, particularly in rural charges, cultivate acquaintance with the members of his flock, by occasionally entering into their dwellings, though it should be only for a few minutes, and while his more immediate object, perhaps, is to obtain the exercise he needs, or to transact some little piece of business. In certain situations, where the field is extensive and the congregation numerous, it may be a considerable advantage both for himself and his people, on his own part a great saving of time and labour, to appoint occasionally times and places where he will be ready to see them individually, and to enter into converse with them on any matters on which they might desire to open to him their minds, or to have his advice.

Now, when the pastor is able in one or other of such ways to maintain personal intercourse with a considerable portion of his people, various benefits will accrue, some of them directly relating to himself, though on these it will be unnecessary to dwell. But he will thereby gain much in respect to intimacy with their state and feelings, and so become more skilful in dealing with their spiritual interests. His knowledge of them gets individualized; their distinctive tendencies and characters, their relative degrees of intelligence, the greater or less capacity they may have for understanding the import and profiting by the instruction of the discourses he delivers to them, the special sins and temptations which they need to be warned against, the duties

S

which require to be most urgently pressed : these things and
others of a cognate description will get familiarized to the
mind of the pastor who takes the course indicated, with a
distinctness and particularity which will otherwise be found
unattainable. Acquiring thus a more thorough acquaintance
with their natural and spiritual characteristics, he will be able
in his various ministrations to adapt himself more exactly
and wisely to their particular cases. And while he may
certainly lay his account with having things obtruded upon
him which cause uneasiness and disappointment, he will
also meet with cheering indications, will even occasionally
light upon wells of Christian life and activity, which his own
exhibitions of the truth may have helped to open, and
which will have the effect of sending him on his way
rejoicing.

But while such advantages are not to be overlooked,
they are still inferior to those which the pastor, by such a
course, may be the means of imparting to others, and the
increased moral influence it is fitted to lend to his ministrations. As he comes thereby to a more intimate knowledge
of the people of his charge, so in turn he becomes better
known to them ; and being often touched through the
familiarities of personal intercourse with the proofs of his
kindliness and fellow-feeling, they will be prepared to
mingle with their respect for him as a pastor, affection and
confidence toward him as a friend. The distance and
reserve which the one relation naturally tends to throw
around him, will become lessened and relieved by the free
interchange of thought and feeling fostered by the other ;
and his addresses from the pulpit will assume more the
character of a speaking from heart to heart. They now
know that they are listening to one who really sympathizes
with them and cares for them ; one who unfeignedly seeks
their wellbeing, and delights to go out and in among them.
Besides, by such a course he greatly multiplies his oppor-

tunities of promoting their spiritual good. Though he will often, perhaps, find it impossible to get beneath the surface, or to touch on other than ordinary topics, yet he will again be able, if himself thoroughly in earnest, to direct the conversation into higher channels, and to drop words that shall be like good seed cast into congenial soil. Openings, occasionally at least, will present themselves for suggesting inquiries, tendering cautions, administering reproofs, or giving counsels and encouragements much more special and pointed than could well be addressed from the pulpit. People will get courage to make known their case in times especially of darkness or perplexity, so as to render comparatively easy a suitable application of the healing medicine of the gospel. This is happily noticed by Bengel:[1] 'Friendly intercourse with our people often effects more than all the reasons, demonstrations, and sermons in the world. The traveller unwraps his mantle, not when the cold wind blows strongly, but when the warming sunshine smiles. It is better here to have a single dove flying towards us of its own accord, than to see ever so many driven into the enclosure. How desirable is it to get our people to feel so easy with us, that they can ask or tell us anything with open-heartedness and simplicity!' He adduces, as a more special reason, a consideration which should certainly not be overlooked : ' Many become seriously impressed and " pricked in their hearts" under sermons, who yet derive no special comfort from the word of grace till it is communicated to them in private conversation. Therefore, *visiting* those committed to his charge should be considered by the Christian minister to be anything but a light matter, for he can often do much more good by his private visits than by his public testimony. He should therefore let his people see that he is always willing and ready to attend privately upon any and every one of them.'

[1] *Life*, by Burk, p. 127.

All this, of course, implies a certain unbending on the part of the minister, a frankness and geniality of manner easily distinguished from a politic or forced condescension. Like other personal characteristics, it may exist in very different degrees even in godly ministers, but is also susceptible of great improvement in those who are anxious to cultivate what they have. It implies, too, that the pastor shall not be content with merely speaking to men in the mass, but shall care for them individually, a matter often too little regarded by men otherwise distinguished for their ministerial gifts. 'As fishers of men, they are too exclusively bent,' Mr. James of Birmingham remarks,[1] 'on casting their net among a shoal, and drawing many at one throw, and are not given enough to patiently angling for the solitary fish. Single souls are thought, if not beneath our notice, yet below our zeal. Have we forgotten our great Pattern, who sat for a whole hour, perhaps, or even more, on the side of a well, and laboured kindly and condescendingly for the salvation of one individual, and that a female of indifferent character? Or may we not receive instruction from the parable of the lost sheep, upon perceiving the solicitude and the toil of the good Shepherd to restore the solitary wanderer to the fold? Or let us learn from the conduct of the blessed angels, who rejoice over one sinner that repenteth. It is this anxiety,' he adds, 'for the conversion of single souls by conversation in private more than the ardour of the pulpit that tests the sincerity of our concern and the purity of our motives. Many things apart from the higher objects of pulpit ministration concur to excite our zeal in public; only one, and that of a right kind, can be supposed to operate in private.' There is, undoubtedly, much truth in this representation; and very few pastors who have been long in the ministry will be able to reflect on it without painful and humbling recollections.

[1] Introduction to Spencer's *Sketches*, p. xlv.

It is not unimportant to notice, however, that the same esteemed and earnest minister, in his anxiety to get more into this individual mode of dealing with his people, and deepening on particular minds the impressions which may have been made upon them by the services of the sanctuary, fell upon a plan in the latter years of his ministry which was attended with considerable success, and which doubtless, at particular seasons, has often in substance been adopted elsewhere. The plan was this : He made very special preparation for his pulpit services on one, or perhaps two Sabbaths, with the view of awakening in the minds of his congregation a deep and solemn concern for salvation, and then gave intimation at the close that, on a particular evening shortly after, he would be at the vestry or schoolroom, for the purpose of meeting any one who might have been affected by what they had heard, or who by any means had been brought into concern regarding the things of their peace. He made them very distinctly to understand that his object was not to interrogate or converse with such persons individually, the apprehension of which, he was sure, would have deterred many from coming, but to speak to them and pray with them collectively. The proposal on the first occasion of its announcement was so largely responded to, that Mr. James felt quite overpowered by the greatness and solemnity of the scene ; and from that moment, he says, he felt that a new view of his pastoral office had been opened to him, and a new means of usefulness had been put into his hands. At the evening meeting, in addition to exercises of devotion, he endeavoured to address those present in such a manner as to deepen their feelings of thoughtfulness and spiritual concern, also to impart to them clear views of the way of salvation ; for which purpose he would sometimes distribute an appropriate tract, and request them to peruse it at leisure, while the instructions given by himself were still fresh upon their minds. Meetings of this sort were renewed for six or seven times in successive weeks, when it was intimated that for the present they would cease, and that the pastor would be ready to converse with persons individually at certain times and places mentioned. Usually a very considerable number availed themselves of the opportunity, and about a half of the whole were added to the membership of the church. The plan, with little variation, was repeated at intervals during the remainder of Mr. James' ministry, and always with considerable success.

It should, of course, be understood that such a plan is neither adapted to all situations, nor suited to every one's ministerial gifts; and wherever it is tried, the greatest care should be taken beforehand in feeling one's way as to the probability at least of the effort meeting with an adequate response. It should also be understood that even where things seem, upon the whole, favourable to the attempt being made, the whole issue, humanly speaking, will depend upon the spirit, the earnestness, the tact of the minister; and while he should never trust to these, or think for a moment that the possession of them in the largest measure would be of itself sufficient, still it must be through them instrumentally that the impression in ordinary cases is to be produced and lasting results reached. In such a line of operations nothing of any moment can be effected unless the chief agent in them is profoundly conscious of a desire for the salvation of men, unless he is ready also for this end to come into close fellowship with them, and be willing to labour both in pains and prayer to have them brought to a state of peace and acceptance in the Saviour. On the other hand, there may be a danger in waiting too long for what are supposed to be the requisite gifts and fitting opportunities; a certain courageous boldness, in the name of the Lord, venturing for His sake on new lines of action, may sometimes be the truest wisdom. If one in such a spirit but conscientiously uses what he has and does what he can,

it may not be in vain ; and in this, as in other departments
of spiritual labour, experience will of itself bring increased
skill and fitness for the work.

In regard to the bearing generally of what may be called
individual cases of spiritual awakening brought under the
cognizance of the pastor on his whole work in any particular
place, it is necessary to judge cautiously ; for, though important evidences of a spiritual movement, they are not by
any means the only, or in themselves infallible, tests of its
reality and power.   Various circumstances may operate in
particular localities to modify the number of such cases, and
make them relatively more or fewer than the actual work of
grace which is proceeding at the time might of itself seem
to warrant.   The manners of society must here be taken
into account, which have their characteristic differences in
persons of higher and lower degree ; in the one more quiet
and self-possessed, in the other more free and demonstrative ;
whence, in times of excitement, of *religious* excitement as well
as excitement of any other kind, while the feelings of persons
in the humbler ranks of life will burst forth like new wine,
those of a more refined and cultivated class, though perhaps
equally strong, and even more deep and lasting, are held
under self-control, and flow on like a silent but powerful
current in the underground of their souls.   In a congregation derived mainly from this higher class there will be
nothing like the same exhibition of emotional feeling as in
one of a different description, though the regenerating influence experienced may not be less general and pervading
in the one case than in the other.   The pastor therefore
must, to a considerable extent, judge by other and less
palpable manifestations.   Another element also, the comparative amount of religious knowledge, the measure that
is possessed of an intelligent acquaintance with the word of
God, must not be overlooked ; for this of itself, when possessed in any competent degree, renders the way of peace

perfectly plain to such as have become really in earnest to find it. Their understandings are already full of light ; they have but to realize what they know, to practise what they believe, and in many cases may find no occasion or need to go to the pastor for special direction or comfort. It will naturally, however, be otherwise where people have grown up in ignorance and neglect, estranged in great measure from the ordinances of religion, and hence requiring to be taught what are the first principles of the oracles of God. Deep conviction of sin with such persons will need to be followed up with special efforts to impart a sufficient knowledge of the truth as it is in Christ ; and in *their* case the expressed desire to obtain what in this respect is needed, and the progress made in acquiring it, may commonly be taken as the evidence and measure of a truly awakened condition. It is still further to be borne in mind, that there are *constitutional*, one may even say *national*, idiosyncrasies, which cannot fail to discover themselves in such matters ; and among these may certainly be reckoned a kind of natural shyness or reserve in the Scottish mind. Taken as a class, devout and serious Christians in Scotland are less communicative in regard to the frames and movements of their inner life than in most other countries. I believe it would often be better both for themselves and others if they revealed more of the currents of thought and feeling, the anxieties, joys, and sorrows of which they are conscious, as they might thus know more of the blessed communion of saints, and in their darker moments might more readily obtain the comfort and consolation of which they stand in need. Yet, if there is to be excess on the one side or the other, that which cleaves to us as a people is at least the safer : rather grave, quiet, earnest thought about spiritual things struggling with itself in the chambers of imagery, than much communicativeness with a deficiency of depth and solidity of thought. And then, for the most part, hearts *will* one time or another open ; circumstances will arise which in a manner compel the reserve to give way, and lead to spiritual communings, especially on the part of genuine believers, with their pastor.   And it may, perhaps, help to reconcile him to a little delay in the matter, and dispose him to avoid anything like undue haste or urgency, when it is considered how often it happens that the readiest to disclose their spiritual feelings, the most talkative about their soul-experiences, are the most apt to yield under the pressure of outward difficulties, and commonly the least satisfactory in respect to consistency of character and steadiness of growth in the divine life.[1]

II. *Dealings with Special Cases.*—The preceding remarks will be misunderstood, if they are conceived to indicate a

[1] The following statement, made several years ago by a minister of the Free Church, formerly of the Scottish Establishment, lends confirmation in one or two points to what has just been stated : ' We must not expect from our people that they shall tell us at what time and in what way they were brought to serious thought.   There is on the part of many a dread lest their goodness should be as the morning cloud ; and if one is to be happy only when he hears his people telling him that such and such a sermon or address brought them to Christ, he will assuredly be disappointed.   Let me tell of the manner in which three cases of, I hope, something better than mere improvement were brought about.   The first was a farm-servant, who had been reared in a very careless family, and whose marriage was not carried through so as to approve itself to me.   Visiting him one day, I was struck with his remark, " You said there was not a more pleasant sight than to see the labouring man sitting down on the Sabbath evening and teaching his children the word of God ; I find it very pleasant."   This was the first intimation of a change.   From that day the man took a new position in the parish.   He had much family affliction, which he bore with a most submissive spirit, and his worldly circumstances have so improved that I found him lately in possession of a small farm, and highly respected. The second case was one of our most "well-to-do" farmers.   Often had this man been approached, but he invariably shied all close deal-

disposition to set little by the occurrence of particular cases, as subjects for more exact inquiry and specific treatment, either to discourage the desire for them, or to account their occasional occurrence of little moment. On the contrary, I am persuaded it would argue ill for the character of any Christian pastorate if such were not both expected and found; only some discrimination should be exercised in the matter, if men would save themselves from needless disappointments; and a rule of judgment suitable enough for one sphere of action should not be applied without qualification to another materially different. In almost every field of ministerial labour, though in some greatly more than in others, there will be found exemplifications of the truth so beautifully set forth in the parable: ' So is the kingdom of God, as if a man should cast seed into the ground; and

---

ings; an " Ay" or a " No" was the sum of what could be got out of him. At length, one day he asked me if I could lend him, or would buy for him, a book of prayers, as such a thing "was a help to the like of him." From that day he presented a new character to the parish, and spoke and acted as one interested in the truth. In another case, an individual in the upper ranks of life, after having kept a thorough silence as to the means of her change from a system of self-righteousness to one of simple dependence on the grace of God in Christ, when expecting death, felt it would not be right to conceal the instrumentality by which she had been brought to entertain serious views. This often occurs. The Lord graciously keeps from His servant the knowledge of what He is doing through him ; it may be, lest he should be unduly exalted.' These cases are contrasted by the writer with two others, the subjects of which were persons in the better classes of society ; one that of a lady, who was often seen to be much impressed by public addresses, affected even to tears ; but when laid on a sick-bed was brought to confess that she had till then never prayed. The other was that of a young man, who became apparently a decided convert, and exposed himself to considerable mockery on account of the truth from friends and relatives, but began to decline in his fidelity and zeal, and ultimately sunk into the lowest depths of profligacy and shame.—*Free Church Magazine*, vol. viii. p. 347.

should sleep, and rise night and day, and the seed should spring and grow up, *he knoweth not how;*[1] a silent, gradual, progressive unfolding, rendering itself distinctly manifest only in the result.

Cases will still arise, however, calling for special treatment; and a good deal of a minister's usefulness and adaptation to his particular sphere may often depend upon his qualifications for making the treatment such as it ought to be. They naturally fall into two classes : first, those which have simply to be met with, the cases of persons roused somehow to spiritual concern, or involved in doubt and perplexity about the interests of their souls, and coming to the pastor for comfort and direction ; and second, those whom the pastor should endeavour to seek out, for the purpose of reclaiming them from indifference, or bringing them to a right sense of their state and duty.

1. In regard to the former class, no great difficulty is likely to be occasioned by them, on the supposition that the pastor is a man of sound Scriptural knowledge, spiritual discernment, and hearty zeal in his work. The vast majority of cases that present themselves will be such as require at his hands the exercise only of a sympathizing spirit, prompting him to listen with attention and interest to the details of each ; skill in the application of the word of truth, according to the varieties of spiritual want and danger that come before him ; and faith, living faith, to lay hold of and press upon the awakened and troubled conscience the promises more especially adapted to conduct it to rest. Prayer, I need scarcely say, should accompany all, prayer for direction how to speak, and for a blessing on what is spoken ; prayer also at times during the conference, as well as before or after it. Usually, the main difficulty experienced is in respect to the persons most deeply pierced with convictions of sin, how to get them brought into such clear views of the

[1] Mark iv. 26, 27.

scheme of grace, and such a realizing sense of the offered forgiveness of the gospel, as will enable them to lay aside their fears, and with a trustful confidence commit themselves to the covenant faithfulness of God. The transition seems so great from the one state to the other, that they are not easy to be convinced of its immediate practicability. And in the case of some, there are constitutional difficulties which serve to aggravate the difficulty, nervous debility, melancholic temperaments, dyspeptic or other bodily derangements, in which material elements become strangely intermingled with spiritual; and something like physical hindrances for a time bar the way to a comfortable assurance. For such cases it is impossible to lay down definite prescriptions, or give instructions that can be of much practical avail. Experience must be the chief guide; and they who cannot find their way thus to the proper mode of treatment, will derive little help either from the lecture-room or the written page.

There are cases, however, occasionally occurring in times of religious awakening, and assuming the aspect of a hopeful concern about salvation, in dealing with which the pastor will have need of other qualities than those which may suffice for guiding ordinary inquirers into the way of peace and safety. It is quite possible that persons may become disquieted in conscience, and exhibit considerable marks of a penitent and changed condition, who still have never become properly alive to their condition as sinners, who are not prepared either to confess or to forsake all that is evil in their temper and conduct, and who, therefore, if they should be plied merely with the consolations of the gospel, might readily solace themselves with a peace which is not of God. Such persons need to be dealt with first in a spirit of faithful severity; they must be made to know themselves better before they can apprehend Christ aright as their Saviour, and enter into the participation of His risen life. We meet with cases of this description in the New Testament; for example, in the scribes and Pharisees as a class; in Nicodemus most especially; in the rich young ruler; and in the method of treatment adopted toward them by John the Baptist and our Lord, searching, wise, faithful, we have the line marked out which, in similar circumstances, we ought to follow. It may not be quite easy to detect the lurking evil, or descry amid the signs of apparent life and hopefulness the indications of a want of thorough earnestness and sincerity; but possibly something in the manner, if carefully watched, may discover it, or it may come out as the result of personal inquiries or incidental means of information. When once ascertained, there should be no dallying with the spiritual sore in their condition; no false delicacy in bringing the truth of God to bear upon it; faithfulness, applying the axe to the root of the tree, is the real kindness. Take as a good illustrative example the following case which occurred in connection with the ministry of an evangelical minister of the Church of England in last century, Mr. Walker of Truro:—'One of his visitors for private instruction was a young man, who stated that he called to thank him for the benefit he had received from his ministry, and to beg his advice. Mr. Walker immediately questioned him as to the knowledge he possessed of his own heart, when the youth expressed in general terms a conviction that he was an unworthy sinner. Perceiving by his manner that he had never duly experienced that conviction, Mr. Walker at once entered into an explanation of the sinner's character, with a personal reference to the individual before him. He dwelt upon his ingratitude to God, the evil nature of the motives which had influenced all his actions, the fruitlessness of his life, the defilement even of his best deeds, and then added, " I fear you are secretly displeased with me, because I have not commended your good intentions and flattered your vanity." " No indeed, sir," said the young man, " I feel extremely thankful for this striking proof of your kindness and regard." ' Yet even this was feigned ; for the young man himself next day confessed that he felt inwardly chagrined at the small account Mr. Walker seemed to make of his professions, and had even secretly determined to encounter no more the searching questions which had exposed his shallowness and wounded his pride. But he could not carry out his purpose of forsaking his instructor ; the arrow of divine truth had entered his heart, he submitted himself to the righteousness of God in Christ, and ever afterwards led an exemplary Christian life. But under a less discerning and faithful minister, who can tell what might have been the result? Most probably a fresh increase to his self-complacency, followed by future backslidings, ever-recurring inconsistencies, and much that betokened the form rather than the life of godliness.[1]

Cases of this description render it manifest that all is by no means accomplished when personal concern is awakened, or when the sinner assumes the position of an inquirer, and that a pastor has often much more to do with those who seek advice from him regarding their soul's interests than quote a few passages of Scripture and point their way to the Saviour. Nor does the difficulty always arise from some latent insincerity or deep-rooted contrariety in some respect to the humbling tenets of the gospel. It may come in great part from the relations of social or domestic life, from embarrassments created by the rival claims of affections and interests, which in themselves are good, and in respect to which it is no easy matter to decide when they compete for the precedency. That which, if one of these claims stood alone, might commend itself to approval, may appear, when relatively considered, to be attended with so many risks and

---

[1] See also some other illustrative cases remarkably well conducted in Spencer's *Sketches*, particularly the one entitled ' Delay ; or, The Accepted Time.'

hazards to interests naturally esteemed precious, that a man may be tempted to pause before making the venture, and to ask whether, meanwhile at least, something less might not be held reasonable and proper.   Perplexing cases of this sort will sometimes present themselves, for which, either to choose oneself the right path, or to counsel others in regard to it, there is needed a spirit of discretion as well as of godly simplicity, and still more perhaps even than that, a strong, reliant faith in God's word, the faith which can remove mountains, and which can fearlessly take the course of lofty principle in the calm assurance that God will stand by the right, and, in spite of all that seems adverse or perilous, will cause it to become the best for present peace and blessing as well as for ultimate good.   The history of Providence is ever furnishing exemplifications of this, and with such the prudent and conscientious pastor will do well to keep himself acquainted, in order that, from the experience of others as well as from his own observation and knowledge of the way of life, he may be able to guide his people through the more trying emergencies of their lot.[1]

2. The earnest and devoted pastor, however, must not be satisfied with simply meeting such cases as come of their own accord to him for counsel and direction ; he must himself assume the part of an inquirer in regard to some, whether formally connected with his congregation or lying on its outskirts, endeavouring by one method or another to get into personal contact with them, and bring them to a sense of what seems unrighteous in their course and perilous in their condition.   I have already noticed the temptations there are with many ministers of the gospel for neglecting this part of pastoral duty, and of the difficulties attending its discharge.   Indeed, these are altogether so peculiar and

[1] Some excellent specimens of what is referred to may be found in Spencer's *Sketches*, especially ' The Persecuted Wife ;' also one or two in Warton's *Deathbed Scenes and Past Conversations*.

so various, that I should only, I fear, spend time to little purpose by going at any length into the subject. It is not so properly a science to be studied as an art to be learned; and, like all other arts, to be learned to purpose, it must be pursued amid the objects of real life. The felt responsibility of being put in charge with immortal souls, among whom there appear to be some perishing for lack of knowledge, and incapable of being effectually reached by public ministrations—this, to awaken the desire for putting forth special efforts in their behalf, and such works as those already referred to suggest practical hints for the most likely methods of accomplishing the end in view, will do more than the most elaborate prelections on the general nature and objects of the duty. I indicate only a few essential points.

First, all reasonable care should be taken beforehand to know the real state and character of the parties intended to be dealt with. There should always be more to go upon than vague impressions or general rumours. Knowledge here, of a circumstantial and definite nature, may truly be designated a key to at least a certain measure of success; for it lays open to us the realities of the case we have to deal with, and so both prevents us from stumbling upon imaginary evils, the bare suspicion of which might lead us astray, and brings us acquainted with the precise evils which have, if possible, to be mastered.

Secondly, we should prepare for the dealing, by considering well the forms of evil or aspects of character to which we mean to address ourselves in the way of reform, the thoughts and considerations which it might be best to urge on the notice of the persons concerned, the very passages of Scripture also we would lodge in their memory; and prepare, moreover, by invoking the guidance and blessing of Him in whose name alone everything should be done that touches the interests of salvation.

Thirdly, this which I have just mentioned, salvation, is the end that should be kept steadily in view, in our private dealings with individual souls, as well as in our public ministrations.   Nothing less ; for short of this nothing will avail to their real wellbeing, or fulfil the design of a gospel ministry. Slighter reforms, however proper to be mentioned, and made perhaps the starting-point of our remarks, should still only be regarded as the preliminary stages to be gained, the soul's surrender to Christ and appropriation of His purchased redemption being ever kept in view as the proper landing-place we desire to reach.   It is this high aim, also, which best nerves the mind to such close and often delicate intermeddling with other men's states and modes of life ; for, when such mighty interests are seen to be at stake, what practical difficulties should not the servant of Christ be ready to encounter !

Finally, while a spirit of profound earnestness and fidelity to the cause of truth should constitute the ground of the whole proceeding, sincere and fervent love should animate and characterize the mode of conducting it, love that may be felt ; for this will soften every stroke, and lend weight to every argument and appeal we make.   ' I cannot think,' said one to a truly evangelical pastor, ' how your people bear such plain speaking ;' to which the reply was, ' It is because they know I love them.'   And of the love itself, which bears such blessed fruit, it has been justly said, that ' it is not the addressing people with epithets of endearment and words of tenderness which proves its existence and secures its objects ; it must be a deep, inward love of souls, learned beneath the cross of Christ; it should manifest itself rather in the actions of a loving life than in ready and apparent demonstrations ; and when it is real, it will lead to the self-denying abandonment of ease, favourite pursuits, and of pleasant company, that in the morning, and at noon-day, and at evening-tide, whenever we can best reach them,

T

we may be with the sick and with the whole, teaching the young, and comforting the mourners, and recalling the wanderers, and building up the weak. Such love as this will impart to the true pastor a character which all can understand, and which, in the long run, few can resist.'[1]

III. *Pastoral Visitations.*—A considerable part of the delicacy connected with a portion of the cases which call for special dealing is in great measure avoided by the practice known among us by the name of *pastoral visitations;* that is, stated official visits, once a year in congregations or parishes of moderate size, to the various households more or less connected with the particular pastorate. No one who is really bent on winning souls will ever think of limiting his intercourse with the families of his flock to such visitations, unless, indeed, the magnitude of his charge or infirm health in a manner oblige him to do so. Yet, even if he should be able to do not a little in that casual and incidental way to keep up a certain intercourse with them, the practice of regular household visitations is in itself a good one, and for various reasons ought to be maintained. It tends, first of all, in a very natural and appropriate manner to keep alive in the minds of the people the feeling that they are under pastoral oversight. For, by such visitations, the fact is ever and anon brought prominently before them, that it is a recognised part of ministerial duty to take cognizance of the families and individuals belonging to a pastorate, and from house to house as well as in the sanctuary speak to them of the things pertaining to the kingdom of God. The practice, besides, furnishes the pastor with an excellent opportunity, perpetually recurring, of breaking the bread of life to the families of the flock in a more homely manner than can be done from the pulpit, and of engaging in acts of devotion with them as one of themselves.

[1] Bishop of Oxford's (Wilberforce) *Addresses*, p. 93.

But in addition to all this, it carries with it the great advantage of providing him with an occasion for noticing anything that may have appeared to him amiss in particular families or individuals without seeming to go out of his way for the purpose. If he has observed symptoms of ungodliness to be growing upon them, if attendance upon ordinances has begun to be less regular and serious than it formerly was, if questionable courses are known to have been entered on, improper companionships formed, scandalous outbreaks of temper exhibited, whatever it may be that has given occasion for anxiety concerning them, the practice of regular pastoral visitations enables the pastor, in a quiet and unobtrusive manner, to bring his Christian influence and counsel to bear on the incipient evil, and perhaps prevent it from going further. There may possibly be only a few things of the kind referred to calling for notice in each round of pastoral visitation ; but it may, notwithstanding, be found of considerable moment, in a practical point of view, to have such a method of dealing with them.

If it is asked, after what manner should the visitation be conducted ? or, at what times ? nothing very explicit can be indicated in the way of answer, nor should anything like unbending uniformity be attempted ; the diversified circumstances of congregations and families call for a corresponding variety. Indeed, amid the artificial arrangements of modern society, the great difficulty often is to find any time suitable for such visitations, families being so variously occupied with the employments of active life, and so seldom for any length of time gathered together in their respective homes. In such cases almost the only practicable method is for the pastor to make a brief visit to the nearly empty households at some convenient season during the day, and appointing a particular dwelling in which to meet them together in the evening ; a method that may occasionally be adopted as a variation, even where not absolutely necessary; but which always carries the relative disadvantage of losing, to some extent, the more private and special in the general.   Usually, where it can be done, the most effective method is to take each family apart, and either draw them into conversation on spiritual matters, such as we have reason to think likely to prove instructive and edifying to the family ; or give a short exposition of some passage of Scripture, with such directness and point in the application as may be fitted to tell beneficially on the hearts of those we seek to impress ; or, still again, where there are several young persons in the family, put a few questions to them from the Catechism, with subordinate questions and illustrations calculated to bring out the meaning, and then turn the points of doctrine or duty thus elucidated to prac-tical account for the older as well as the younger members of the family.   Prayer should always conclude the exercise, and prayer so constructed as to bear specific reference to the several classes composing the membership of the house-hold and the duties respectively devolving on them.   Which-ever method be adopted, nothing should be done in a rapid and perfunctory manner, as if the object were merely to perform a certain amount of work in a definite portion of time.   Work so done is not likely to yield much return of spiritual good.   We must throw our souls into it ; and if we do so, we shall find that a comparatively small number of families is as much as can be satisfactorily overtaken in a day, as it necessarily involves a considerable degree of mental labour and spiritual anxiety.   And here, as in other things, he who would win the blessing must not grudge the cost.

It is impossible, as I have said, to prescribe for work of this description any uniform rule ; nor can the example of any single individual, however eminent in ministerial gifts, or honoured in the work itself, be fitly set up as a kind of universal pattern.   Yet it may not be without benefit to set before one's mind occasionally a higher specimen of skill and devotedness in this department of pastoral labour, if not for the purpose of copying it, which may now be impracticable, yet as an elevated ideal, which may serve to stimulate one's exertions, and lead to greater things being aimed at than might otherwise be thought of. Such an ideal we undoubtedly have in the account given by Richard Baxter of the practice of the well-known Joseph Alleine, when assistant parish minister of Taunton.   ' He would,' says Baxter, ' give families notice of his coming, the day before, desiring that he might have admittance to their houses, to converse with them about their soul-concerns, and that they would have the whole family together against he came.   When he came, and the family were called together, he would be instructing the younger sort in the principles of religion by asking several questions out of the Catechism, the answers to which he would be opening and explaining to them.   Also, he would be inquiring of them about their spiritual state and condition, labouring to make them sensible of the evil and danger of sin, the corruption and wickedness of our natures, the misery of an unconverted state; stirring them to look after the true remedy proposed in the gospel, to turn from all their sins unto God, to close with Christ upon His own terms ; to follow after holiness, to watch over their hearts and lives, to mortify their lusts, to redeem their time, to prepare for eternity.   These things, as he would be explaining them to their understandings, so he would be pressing the practice of them on their consciences with the most cogent arguments and considerations. Besides, he would leave with them several counsels and directions to be carefully remembered and practised for the good of their souls. Those that were serious and religious he would labour to help forward in holiness by answering their doubts, resolving their cases, encouraging them under their difficulties.   And before he did go from any family he would deal with the heads of that family, and such others as were grown to the years of discretion, singly and apart ; that so he might, as much as possibly he could, come to know the condition of each particular person in his flock, and address himself in his discourses as might be suitable to every one of them. If he perceived they did live in the neglect of family duties, he would exhort and press them to set up the worship of God in their families, and directing them how to set about it, and to take time for secret duties too. Such as were masters of families he would earnestly persuade and desire, as they did tender the honour of Christ and the welfare of their children and servants' souls, to let them have some time every day for such private duties, and to encourage them in the performance of them ; nor would he leave them till he had a promise of them so to do. Sometimes, also, he would himself go to prayer before his departure. This was his method,' Baxter adds, 'in the general, although with such necessary variation in his particular visits as the various state and condition of the several families did require.   If the family where he came were ignorant, he would insist the longer in instructing and catechizing ; if loose, in reproving and convincing ; if godly, in encouraging and directing.   He did use to spend five afternoons every week in such exercise, from one or two o'clock till seven in the evening.   In which space of time he would visit sometimes three or four families, and sometimes more, according as they were greater or less.   This course he would take throughout the town ; and when he had gone through, he would presently begin again, that he might visit every family as often as he could.   He often did bless God for the great success he had in these exercises, saying that God had made him as instrumental of good to souls this way as by his public preaching, if not more.'

Pastoral visitations conducted after this fashion might justly be termed a doing business with people about the salvation of their souls; it displayed such laborious pains-taking for their spiritual good, such earnest travailing in birth for its accomplishment, as bespoke a man of apostolic zeal to whom ' to live was Christ;' and it was but a specimen, though doubtless one of the more distinguished specimens of what about the same period was pursued by the Puritan ministers in many an English parish, and very generally in Scotland. In Scotland it was both more generally followed and longer continued; and it undoubtedly contributed much to that wide diffusion of religious knowledge and observance which, in the better periods of their history, has been the cha-racteristic of the Scottish people. The instructions issued by the General Assembly on ministerial visitations in 1708,[1] if

---

[1] *Act of Assembly* 1708 *respecting Ministerial Visitations.*

' 1. After the minister has got an account of the persons dwelling in the family, he may speak to them *all* in general of the necessity of re-generation, and the advantages of serious religion and godliness, of piety towards God, and justice and charity towards man.

' 2. And next more particularly to the *servants;* of their duty to fear and serve God, and to be dutiful, faithful, and obedient servants, and of the promises made to such; commending to them the reading of the Scriptures as they can, and prayer in secret, and love and concord among themselves, and, in particular, a holy care of sanctifying the Lord's day.

' 3. The minister may apply his discourse to the *children,* as they are capable, with affectionate seriousness, showing them the advantage of knowing, loving, seeking, and serving God, and remembering their Creator and Redeemer in the days of their youth, and honouring their parents, and to mind them how they were dedicated to God in bap-tism; and when of age and fit, and after due instruction of the nature of the covenant of grace and the seals thereof, to excite them to engage themselves personally to the Lord, and to desire, and prepare for, and take the first opportunity they can of partaking of the Lord's Supper; to be especially careful how they communicate at first, much depending thereon (and such of the servants as are young are to be exhorted hereto in like manner); exciting them also to daily reading of the Scriptures, and to secret prayer, and sanctifying the Lord's day.

' 4. After the minister has spoken to servants and children, he should

properly carried out, must have required a substantial repetition of the method practised by Alleine. As a rule, it can be but occasionally and partially followed now ; there has come, along with other changes in the course of time, such a divided state of things in parishes and families, such an impatience of authority and whatever in matters of religion wears an inquisitorial aspect, such a want of repose also for the quiet and thoughtful handling of spiritual concerns, as

speak privately to the *master and mistress* of the family about their personal duty toward God, and the care of their own soul's salvation, and their obligation to promote religion and the worship of God in their family, and to restrain and punish vice and encourage piety, and to be careful that they and their house serve the Lord and sanctify the Lord's day. And after this it may be fit to exhort masters to take care that God be worshipped daily in the family by prayer, and praise, and the reading of the Scriptures. *2d.* Concerning the behaviour and conversation of the servants, and their duty towards God and man, and how they attend the worship of God in the family, how they attend the public worship on the Lord's day, and how they behave after sermons ; if any of them be piously inclined; if they make conscience of secret prayer and reading the Scriptures. *3d.* If there be catechizing and instructing the ignorant and weak ; if due care be taken in educating the children; and particularly, if they be put timeously to school, and how they profit thereat, and how the Lord's day is spent after sermons in the family and in secret : in all which the minister may mix in suitable directions, encouragements, and admonitions as he shall see cause, and most for edification.

' 5. (Directs inquiry as to the supply of Bibles.)

' 6. (To exhort communicants to remember and pay their vows.)

' 7. Seeing there is need for all this of much prudence, zeal for God, and love to souls, and affectionate seriousness, all this should be carried on with dependence on God and fervent prayer to Him, both before a minister sets forth for such work, and with the visited, as there shall be access to and opportunity for it.'

[Sensible and good in the main, but somewhat too formal, dwelling proportionally too much on externals, and carrying the appearance of a degree of inquisitoriousness; the great object better gained by going more into the spirit and life of religion.]

renders the spirit only, not the precise form, of the good old practice for the most part applicable in our generation. Ministers of the gospel, therefore, must here endeavour to adapt themselves to circumstances, and follow the example of her who is commended for having done simply what she could.

IV. *Catechetical Instruction.*—One part of the object intended to be gained by pastoral visitations has been often sought by means of meetings for catechetical instruction; diets for catechizing, as they used to be called among us. No method, certainly, is so well calculated as that of communication by means of question and answer, for enabling the pastor to get at the real state of knowledge in those who are committed to him for instruction in divine things; none also better adapted for bringing such as are imperfectly enlightened in the truth to clear and definite views of it, and exercising their faculties to a proper discrimination between the doctrines of God and the errors and corruptions with which they have been overlaid by men; and when regularly carried out by special meetings for the purpose, held from year to year and from place to place, as was once the common practice in Scotland, it must have had a considerable effect in sharpening the intellects of the people in connection with religious subjects, and raising them to a relatively high place as to the possession of doctrinal knowledge.

That, however, was probably about the whole of the result that came out of the yearly catechizings as they were wont to be conducted, an increase of head knowledge; so far, indeed, good if kept in its proper place, and used chiefly as the means to a higher end, but a very inferior good if rested in as an end of its own, or held merely as the buttress and ornament of a lifeless orthodoxy. There is some reason to fear that this, latterly at least, was the turn things in great measure took, especially when persons in full communion with the Church, as well as those in training for it, were subjected to the process (a thing scarcely capable of justification in an ecclesiastical respect); and the growing conviction of the general inefficiency of the practice with reference to the higher interests of religion, coupled with the somewhat awkward exhibitions not unfrequently made at them by the more bashful and retiring portions of the flock, tended to bring on a disrelish for such catechizings, and ultimately, in most parts of the country, led to their discontinuance.

The tendencies in this direction were considerably strengthened by the passing away of the old simplicity of manners, the gradual introduction of a more artificial state of society, accompanied by a greater diversity of rank and position among the people. The minister could not well be catechizing before others ladies and gentlemen, or persons who would not be quite pleased if they were not reckoned such; and then, if *they* were exempted as belonging to a higher grade, others not very far beneath them in circumstances, possibly in religious knowledge and character superior, could scarcely deem themselves treated with due regard if they should seem to be kept in a sort of leading-strings. Were it only, therefore, to avoid the appearance of partiality, it became in a manner necessary to grant to others the exemption which had already been conceded to some. And another thing which might be said to consummate the change, and to do so without any real loss, was the general establishment of Sabbath schools and of Bible classes for the young. These being usually placed under the superintendence of the pastor, and bringing him more or less into intelligent contact with the minds of the young when ripening to manhood and womanhood, very much superseded the necessity of stated examinations for the congregation as such. At the proper period for acquiring the elements of religious knowledge the pastor has taken cognizance of at least the greater number of those who ultimately form the congregation ; so that, in ordinary circumstances, the work of the pastorate in this particular line might be fairly regarded as done.

It is not, therefore, by any means an absolute loss that has here to be thought of, but rather the dropping of one mode of action for another, which is even in some respects better, because when rightly managed more thorough and complete. Regularly conducted and well-organized Sabbath schools, followed up, wherever practicable, by Bible classes for the more advanced, may be made most effective instruments for the godly instruction and upbringing of the young ; and they have this advantage, that while they afford ample opportunities for pastoral inspection and oversight, they also serve to call into play the available Christian agencies belonging to the congregation ; others, with capacities of service differing according to the gift of Christ, become fellow-workers with the pastor in sowing the gospel seed. But the pastor must keep his hand at the plough also here ; especially in rural situations, where the supply of teachers is usually most imperfect, and the presence of the pastor is needed to give life and direction to the whole. And he may find it useful—useful to the older as well as to the younger portions of the congregation—to have occasional, quarterly perhaps, or half-yearly, examinations of the Sabbath school in the church ; taking care, through the examinations, to bring clearly out to all present the great facts and principles of the gospel of Christ, and to enforce the lessons taught by such illustrative examples and appeals as may prove interesting and instructive to all classes. Methods of this nature wisely planned, and diligently carried out, will in most situations be sufficient to compensate for what has been lost.[1]

[1] It is scarcely necessary to add, that the personal catechizings which

V. *Visitation of the Sick and Afflicted.*—The only point that remains to be noticed under this general division has respect to the case of those who are in circumstances of distress—the diseased, the dying, or the bereaved. The ministration of counsel and comfort to these is undoubtedly a most important branch of pastoral duty. It is such, indeed, that the neglect or slovenly discharge of it will go far to neutralize the effect of all other services. For the pastor who makes himself strange in the households of his flock, while they are involved in sorrow or stricken with disease and death, will invariably be regarded as devoid of the tenderness and consideration which are the most appropriate characteristics of his calling ; also, as letting most precious opportunities slip for prosecuting his high commission. He will be regarded as one more intent on his own ease or gratification than on the business of his spiritual vocation, and even as doing what he may otherwise perform in the fulfilment of its duties, rather out of respect to worldly motives and inducements, than from zeal to the glory of God, and love to the souls of men. So strong is the general feeling among Christian people on this point, that they will hardly allow cases of fever, or other diseases supposed to be infectious, to form a just ground of absence at such times. Unless in very extreme cases, the shrinking of the minister from the region of danger is viewed as a dereliction of duty, since there appears in it an unwillingness to adventure for the sake of men's souls where others readily go for the sake of their bodies. He should therefore consider well how much the course of procedure he follows here may tell upon his general standing and usefulness. If he might be disposed, from a nervous dread of

it was the more immediate object of Baxter in his *Reformed Pastor* to recommend, are no longer suitable or practicable ; they never were so except in part, or in some particular situations ; but the work itself is in other respects of great practical value, and well deserves perusal.

infection, or from what may seem a becoming regard to the welfare of his family, to stand aloof, he should reflect that disease—possibly the very form of disease he seeks most anxiously to avert—may reach him by ways he cannot anticipate or prevent ; and that it were unspeakably better the visitation should find him while faithfully pursuing the path of duty than when timidly deserting it. It is a happy thing, in such times, when one can attain to the conviction, that in all ordinary cases the path of duty is more than any other the path of safety ; because, when followed with due precautions, and in a spirit of unshrinking fidelity, it is that in which one can most confidently look for the divine protection and blessing. Not that, even when he has attained to the conviction and is prepared to act on it, the pastor should feel himself obliged to visit the infected chamber, when it is clear he can minister no spiritual benefit, or when he is himself in a state of bodily exhaustion ; but merely that inferior considerations should be kept in their proper place, and no one should have just reason to say that for certain by-ends of his own he allowed the solemn calls of duty to fall into abeyance.

It is possible, however, at such times to show much sympathy and attention, and still fail miserably in the discharge of duty ; never, indeed, rise to any due conception of it. There is a natural feeling in the minds even of the careless and ungodly, which prompts them to desire the visit of a minister when trouble and sickness lie heavy upon them ; they are for the time checked in their worldly course ; ordinary comforts and supports fail them ; their minds are involuntarily thrown into a sombre mood ; and they are hence prepared to welcome into their habitation one who comes as the ,peculiar representative of religion. His very presence is by some thought to carry a blessing with it ; and to hear from his lips a few words of consolation, or obtain the benefit of his prayers, is too often deemed sufficient to atone for many a past neglect. Now, a minister may fall in with this state of feeling, and by so doing greatly endear himself to his people ; while still nothing after all may be done which the occasion properly demands, and the parties concerned may presently again move on, as before, in their course of worldliness or indifference. Personally, the pastor may have grown in their affection and esteem ; but they are not the less settled on their lees.

It is in another spirit, and for other ends, that the true servant of Christ will endeavour to discharge the duty devolving on him in the season of trouble. His behaviour will certainly be marked by such kindness and sympathy as will give him a firmer hold of the affection and confidence of his people ; but his great concern will be to deal faithfully with their souls, and turn the time of their special visitation into a season of grace and blessing. Personal illness or family trouble is a favourable opportunity for getting nearer to them in a spiritual respect than can usually be done at other times, and pressing home upon them the words of soberness and truth. It is with such words especially they should then be plied ; and it were better one should abstain from attempting to act the part of a comforter, than leave them mistaken or in doubt as to the way in which it is to be found. Should the general tenor of their life have been manifestly wrong, and one has reason to fear that they are still in alienation from the life of God, it were kindness altogether misplaced, cruelty, indeed, rather than kindness, to refrain from touching the great sore in their condition, and bringing it into contact with the true, healing balsam of the gospel. The task may often be alike delicate and difficult ; it may even exceed all the skill and consideration which we are able to muster for the occasion, or cause us at least to feel in doubt whether we had actually reached the bottom of the matter ; but this, at all events, is the great point to be aimed at ; and above and beyond the common

sympathy we may cherish, and the ordinary acts of kindness in which we may express it toward them, we should
set our hearts on the object of having them brought to
know and partake of the good part which cannot be taken
from them.

Such, in particular, should be the spirit and character of
our procedure with those who are themselves stricken with
disease, and may possibly be trembling on the brink of
eternity.   It is a solemn thing to have to deal, in God's
stead, with persons who are lying under the shadow of
death ; in a few brief hours, perhaps, destined to give in their
final account.   'There are two classes,' Bengel remarked,[1]
' which a minister of souls should make his especial care :
those which may be called the first and the last, the children
and the dying.   The first, because in them he may look for
the largest outpouring of blessing on his labours ; the last,
because so little time remains for the fulfilment of his ministry to *them.*'   In their case it is indeed now or never ; and
many a time, when the knell of death has finally rung out
the season of opportunity, the spiritually-minded pastor will
see cause to reproach himself for not being more frequent
in his visits, and more earnest in his pleadings with them,
while they still were within the offer of mercy.   It is true,
probably, that the actual number of conversions on the bed
of death is not very great ; few, it may be, compared with
the whole of those who have exhibited some evidence of
an awakened concern about their souls, and of a hopeful
trust in Christ.   There must always, when the concern or
hope has begun only then, be a want of full satisfaction as
to the result ; since the grand test necessarily fails of a work
of grace, namely, a stedfast adherence to Christ amid the
trials and temptations of life.   And the sad relapses often
made into the ways of vanity and sin by those who have
awoke apparently to righteousness under the momentary

[1] *Life*, p. 147.

apprehension of death, when the danger which produced it
has passed away, leaves no room to doubt that the same
results would have happened in the case of many others
who, after undergoing similar experiences, passed into their
final home. Still, there are doubtless some whom the grace
of God reaches even then for the first time ; and the bare
possibility of being the instrument of rescuing so much as
one, or a very few, amid the last flickering moments of life,
cannot but dispose the faithful pastor to seize with all readiness the opportunities presented by such solemn emergencies
to do the work of an evangelist.

It is, however, to be borne in mind, that though there
may not be many actual conversions in the time of severe
sickness or approaching death, there are many cases in
which these prove seasons of peculiar blessing ; cases ever
and anon occurring, in which the already existing germ of
life, comparatively latent before, becomes quickened by the
stirring experiences of the time, and developes into full consciousness of vitality and strength ; and cases, again, in
which where life has distinctly appeared, though compassed
about with obvious failings and infirmities, a fresh start is
taken, and presently a more healthful, vigorous, and decided
tone discovers itself in all that is thought and done. The
valley of Achor is thus found a door of hope—of hope, at
least, as a distinctly realized and conscious power, or a
sustaining and governing principle of action ; and the
diligent pastor, like the wise and skilful physician, should
endeavour so to tend, and guide, and nourish the reviving
energies of life, while still labouring in the valley, as to help
forward the desired result. He should not imagine that for
this end much speaking on divine things will always be
requisite. Not unfrequently the individual is incapable
from bodily prostration to follow that sufficiently ; and even
when capable, would probably be less benefited by it than
by something short, if only earnest, thoughtful, and suited

to his spiritual condition. A single verse or brief passage of Scripture, uttered in a serious, affectionate, and believing manner; or the same in a few appropriate sentences, explained and applied, will often do more than a multitude of words. For the thing chiefly needed is to get the heart first to know itself, and then to apprehend and grasp by a living faith, as suited to its wants and weaknesses, the word of God's faithfulness and truth; when this is done, all in a manner is gained. And very commonly, as I have said, it will be most readily gained, not by lengthened addresses, or by long prayers; but by tenderness of spirit, sympathetic feeling, discriminating fidelity; faith mingling with all, and giving point and impressiveness to the sayings it brings forth from the oracles of God.

In regard to experienced believers the method pursued will naturally differ, according as they are themselves exercised under their affliction. If their faith continues living, and death itself is anticipated without alarm, the pastor will often feel that he has little to do as a guide or instructor, but has himself to learn rather than to teach; and has only as a sympathizing friend to mingle his expressions of faith and hope, his tears and prayers, with those of the afflicted to whom he ministers. Cases, however, will occur in which he will find other work to do; to re-assure hearts that in the hour of trial have begun to lose the hold they were wont to have of the Saviour; to strengthen the fainting spirit, and allay vexing doubts and fears which, perhaps, were little known till the waves of sore trouble began to beat upon them. In dealing with cases of this sort, the pastor will sometimes find his own spirit not a little tried; he will be made to see how impotent man's word is to calm such perturbations of soul, and restore it to confidence in God; how little even God's word may avail, unless it be handled with a realizing sense of its power and sufficiency, as well as skilfully applied to the particular moods and trials of the

U

persons concerned. Prayerful consideration, therefore, seriousness of spirit, and special preparation as to the most effective mode of reaching the springs of thought and feeling in the bosom, may be needed for the pastor, if he is to do the part of a true spiritual physician. And for this, whatever help he may derive from human compositions, he will still repair as his chief armoury to the word of God ; for only on the sure sayings of that word can the troubled soul be really brought to anchor itself in the near prospect of eternity.

Times of sickness and bereavement, it should further be remembered, are fraught with solemn lessons to the other members of the family beside those more immediately affected. And these the pastor should also keep in his eye, and help as much as possible to a right improvement of the dispensations of God toward them. He should try to impress them with the conviction that seasons of severe affliction are seasons of special dealing on the part of God, who doubtless watches with peculiar interest for the proper result. And it will also be well for him to urge on them the important consideration, that it is not so much by the outward circumstances of one's death, or the precise shade of feeling in which it is met, that the final issue for each shall be determined, as rather by the treatment he has given through life to God's manifestation of Himself in His Son, and the evidence borne by his daily walk and conduct to the reality of his faith and the sincerity of his love.

CHAPTER VII.

PUBLIC PRAYER AND OTHER DEVOTIONAL SERVICES.

IT is necessary to give so much space to the function of preaching and other collateral duties in treating of a pastor's ministrations, that a comparatively brief discussion must suffice for what concerns the devotional part of the church-service.[1] It scarcely, indeed, admits of prolonged discussion, unless where the service has been permitted to grow into a mass of liturgical observances. A certain measure of simplicity of worship may still be preserved, though a liturgy is used in the main parts of the service, as is the case in some of the churches of the Reformation, Presbyterian as well as Episcopal. But in these cases the responsibility and the power of the pastor are of a very limited nature. He has the *matériel* of the service prepared to his hand; and to give the proper tone and character to this, is the whole that can justly be expected of him. Even that, however, is not so easy as might at first sight appear; for though it neither demands nor admits of any fresh thoughts or independent manifestations of pious feeling, it necessarily owes much of whatever interest or impressiveness may belong to it to the manner in which it is performed. If the officiating minister should go through this department of his work in a dull and spiritless style, like one treading the routine of a prescribed formalism, the performance is sure to repress and deaden the devotional feelings of the people rather than stir and quicken them into lively exercise. Let the mode of conducting divine worship be what it may,

[1] Compare Allon's Essay on Worship, in *Ecclesia*.

if it is to be for a congregation of believers a worship in spirit and in truth, the person who conducts it must himself enter into the spirit of the service, uttering from his own heart what he would have re-echoed from the hearts of others. And, obviously, the more beaten the track that is to be followed, the more familiar to all the specific forms of devotion, the greater at once must be the need of a lively devotional sentiment to inspirit them with life, and the difficulty also of expressing it through the appointed channels.

But with liturgical services we have at present nothing to do, as they have been rejected from a place in our public worship. With us the minister who has to address the people on God's behalf has also to address God in behalf, and indeed in the name, of the people. The responsibility here, therefore, is considerably greater. The matter of devotion, as well as its manner and the fitting adaptation of one part of it to another, are left entirely in his hands ; so that, according as he possesses or wants the requisite qualifications for the work assigned him, must the edification and comfort of the worshippers be promoted or marred in the service. It is chiefly, of course, in connection with the prayers offered in the sanctuary that these qualifications will be brought into play, but other parts of the service will also afford a certain scope for their exercise. The psalmody of the congregation is always so far under the pastor's control, that to him belongs the selection of the pieces to be sung ; consequently it is his part to see that they are appropriate to the lessons of the day, and of a kind fitted to sustain and raise the devotional spirit of the worshippers. In the majority of cases, perhaps, he may not be able to do much more directly in this line, as the musical accompaniment must be managed by others. He should, however, take an interest in this, and endeavour to diffuse a sense of its importance in the congregation, and encourage by every

legitimate means its due cultivation.   The remarks of Baxter
on the general subject are nearly as applicable now as when
they were originally penned : ' A great part,' says he, ' of
God's service in the Church assemblies was wont in all ages
of the Church till of late to consist in public praises and
eucharistical acts, and the Lord's day was still kept as a day
of thanksgiving in the hymns and common rejoicings of the
faithful, in special commemoration of the work of redemption, and the happy condition of the gospel Church.   I am
as apprehensive of the necessity of preaching as some
others, but yet methinks the solemn praises of God should
take up much more of the Lord's day than in most places
they do.'

It is not, however, the comparatively small space given
to the celebration of God's praise in public song, so much as
the imperfect and unsatisfactory manner in which it is often
performed, that is cause of regret. A prolonged singing of
praise soon becomes wearisome, unless it is peculiarly varied
and finely adjusted as to the mode of execution ; and then
comes the danger of allowing it to degenerate into a mere
artistic display.   The happy medium is to have the singing
arranged and modulated, so as at fitting intervals to relieve
the service, and by the lyrical fervour of sacred song, chanted
to appropriate melodies, to give vent to the devotional feelings and aspirations of the worshippers.   For this, unquestionably, a certain attention must be paid to the æsthetical
element, to the cultivation of sacred music as an art, without
which there never can be anything like a properly varied
and effective psalmody ; and the pastor should exert his
influence, especially on the younger members of his congregation, for the purpose of inducing them to lend their
efforts in this direction.   Still, of course, the mere mechanical part of the work, even though it were performed with
the most correct taste and propriety, is but, as it were, the
shell of the service of praise ; the kernel must be sought in

something higher, in the spirit and life that are infused into it on the part of those who chiefly engage in it. Everything here in a manner depends on the state of devotional feeling in the congregation, which, when lively and strong, never fails to impart a freshness and fervour to the singing which would be sought in vain from simply artistic cultivation. It is therefore the primary duty of the pastor, with respect to this department of public worship, to endeavour to awaken and foster the devotional element among his people; and this will of itself, if wisely directed, dispose them to give the requisite heed and application to the subsidiary means, which, in their own place, are capable of rendering important service toward the perfecting of praise.

It is further to be remembered, that the celebration of divine praise in the sanctuary is only in part to be identified with the congregational psalmody. Formally, the chief part is to be found there; but the praise of God should also have expression given to it in the portions of Scripture read, which will sometimes, at least, contain what is pre-eminently matter of praise, and still more in the direct addresses made to the throne of grace. In what is called common or public prayer, thanksgivings and adorations should ever form a prominent part. And they will be a fit expression of the general sentiments of devout acknowledgment and grateful feeling, cherished by the better portion of the assembled people, only when the pastor who represents them, and speaks in their stead, is in his own soul properly responsive to the infinite goodness and manifold grace and wisdom of God. In this alone there is matter of serious concern to the pastor; and the more so when the further consideration is added, that not merely the united weekly ascription of a people's thank-offerings to God, but also their collective experiences and desires, their confessions of sin, their sense of want and danger, their fears, temptations, hopes, deliverances, must all, in like manner, find their

utterance through his lips.   To be thus the representative
and organ of a religious community in their stated meetings
for intercourse with Heaven, is to occupy one of the highest
positions at once of privilege and responsibility ; and in no
part of his vocation more than in this is it desirable that
the pastor should be a kind of typal Christian ; one in whose
bosom every pious thought and feeling may lodge as in its
proper home, and come forth in suitable times and ways for
the glory of God and the edification of His Church.   It
will be a grievous mistake if this should be supposed to be
a simple thing ; for there can be no reasonable doubt that
the difficulty of doing it aright, and doing it with some
degree of regularity, is what originally led to the use of
liturgies, and what still leads many persons of unquestionably sincere and earnest piety to prefer them to extempore
prayer in the sanctuary.[1]

1. The primary requisite, therefore, for pastoral work
here, as for the preaching of the gospel, and, if possible,
still more here, consists in the pastor's own state, in the
qualities which go to constitute a man of God.   There must
be an enlightened discernment and appreciation of the truth
as it is in Jesus ; and along with that, an experimental
acquaintance with the heart, so that he may be able to
hold communion with God as one who is in a sense
familiar with the divine presence, and has known what it is
to transact with God for his own salvation.   Yet, standing
as he does in the room of so many others, and pleading
with God for them, he must be able to combine with a
regard to self in the matters of religion a regard also to the
state of those around him, repressing what is more peculiar
to himself where it might fail to meet with sympathy in his
fellow-worshippers.   A man *may* not, in public prayer any
more than in private, indeed he *cannot*, if he throws his

[1] See Shield's edition of the *Book of Common Prayer*, as to the relative place of prayer and praise.

soul into the exercise, lose his proper individuality.   Both
in the things he utters and the manner in which he utters
them, there will undoubtedly be the impress of his own cast
of thought and feeling, and *in that*, what will, no doubt,
serve to distinguish his prayers from those of other men.
Yet in public prayer this individuality should be kept within
comparatively narrow bounds ; since it is only what is proper
to the individual believer, in so far as it is in a measure
shared in, and is capable of being sympathized with, by the
company of believers whom the minister for the time
represents, that should find articulate expression before the
throne of the Majesty on high.   It is what is *common* to
the heart of faith and love, rather than what is *peculiar* to
one or a few, which should at such times be brought into
notice.   The tendency which minds of strong individuality
have to run out into veins of thought and forms of expression which carry an air of extravagance to ordinary men,
should here especially be kept in check.   The thought of
the awful presence in which we stand, and of the feelings
and necessities of those who are partaking with us in the
exercise, should of themselves shame into silence every idea
or word which might seem to others forced and unnatural,
and aimed, perhaps, at display.[1]

2. If the possession of a Christian state and sympathy
with the Christian mind of a congregation be the primary
element in a minister's qualifications for conducting aright

---

[1] There could scarcely, perhaps, be found a better description of
what is here meant than is given by Jonathan Edwards in his account
of the eminently devout David Brainerd's manner in prayer : ' This,' he
says, ' was very agreeable ; most becoming a worm of the dust, and a
disciple of Christ addressing an infinitely great and holy God and
Father of mercies, not with florid expressions, or a studied eloquence,
not with any intemperate vehemence, or indecent boldness.   It was
at the greatest possible distance from any appearance of ostentation,
and from anything that might look as though he meant to recommend
himself to those that were about him, or set himself off to their accept-

the united prayers and thanksgivings of those among whom he ministers, the cultivation of an appropriate manner may certainly be placed next. It is of importance that the devotional spirit should give vent to itself in a natural and becoming mode of expression. For devotion, as well as popular speech, has a style of its own, though the one is no more than the other a uniform style. There may be as many shades of difference in the mode of presenting prayer to God, as in the sacred oratory which aims at instructing and convincing a fellow-creature. But never, when sincere and genuine, will the one take precisely the hue and tone of the other ; since no truly humble and enlightened Christian can speak forth his feelings to God after the same manner that he would utter his mind to one of like passions and infirmities with himself. The former kind of address will naturally be pervaded by a subdued, reverential, hallowed air, which, if not wholly wanting in the other, will not at least be found in anything like the same measure ; and the perfection in this respect may be said to be reached when the feeling instinctively arises which has been known to be expressed respecting an exemplary pastor, ' The man prays as if he *lived* at the throne of grace.'

Let it not be imagined, however, that there is any need for the manner being artificial or stereotyped, as if some peculiar pitch of voice, or a kind of tone and cadence essentially different from that of ordinary discourse, were

ance. It was free also from vain repetitions. He expressed himself with the strictest propriety, with weight and pungency ; and yet what his lips uttered seemed to flow from the fulness of his heart.' A very different sort of praying, therefore, from that mentioned by an American periodical not long ago of a Mr. Everett, and characterized as ' the most eloquent prayer ever addressed to a Boston audience ; ' a rhetorical effusion, formally, no doubt, addressed to God ; but in reality, as the paper stated, to the audience that listened to it with such admiration. Prayers of that description do not reach beyond the place of meeting where they are spoken.

required to give to prayer its appropriate devotional impress. There are cases, no doubt, in which the devotional spirit does clothe itself with some such peculiarity, and does so, possibly, without the effect being sensibly marred in the experience of those whom use has familiarized to the distinctive habit. It is still, however, a defect, as all mannerism is; and in the great majority of cases it will be found, if closely investigated, to prove more or less an impediment to the proper efficiency of the service. The artificial form insensibly usurps to a certain extent the genuine spirit of devotion. Some please themselves with the tones of a sanctimonious manner, instead of pressing into the realities of a true spiritual intercourse with Heaven; while others, perhaps, suffer themselves to be arrested by the peculiarity of the manner, instead of being silently and powerfully borne along with the stream of spiritual thoughts and aspirations expressed. To aid this concurrence of devotional sentiment, an agreeable simplicity and naturalness of manner in the officiating minister is of great service; it should be such as befits one with his habits of thought and feeling when assuming the attitude of profound reverence and holy earnestness. Such a manner, however, though in itself only what might be deemed natural, may not be quite easily arrived at; in certain cases, at least, it may call for a good deal of patient and assiduous effort, but it is what no one should rest satisfied without having in good measure attained. And even when attained, it is of real avail only when it is the vehicle of a quickened spirit.[1]

Perhaps more pains should be taken in this direction

[1] Two things may be mentioned in particular as desirable to be avoided in prayer. One is quickness and rapidity of utterance, a fault young preachers are very apt to fall into; and objectionable, both because it has an irreverent appearance, and also because the people cannot intelligently follow. The other is boisterousness, which Mr. James justly discriminates from earnestness; the confounding of the two

than is commonly done even by the more pious portion of evangelical ministers.   Cecil has noted it as a defect that appeared among them in his time, although his mode of doing so, as it appears in his *Remains*, is by no means free from exception.   He is reported to have said, ' The *leading* defect in Christian ministers is want of devotional habit. The Church of Rome made much of this habit.   The contests accompanying and following the Reformation, with something of an indiscriminate enmity against some of the good of that Church as well as the evil, combined to repress this spirit in the Protestant writings ; whereas the mind of Christ seems to be, in fact, the grand end of Christianity in its operation upon man.'   There is an element of truth undoubtedly in the remark, both on the Protestant and the Romish side ; but it is too broadly announced, and with less of the clearness and discrimination which usually distinguish Mr. Cecil's remarks.   He could scarcely have meant, though the words ascribed to him seem to imply as much, that there is more either of the mind of Christ or of true devotion among Popish priests than with evangelical ministers as a class.   The whole that could justly be said, and probably the whole really meant by Mr. Cecil, is that the devotional element has had a more prominent place assigned to it in the system represented by the one class than in that represented by the other, and that in this relative prominence the Romish party have acted more in accordance with the mind of Christ.   But in such a matter the appearance must not be taken for the measure of the reality.   In the public services of the Church of Rome, the devotional form has become well-nigh the one and all ; and

he characterizes as ' a mistake too commonly made by many, who work themselves up into vociferation and actual contortion. Such vehemence,' he properly adds, ' like a violent blast of wind, puts out the languid flame of devotion, when a gentle breeze would fan it into greater intensity.'—*Earnest Ministry*, p. 125 sq.

the officiating priests, who are constantly employed about the services, naturally acquire much of the devotional *habit;* though, as possessed and exercised by *them*, one would never think of characterizing it as a nearer approach to the mind of Christ than what is to be met with in Protestant worship. Still something may be learned from them in respect to the point to which they have given their chief attention ; and however little the devotional habit may be worth, when unaccompanied by the devotional spirit, it is not in itself to be undervalued.

3. Another thing requiring careful attention in respect to public prayer is the selection of appropriate language, the use of a suitable and becoming phraseology. Very commonly this may be assumed as a thing almost certain to follow from the possession, in any adequate measure, of the spirit and manner already adverted to. But such is not uniformly the case ; and by ministers themselves it should never be regarded as a matter of course, coming without pains or consideration on their part ; it should engage more or less of their attention. And the fundamental ground on which they should proceed is the representative position they are called to occupy in presenting the adorations and prayers of the congregation. The officiating minister personates a body of worshippers; he must therefore endeavour to give his ideas the form and clothing which they can readily understand and appropriate as their own. If the language is too ornate, if it is such as would appear to them artificial and far-fetched, it will inevitably jar upon their feelings, and disturb the heavenward flow of their thoughts and desires ; to suit its purpose, it must, in general, be embodied in such a mode of expression as they are wont to associate with the exercises of devotion.

Now, to this nothing is more indispensable than simplicity ; it is an unfailing characteristic of all profound and earnest devotional utterances. It is so even when these take a poetical form, and appear in psalms and hymns, though from the demands of the verse a certain freedom in respect to language is easily conceded to them. But only within comparatively narrow limits ; for in such compositions unusual forms of expression, remote or technical terms, and pompous phraseology are fatal to success. ' Of sentiments purely religious, it will be found that the simplest expression is the most sublime,' said Samuel Johnson truly, though he made a wrong application of it, when on the ground of this thought he argued against the possibility of a high religious poetry. But the fact is decisive as to the proper style and diction of prayer ; if it wants simplicity, it wants the most essential element of adaptation to the minds of a Christian congregation. And for more effectually securing this element, or securing it in the best possible form, the whole should be cast much in the mould of Scripture, and should be marked by a free use of its language. For, being the storehouse alike of God's more special communications to men, and of the returns made to Him by His more elect worshippers, Scripture provides, not merely in the matter of its contents, but also in the very form into which they are thrown, the best directory and most fitting vehicle of devotion. Its utterances of faith, of desire and hope, were in a peculiar sense prompted by the Spirit of God ; and the more that believers are under the power of His grace, the more will they ever be disposed to pour out their hearts before God in what may justly be termed the Spirit's own style. I am not, however, to be understood as indicating that passages of Scripture alone should be employed in prayer ; this is neither necessary nor is it expedient. A prayer simply and wholly composed of such passages cannot fail to wear a sort of borrowed, miscellaneous, and commonplace character. It will seem as if the mind, when speaking only in forms prepared to its hand and culled from all parts of Scripture, were somewhat formal and apathetic in its own frame. Yet, while Scripture should not constitute all, it should undoubtedly give the tone and character to all. And he who would excel in this spiritual gift must be at pains to have the word of Christ dwelling in him richly.[1]

4. In addition to these general prescriptions, which have respect to the matter as a whole, I would earnestly advise a certain measure of special preparation for the devotional work of the sanctuary. The preparation, indeed, should be twofold, consisting partly in having the heart brought into a suitable frame for the exercise, and partly in having it provided with fitting materials of thought and expression. The former is also, no doubt, somewhat general; it must be in a great degree habitual to the minister; and yet, even where it is so, he will rarely find that he can safely dispense with some special pains of a preparatory nature before actually proceeding to the duty. The bustle and anxiety connected with the working out of his discourses for the Sabbath, will naturally have the effect of repressing the immediate outgoing of devotional sentiment, will even occasionally

[1] In addition to the more general directions given above, I would notice a few things which ought to be avoided in prayer. 1. Ungrammatical or vulgar expressions, such as 'Grant to impart unto us;' 'We commit us unto Thee,' 'We commend us unto Thee, and to the word of Thy grace.' Now we may commend others to God and His Word, but it is a very inaccurate, and indeed scarcely intelligible mode of speech to say that we commend ourselves to these. And I confess I do not like the expression, 'Come into our midst,' or 'Be in our midst.' 2. The too frequent use of the same forms of expression, such as Heavenly Father, or any particular name of God, when almost solely used, has the appearance of a kind of mannerism; and *Oh!* much repeated, becomes a mere expletive. Scripture is in this a fine example. 3. Amatory language, such as 'Lovely Jesus,' 'Dear Lord,' 'Sweet Saviour.' Here, again, Scripture is the best model. 4. Undue familiarities, which may take different forms, such as 'metrical quotations,' extreme professions of unworthiness, personalities either of a flattering or sarcastic kind; all such things are in bad taste.

render the mind less apt to cherish it; and a little time will be needed to get the desires of the heart back, and the mind raised to such a spiritual tone, as will render the work of communion with God altogether congenial to its existing state.

In regard, however, to the other kind of preparation, that which refers to the providing of materials of thought and expression suited for the occasion, something more precise and definite may be said. For, as the pastor, when going to conduct the services of the sanctuary, has to bear on his heart various interests and relations, none of which should be overlooked or passed slightly over, he both may and should have in his eye distinct topics for notice in prayer, and particular trains of thought to be pursued. Not otherwise will he be able to give sufficient freshness and point to his supplications, or present them in a form altogether appropriate to the occasion. Entirely unpremeditated prayers will usually partake much of the character of unpremeditated discourses; they will consist chiefly of commonplaces which float upon the memory, rather than of thoughts and feelings that well up from the hidden man of the heart; and as they have stirred no depths in the bosom of the speaker, so they naturally awaken but a feeble response in the minds of the hearers. Nor can it fail, when this offhand method is systematically pursued, that sentiments and expressions will occasionally come out which are in bad taste, or palpably wanting in adaptation to the time and circumstances wherein they are employed. Hence, I fear, it is that there is so often a marked difference in the interest felt, even by good people, in the prayers offered at their stated meetings for worship, as compared with that arising from the sermons delivered; the one does not, while the other does, spring from a background of well-arranged thought and spiritual consideration.

A sensible American writer in the *Princeton Review*, some

time ago gave expression to the same view of the subject, and supported it by some remarks that are well deserving of consideration. ' Ministers,' he says, ' labour hard to prepare to address the people, but venture on addressing God without premeditation.'[1] Dr. Witherspoon says, 'that the Rev. Dr. Gillies of Glasgow, who in his judgment exceeded any man he had ever heard in the excellency of his prayers, was accustomed to devote unwearied pains to preparation for this part of his ministerial work ; and for the first ten years of his ministry never wrote a sermon without writing a prayer appropriate to it. This was also Calvin's habit ; and many of the sermons printed in his works have prayers annexed. An aid which Calvin found needful, no man living need be ashamed of employing.'

It is true that most of the prayers appended to Calvin's printed sermons are very short, more like brief collects than regularly constructed prayers, expressing in a few pregnant words the thoughts and desires naturally suggested by the subject which had formed the matter of discourse. But the mind which was habituated to such pieces of devotional writing could not be negligent of preparation for more lengthened services of the same description, whether they might take the form or not of written compositions. Probably the more advisable course for ministers of settled congregations will be to meditate, rather than formally commit to writing, the chief prayers they are going to offer in the public meetings for worship ; to think carefully over, occasionally also to note down, the train of thought, or the special topics and petitions they mean to introduce, with such passages of Scripture as are appropriate to the occasion. The mind will thus be kept from wandering at large in the exercise, and yet will move with more freedom than if it were trammelled by the formality of a written form ; will be able more readily to surrender itself to the hallowed influ-

[1] Quoted in *British and Foreign Evang. Review*, p. 14.

ences of the moment. At the same time, I cannot but regard it as a good exercise for the pastor, calculated to improve his gifts in this direction, and to render him more apt and felicitous in his method of conducting public prayer, if he should accustom himself, not only to peruse some of the best models of devotional utterance, but also to compose particular forms for his own use. Such a practice, though only pursued at intervals, will bring here also a measure of that advantage which always springs from sustained application and cultivated skill ; and cannot but help to check the tendency, which is so apt of itself to grow, of doing little beforehand even by way of premeditation, and of performing the service in a kind of slovenly and conventional manner.

5. Nothing has yet been said as to the length of time proper to be spent in public prayer, or to the greater or less frequency with which it should be introduced into the regular services of the sanctuary. But these are obviously points which call for some consideration. They are also closely connected with each other ; for the less frequent the acts of common prayer are, the more protracted will each particular exercise naturally be. It has been for long a very common practice in Scotland to have only two prayers at each meeting for public worship ; and to make the first prayer, the one before sermon, by much the longer of the two, so that it not unusually runs out into a continuous address to God of twenty minutes or upwards. I cannot but think this practice unhappy, since it necessarily tends to fatigue the mind by too long a strain in this one direction, and to leave the service of the sanctuary bereft of that variety of relief which, within certain limits, are not only allowable, but of material use, as helping to sustain the attention and keep alive the devotion of the worshippers. A measure of respect is due to an established practice in worship, even though, abstractedly considered, it may not approve itself as in all

X

respects the best; and it would be unwise rashly to interfere with it, or strike at once into a path altogether new. It is right, however, to bear in mind, that the usage in question rests upon no proper authority; that it is, indeed, an innovation of comparatively late times; for, according to the authorized Directory for public worship, there should be at the principal meeting of the congregation each Lord's day three several prayers, and, with the Lord's prayer, four; for the latter, though not authoritatively enjoined, is yet recommended as deserving a place in the stated observances of worship.[1] The order there set forth as the most fitting to be observed consists, first, of a brief prayer as soon as the minister enters the pulpit, composed chiefly of adoration and invocation; then the singing of Psalms and the reading of sacred Scripture, of which a portion is to be taken as well from the Old as from the New Testament; after this comes another prayer of greater length, in which there should be made humble confession of sin, also acknowledgment of the loving-kindness and mercy of God in providing the blessings of salvation, with an earnest and varied supplication of an interest in these for different ranks and conditions of men; then the discourse, which is again to be followed by prayer, singing of Psalms, and the benediction. No particular place is assigned for the introduction of the Lord's prayer; this was left to the discretion of the minister, as was the place also for supplicating the divine blessing on magistrates, rulers, and other subjects of public interest; they might be noticed before or after sermon, as appeared most suitable and convenient. As a whole, this order is undoubtedly better than the one previously referred to, though I am not inclined to advocate a uniform and rigid adherence even to it; and whenever a change is deemed

[1] 'And because the prayer which Christ taught His disciples is not only a pattern of prayer, but itself a most comprehensive prayer, we recommend it also to be used in the prayers of the Church Directory.'

desirable on the mode of service that has been in use in any congregation, care should always be taken to carry the feelings and inclinations of the people along with us.

Perhaps the chief point in respect to which a nearer approach to the Directory should be generally aimed at, is the introduction of two prayers before sermon in the principal service instead of one.   The advantage of this will be, that the devotional element will obtain a more prominent place, and also that, by dividing into two what otherwise would need to be compressed into one, each exercise will be less protracted, and the attention, especially of the young and the less informed, will be more easily sustained.   But whatever may be the precise number of devotional services, public prayer should never be much protracted, should rarely if ever, I would say, exceed at a stretch a quarter of an hour, and, as a general rule, two prayers within that limit would be greatly preferable to one going beyond it. For, if a few individuals in a congregation of strong intellects and ardent piety might be found capable of enjoying and profiting by a more prolonged exercise of devotion, with the great majority it will certainly be quite otherwise.   And in nothing does undue protraction more infallibly defeat itself than in prayer ; for if once the minds of the worshippers relax their attention and get into a wandering mood, the proper frame is gone, and it will rarely be possible to have it again restored by subsequent effort.

Further specification or more minute detail on such a subject seems to be unnecessary.   A right state of feeling regarding it, with some measure of common sense, will be of much more avail than a thousand specific rules and directions.   Let the pastor, first of all, place this branch of public duty among the things which demand his earnest consideration, and which, with regard alike to the substance and manner of the exercise, call for serious forethought and application.   Let him also bear in mind that the spirit manifested by him, and the power put forth in the devotional parts of the service, will be sure to leave its impression on the minds of his people; and that, according as he rises toward the proper measure of excellence, so are they likely to become elevated in their tone and practice as worshippers. Let him still further bear in mind that, for the character of other parts of the service, and especially for the effect of the discourses he may deliver, much depends on the interest he throws into the work of prayer, and the spirit of devotion thereby evoked on the part of the people. For when the result in this respect is as it should be, when the hearts of the people have really been borne along with the pastor in his supplications at the throne of grace, and a profound sense of God's presence is in consequence awakened in them, vast preparation is made for the earnest consideration and belief of the truth. They are thus brought to feel that it is with God rather than with man they have to do in the treatment they give to the preached gospel, and that the matter demands their most serious thought. On this account, no doubt, it partly is that the ministrations of deeply pious, though comparatively weak or unlettered men, have often been accompanied with results upon the hearers more lasting and productive of spiritual good than by the exertions of those who have been able to bring the highest powers and attainments to the work. The spirit of prayer resting upon them diffuses itself among the audience, and disposes them to receive the word as it is preached in simplicity and godly sincerity. Hence, seasons that have been remarkable for the spirit of grace and supplication have also been the most noted for the successful preaching of the gospel, even sometimes when the style of preaching has been by no means distinguished for the graces of pulpit oratory. Nor is the fact unworthy of notice which is reported by Gillies[1] to have been observed by a Mr. Hutcheson, minister of

[1] *Historical Collections*, p. 201.

Killellan : 'When I compare,' he said, ' the times before the Restoration with the times since the Revolution, I must own that the young ministers preach accurately and methodically ; but far more of the power and efficacy of the Spirit and grace of God went along with sermons in those days than now. And for my own part (all the glory be to God), I seldom set my foot in a pulpit in those times but I had notice of some blessed effects of the word.' It were wrong, perhaps, to ascribe the whole of this difference to the greater prevalence of the spirit of prayer at the one period as compared with the other ; for various things of a peculiarly grave and stirring kind undoubtedly contributed to make the period before the Restoration and that also preceding the Revolution times of great moral earnestness and awakened interest about the concerns of salvation in Scotland ; but it assuredly had an important bearing on the matter. The public troubles and convulsions then constantly transpiring drove the hearts alike of pastors and people to close communion with God, and prompted the one to preach and the others to hear in a different manner from what is too often witnessed in more quiet and easy-going times. Such things are lessons in Providence to us, and it is our duty to profit by them, yet so as to make due allowance for circumstances of place and time, and thinking rather of the general principles of instruction furnished by them than of simply adopting them as patterns for servile imitation.

CHAPTER VIII.

THE ADMINISTRATION OF DISCIPLINE.

I F we take our views of the Christian Church from what is written in Scripture of the nature and ends of the Christian calling, as well as of the pains taken by the apostles to reprove and cast out whatever was palpably opposed to purity of communion, we shall have no doubt that the administration of discipline must be one of its necessary functions.   And from the position of the pastor, as called in a peculiar manner to preside over its affairs, the exercise of this function must specially devolve upon him, although, in rightly constituted churches, there will be others to share with him the responsibility and the burden.   It is a department of pastoral duty which, from its very nature, must involve a good deal that is delicate and irksome, which will even be found occasionally fraught with trouble and perplexity.   For it brings the sword of the Spirit into sharp conflict with man's pride and corruption, and requires unreserved submission to Him of whom, in some respect, they have been practically saying, We will not have this Lord to rule over us.   Here, indeed, there has ever been discovering itself one of the strange inconsistencies that cleave to professing Christians, strange because it is so flatly opposed to the whole spirit and tendency of the gospel, that while they will not only endure, but even insist upon, sound doctrine in the kind of preaching they listen to, they will often not endure sound discipline.   And both from this known reluctance on the part of many to submit to the exercise of spiritual authority, and from the habits of intercourse and mutual good-will subsisting between the administrators of the discipline and the subjects of it, a strong temptation naturally arises to be somewhat slack or partial in its application, to do it in many cases but half, or even to leave it altogether undone.

Symptoms of defection in this respect began to discover themselves at a comparatively early stage of the Church's history, ominous of what might confidently be looked for in the future. The church at Corinth, which started so well, and with such a plenitude of gifts, ere long drew down upon it the severe rebuke of Paul for its want of faithfulness in checking disorder and licentiousness among its members. And of the seven churches of Asia, to whom the glorified Redeemer, as the chief Shepherd and Bishop of souls, sent specific messages, how few escape censure on a similar account? Even in the most favourable circumstances, and in the hands of the most faithful rulers, there will doubtless be occasional failures ; backslidings and disorders will not be met with the corrective discipline that should be applied to them ; and at no period has the Church to any considerable extent approached as nearly the condition of being without spot or wrinkle in the state of her membership as a thoroughly faithful and efficient administration might have made it. In early times, however, it can scarcely be questioned, discipline did in general flourish ; and with its vigorous administration the Church felt her existence of prosperity in a manner bound up. The notices which appear in the history of the times, and the well-known exemplariness of the Christians as a body, furnish on this point the most ample proof. So that it was only expressing the general minds of all the better authorities in the early Church, when Cyprian, for example, spoke of discipline as the 'safety of the Church,' 'the stay of faith and hope,' 'inculcated in all Scripture as necessary to the

order and purity of the Church ;' or when Augustine designates it 'the tutor of religion and of true piety.' Indeed,
the predominant tendency in those times was rather to lay
too much stress on it than too little, to expect from it in
a measure what could only be accomplished through the
direct action of the grace and truth of the gospel. And so,
when the ascetic element diffused itself as a subtle poison
through the leading minds of the Church, and the higher
discipline which it made so much account of came to be
identified with the perfection of the Christian life, discipline
in the Scriptural sense fell into abeyance ; things needful to
the guardianship and maintenance of the common Church
life were neglected, in order that the bodily fastings, the
mortifications, the self-imposed labours and penances of
monkery, might have their due prominence and laudation.
The very name *discipline* came by degrees to be appropriated
to such things ; while, among others who lay beyond its
sphere, hypocrisy, corruption, worldliness of every sort,
flowed in ; and these common forms of evil were, after the
establishment of Christianity, for the most part met with
worldly modes of treatment ; civil pains and penalties, fines
and corporeal inflictions of some sort, too commonly taking
the place of the true, brotherly, spiritual discipline of the
gospel of Christ.

Of this true Christian discipline, as contradistinguished
from all coercive measures of a physical and penal description, Milton has justly said in his own peculiar manner :
' It seeks not to bereave or destroy the body ; it seeks to
save the soul by humbling the body, not by imprisonment
or pecuniary mulct, much less by stripes, or bonds, or disin-
heritance ; but by fatherly admonition and Christian rebuke
to cast it into godly sorrow, whose end is joy, and ingenu-
ous bashfulness to sin. If that cannot be wrought, then as
a tender mother takes her child and holds it over the pit
with scaring words, that it may learn to fear where danger

is ; so does excommunication [*i.e.* discipline] as dearly and as freely without money use her wholesome and saving terrors.   She is instant, she beseeches ; by all the dear and sweet promises of salvation she entices and woos ; by all the threatenings and thunders of law, and a rejected gospel, she charges and adjures.   This is all her armoury, her munition, her artillery.   Then she awaits with long sufferance, and yet ardent zeal.   In brief, there is no act in all the errand of God's ministers to mankind wherein passes more lover-like contestation between Christ and the soul of a regenerate man lapsing, than before, and in, and after the sentence of excommunication.'[1]

The object of such dealing in respect to the Church itself, is to have its actual state brought into as near conformity as possible to its Scriptural idea, by repressing incipient evil within its pale, or casting out of it what gives just occasion of offence.   And in respect to the parties more immediately concerned, its design is to lead them to a right view of their particular case, and produce in them an honourable shame, by bringing to bear upon them the more earnest, spiritual sense of the pastor and those associated with him in the care and oversight of the flock.   And if anything, as again excellently said by Milton in another treatise,[2] 'may be done to inbreed in us this generous and Christianly reverence one of another, the very nurse and guardian of piety and virtue, it cannot sooner be than by such a discipline in the Church as may use us to have in awe the assemblies of the faithful, and to count it a thing most grievous, next to the grieving of God's Spirit, to offend those whom He hath put in authority, as a healing superintendence over our lives and behaviours, both to our own happiness and that we may not give offence to good men, who, without amends by us made, dare not against God's command hold

[1] *Of Reformation in England,* 2d Book.
[2] *The Reason of Church Government,* Book ii. sec. 3.

communion with us in holy things. And this will be accompanied with a religious dread of being outcast from the company of saints, and from the fatherly protection of God in His Church, to consort with the devil and his angels.'

This, undoubtedly, is the correct view of the matter, and the right mode of aiming at its accomplishment. But the churches of the Reformation did not readily find their way to it; many of them, indeed, have never yet succeeded in doing so, or even in earnestly setting about it. The mournful confounding of the civil and spiritual jurisdictions which had existed for ages still lingered in most of them, and disposed them to trust, in part at least, to legal and compulsory measures for effecting what could only be done to purpose by spiritual means.[1] The same disposition lingers still in not a few Protestant churches, which can scarcely be said to have any discipline, except what is secured by the adminis-

---

[1] How much this was the case for a considerable time also in Scotland, even to a period later than that to which the noble treatises of Milton belong, will be evident from the following historical statement by Dr. Lee respecting post-Reformation times :—'Every living soul within the realm must either conform to the same profession, and practise the same worship, and submit to the same discipline, or undergo the vengeance of the law. . . . A stripling or a girl of the examinable age must either communicate in the parish church or else pay a fine according to the rank of the party. In the year 1600, and again in 1641, the Church prevailed on the State to impose fines on all non-communicants of the age of 15 years complete. The fines on people of condition were very heavy ; and every servant contravening the Act was liable to pay one year's fee *toties quoties*. These were powers actually granted to presbyteries, who had a right to crave, receive, and pursue for the penalties ' (Lee's *Lecture on Christian History*, i. p. 204). The zeal of Baxter not only led him to approve of the magistrates obliging people by penalties to attend on ministers for instruction, but also to compel ministers to instruct and subject the people of their charge to discipline. He would not, however, have any forced to the communion. (See his *Confirmation and Restoration*.)

tration of justice through the civil and criminal courts of the lands to which they belong;—a state of things which is deplored by all who know what a Christian Church ought to be, though many, not absolutely ignorant of divine truth, have through the ill effects of custom become habituated to the corruption, and in this particular respect have lost sight of the principles of church order and government.   Baxter speaks of some such in his day in England, whom he once took, he says, for godly divines ; but who afterwards reproached those who endeavoured to maintain discipline, and would not give the sacrament to every one in their parishes, as Sacramentarians or Disciplinarians.   He justly expresses his astonishment that such persons could be found in a Christian Church, and says: 'Sure I am, if it were well understood how much of the pastoral authority and work consisteth in church guidance, it would be almost discerned, that to be against discipline is nearly all one with being against the ministry ; and this, again, nearly all one with being against the Church of Christ.'   For to what end does the Church exist, but to be a witness to the truth, and an organ for diffusing the life of Christ?   In proportion, therefore, as she harbours corruption within her pale, and extends the sacred symbols of the faith to those who practically belie its spirit, she is unfaithful to her trust, and fails in the very object of her mission to the world.

It must be owned, however, that even where there is a just appreciation of the nature and of the importance of a sound discipline, the relative positions of churches, I mean of such churches as have a constitution which makes provision for the maintenance of discipline, and aims at it with more or less of fidelity, interpose certain difficulties in respect to the efficient discharge of the duty which it is not quite easy for individual pastors or even churches to overcome.   These differ in Established Churches and churches independent of the State.   In the former, the territorial principle, which brings along with it a certain advantage and authority, brings also a relative weakness ; since persons, living within the bounds of any particular parish, naturally come to regard their local situation as of itself constituting a right to the ministrations of the parish church, and to the participation of ordinances within its pale. And practically it is very difficult, as those know who have had trial of the system, to restrain this feeling within proper bounds, that is, so to restrain it as to make the membership of a parish church present the appearance of even a tolerably pure communion. The unregenerate, the worldly, the merely nominal professor, who finds the name of Christianity useful to him, but refuses to give any material sacrifice or even renounce objectionable courses for its sake, have advantages for obtaining connection with an Established Church which attach to no other Evangelical Communion, and of which they very readily avail themselves. A parochial economy is thus from its very nature better adapted for diffusing a certain amount of religious knowledge and profession than of exhibiting the pattern of a living, spiritual Christian community. For checking the more flagrant social evils, for removing or preventing the existence of cases of extreme spiritual destitution, for ensuring the diffusion of a general decency of behaviour, and bringing within the reach of all the means and opportunities of grace ;—for such ends and purposes the parish church, with its appropriate machinery, if well wrought, is perfectly adapted. But, excepting in very favourable circumstances, and within comparatively short periods and limited districts, its congregations can seldom be made to assume the aspect of a community of saints.

In non-Established Churches there is, for the most part, a fairer opportunity for making at least an approach to this, although there are discouraging circumstances of a different kind arising out of the divided state of things implied in their very existence. For this provides facilities to offending parties for evading the close dealing and defeating the just ends of discipline, by transferring themselves from a more to a less faithful Communion. Still it is of great importance that churches which know and hold the truth, that the Free Church in particular should, in spite of all hindrances and discouragements, apply herself in earnest to the maintenance of an efficient and godly discipline. Her influence in the land for good, and the measure of blessing she is to receive upon her public ministrations, will to a large extent depend upon her faithfulness in the exercise of this function. If the cause of righteousness thrives among her members, if sin when it breaks out is sorrowed over and rebuked, if the procedure altogether is such as to show that the Church cannot bear them that are evil, then she will command the respect of the community. More than that, the favour of the Lord will rest upon her, she will be both blessed and made a blessing. But if, on the other hand, she should show herself more solicitous about the extent of her membership than the purity of her communion, if backsliders and transgressors are not properly dealt with, and something like a travailing in birth experienced to have them brought to repentance and the knowledge of the truth, we may hold it for certain that her real interest and prosperity as a Church will decline. Not being jealous for the honour of her Lord in respect to the holiness of His house, she will not be honoured of Him.

Considered merely as a means of spiritual instruction, an ordinance for impressing the minds of a people with right views of things, for leading them to distinguish between what may and what should not be tolerated in Christian communities,—for this end alone a well-regulated discipline is of no small importance. There are many, in all ranks of life, who so readily fall in with the stream of custom, and are so difficult to be convinced of the sinfulness of anything however contrary to the spirit of the gospel, if it be but commonly practised in the neighbourhood, that nothing scarcely will rouse them to proper thought and consideration about it but the formal act and procedure of the Church, treating it as inconsistent with the Christian life. This, if only done on fitting occasions, and done with prudence and discretion, will rarely fail to produce its effect. Individual offenders, it is possible, may not be reclaimed by it, they may even at times kick at the attempt made to interfere with their liberty, and only with increased determination adhere to their objectionable course ; but the general conscience of the community will be quickened, inquiry will be awakened, and the things adjudicated upon and pronounced contrary to a sound profession of the faith will be more closely examined by the word of God, and a juster estimate formed respecting them by at least the more thoughtful and serious minds.

It is, however, to be carefully borne in mind, that everything, both as regards the practicability and the effect of a righteous discipline, depends upon the Christian sense and feeling which one has to work upon in those among whom it is exercised. While it rests upon the teaching of God's word as to its *formal* ground and warrant, this can be made valid as a principle of action, in particular congregations, only in so far as it has been wrought into the minds and consciences of a considerable portion of the community, and is responded to by them as right and good. To get this Christian sense and feeling, therefore, widely diffused and firmly maintained, must always be the first care of the pastor. Behind all specific measures of repression or reform, and as the understood basis on which they are to proceed, there must be a solid groundwork of spiritual enlightenment and conviction, otherwise the measures will fail for want of backing, will not carry with them the requisite moral weight.

Passing now from these preliminary considerations to the actual administration of discipline, the first thing that naturally comes into notice is the matter about or upon which discipline should be exercised.   There are things in respect to which no difference of opinion in this respect can well be entertained among evangelical Christians, they are so palpably at variance not only with the precepts of the gospel, but with the findings of the natural conscience, that all will admit them worthy of correction and rebuke. Adultery, for example, fornication, blasphemy, forgery, deliberate fraud or theft, habitual neglect or avowed contempt of divine ordinances, these and such like things leave no room for hesitation or doubt; they are in open contrariety to the Christian character, and no one chargeable with them can be recognised as a proper subject of Christian privilege.   But things are ever and anon appearing of a somewhat indeterminate nature ; indeterminate, that is, as to the degree of guilt they involve, or the measure of contrariety which the performance of them betrays to the faith of the gospel.   With respect to such things great prudence and caution are necessary in determining whether they should be proceeded against by way of discipline, or when.   Even some of those just specified, practices of fraud, for example, or habitual neglect of divine ordinances, while as facts in the behaviour of this or that individual they may admit of no dispute, they may still be found accompanied with so many qualifying circumstances, complicated relationships, and grounds of defence real or imaginary, that it may not be quite easy for the pastor, and those associated with him in the oversight of the church, to come to the conclusion respecting particular parties, that they should be subjected on account of them to disciplinary treatment.   Then there are others ; for example, intemperance, violent, revengeful, or harsh dealing, quarrelsome behaviour, compliance with the follies or questionable customs of the world, which admit of

so many degrees, that the point at which the excess becomes
such as to warrant the interference of church action is a
very variable and shifting one.   Even the most experienced
minister and elders will often find it difficult to arrive at
clear convictions as to the path of duty.   Generally speaking,
where the conduct has been such as to give rise to offence,
and begets serious doubt as to the Christian state of the
parties concerned, though it may still not be chargeable
with deliberate or palpable sin, there should, in the first
instance, be private and personal dealings, which, if wisely
conducted on the one side and properly met on the other,
will very often render any further or more formal proceedings unnecessary.   For such dealings, as stated in another
connection, a calm, earnest, and prayerful spirit is peculiarly
required ; since, if a false step is taken at the outset, or an
undue regard should appear to have been given to unfounded
rumours, all chance of doing good will be lost, and a sense
of wrong evoked on account of the treatment experienced,
rather than of regret or shame at the behaviour which occasioned it.

The difficulties connected with these private efforts to
bring under consideration incipient and less broadly developed forms of evil have led some ministers to avoid
interfering with anything for purposes of admonition or
censure but what may have become matter of public
notoriety, and as such can be taken up in a formal manner
by the Session or other constituted authorities.   It is a
course which will, no doubt, save the pastor a good deal of
anxious thought and occasional acts of annoyance ; but this
personal advantage will be purchased at the heavy cost of
sometimes losing the chance of winning a soul.   For, when
courses of defection like those referred to are censured at a
certain stage, censured when they are still only in the forming, and just beginning to awaken solicitude and concern in
thoughtful minds, there is room to hope that something may

be done to arrest the evil by faithful treatment, the wrong bias may yet be checked before it takes its final set; while, at a more advanced stage, the transgressor may indeed be officially admonished, suspended from his Church privileges, or altogether cut off from the communion of the Church, but with little prospect of any good being thereby effected on his spiritual state. He has become wedded to his idols, and will not be separated from them.

In actual processes of discipline there are three stages, which naturally succeed each other, and which call for separate consideration. The first has respect to the ascertaining of the facts of the case, often a very perplexing part of the process. The party suspected or accused has an obvious interest in disguising them, putting a different face on them from that which they actually wear: other parties, perhaps, have a like interest in overcharging or distorting them; and persons capable of giving important evidence on the matter are either unwilling or afraid to have anything directly to do concerning it. Hence it will sometimes happen that a very general desire may exist among persons of influence in the Church to leave what is likely to prove delicate and irksome in abeyance, or have it summarily huddled up. In such cases it is always of grave moment that the pastor be known to be a perfectly reliable person, one, I mean, who is seen to be actuated by a sincere regard to the spiritual good of the people, and of firmness tempered with discretion in his endeavours to discountenance what is manifestly evil. If he is either too sluggish in bestirring himself about things which call for serious inquiry, or, on the other hand, too hasty and forward in pressing them into notice; above all, if he is of irresolute purpose, moving but with hesitating step, doing somewhat and again undoing it, the result will commonly be, that matters are concealed from him which he ought to be informed of, or evidence that might be forthcoming is withheld from a feeling of

Y

uncertainty as to the use that might be made of it. But even supposing him to possess the proper requisites for inspiring confidence and satisfactorily conducting the inquiries necessary to be instituted, he will often find it extremely difficult, especially in cases connected with uncleanness, to get at the real state of matters ; penetration, caution, judgment, patience also and industry, will be required. Guilty or suspected persons will make the most solemn declarations such as it might seem an act of injustice or hardness of heart to discredit, while yet subsequent discoveries may show them to be essentially false ; or gross misconduct will be covered with most plausible excuses and pretexts which have little foundation in reality. Ministers generally, and especially young ministers, should hear in such cases with a prudent reserve, taking care not to commit themselves to a view or espouse a side till full time has been had for considering the matter, and every accessible means of information has been turned to account. This should be done, yet so as to beware of giving encouragement to busybodies, or granting a kind of delegated authority to inferior parties, who are likely to become too full of their office to manage it discreetly. Occasionally, though not more than occasionally, and only after every attempt has failed to get conclusive evidence, the matter may be put, if not with the form, at least with the solemnity of an oath, to the individual chiefly interested. This is a last alternative, and one that can rarely yield a satisfactory result, because of the strong temptation it affords to lay all to rest by a false asseveration. It should therefore be very rarely resorted to.

The next step in the process has respect to the proper method of dealing with those whose guilt has been admitted or proved, with the view of bringing them to a right sense of their sin and such a state of mind as would justify the Church in restoring them to its communion. This must always form a most important part of the proceedings, since it has respect to that on which the whole issue for the spiritual good of the offending parties may be said to turn.   It will be understood of itself that there should be private personal intercourse held with them.   If the whole that is done is limited to the somewhat formal action of an official procedure, it will but rarely happen that any real good is accomplished.   Yet even in this part of the dealing, especially in the manner in which the parties are received and addressed when making appearance to confess the misdeed laid to their charge, not a little may be done to prepare the way for future action ; that is, if by the proper exercise of the spirit of rebuke the pastor is enabled to penetrate, touch, and soften the heart.

Let it be well considered, however, wherein properly consists the spirit or power of rebuke, and how, in *any* circumstances, it can be made to tell with due effect upon the minds of such as have gone out of the way.   It is very different from a stern and unflinching denunciation of the wrath of God against transgressors, or a fiery ebullition of righteous displeasure at what has appeared of shameful misconduct.   A measure of these occasionally may be pardoned, or even in extreme cases justified ; but the spirit of rebuke, as it should commonly be exercised by the Christian pastor, is something deeper, calmer, more measured and restrained, and hence is neither so readily acquired nor so easy to maintain in efficient exercise.   Indeed, it is hardly too much to say, with Isaac Taylor,[1] that ' every part of the duty of the minister of religion is more easy to maintain in vigour than the spirit he needs as the reprover of sin and the guardian of virtue.'   He runs over the other leading parts of ministerial duty, somewhat certainly under-estimating the facility with which they may be performed, and then, with reference to the point in hand, specifies various things that may be tried as a substitute for it, argument, erudition,

[1] *Saturday Night*, chap. xv.

eloquence, and adds, ' Ah ! but to speak efficaciously of that holiness and justice of Almighty God, and of its future consequences ; to speak in modesty, tenderness, and power of the approaching doom of the impenitent, is altogether another matter, and one that must be left to those whose spirits have had much communion with the dread Majesty on high. As the punishment of sin springs by an ineffable harmony from the first principles of the divine nature, and infringes not at all upon benevolence, so must he who would rightly speak of that punishment have attained to a more intimate perception of the coincidence of holiness and love than language can convey, or than can be made the subject of communication between man and man. This knowledge belongs to the inner circle of the soul, and is only conveyed to it in any considerable degree when much meditation and prayer and abstraction from earthly passions open the way to its reception and entertainment.'

It is the possession and exercise of such a spirit that is required for the discharge, in its higher style, of the duty under consideration. Of course it will differ, not only in different individuals, but even in the same individual from time to time ; and not unfrequently, those who have it most will feel as if they were singularly deficient in the proper manifestation that should be given to it. I speak only of the quality itself, and of what should be aimed at in regard to it ; what also, in proportion as it is brought to bear upon persons whose conduct has subjected them to the discipline of the Church, is likely to have most effect in bringing them to genuine contrition and godly sorrow for sin. Even this, when possessed and exercised with comparative perfection, will not always secure the desired result. The most faithful and spiritually-minded pastors may lay their account to not a few dealings with offenders who, whatever temporary effect may have been wrought upon them, will give afterwards unmistakeable evidence that they have undergone no real

conversion.   Here also, and very peculiarly, the maxim
of our Lord applies, ' The tree is known by its fruits;' for
while there is much in the condition of those whose im-
moral conduct has brought them into reproach and laid
them open to the censure of the Church, to produce a soft-
ened and penitent feeling for the time ; if it is nature only
that works, the recoil of feeling may pass away, and leave
the individual as far as ever from the kingdom of God.

The remaining part of the process has reference to what
is called the satisfaction of the Church and the formal
absolution of the offending parties, or their restoration to
Church privileges.   This is now usually a very brief and
perfunctory thing compared with what it was in the earlier
periods of the Reformed Church, and still more in the
strict disciplinary period of the first centuries. When one
reads the accounts given in Cyprian and Tertullian, for
example, of the penitential acts and humiliating services
through which the subjects of Church discipline had to pass
in their day before they could expect to have their names
restored to the communion-roll of the Church, one is apt to
be struck with the laxity of present times, and to sigh for
the return of such moral strength to spiritual authorities as
might enable them to exact from the lapsed demonstrations
of sorrow and shame so profoundly indicative of their conscious guilt, and expressions of desire so intense of being
re-admitted to a place among the faithful.   In describing
what was termed the *exomologesis* of the penitent, Tertullian
represents them as appearing clothed in the meanest ap-
parel, lying in sackcloth and ashes;[1] either fasting entirely
or living upon bread and water, passing whole days and
nights in tears and lamentations ; embracing the knees of
the presbyters as they entered the church, and entreating
the more honoured brethren to intercede for them ; all this
continuing often for a lengthened period, for years some-

[1] *De Pœnit.* § 9.

times, occasionally even to the point of death; when, the rulers of the Church being satisfied that the repentance was sincere, and that the honour of the Church had been sufficiently vindicated in their contrition, absolution was granted to them, and they received again the right hand of fellowship. But then, as already noticed, this awful stringency, which at first sight carries such an aspect of holiness, at the same time that it tried by vast applications to heal existing sores, was itself indicative of a deep disease; it at once sprung from and fostered a disposition to look to bodily mortifications and self-inflicted penances for what could only be reached through the mercy of God and Christ's work of reconciliation. Hence we find Tertullian speaking of the penances in question as 'mitigating God,' and 'blotting out eternal punishments;' and Cyprian, in like manner, who equally lauds the virtue of such disciplinary treatment, describes the penitent who submits to it as not only satisfying the Church, but appeasing the wrath of God; by means of his prayers, it is said, his tears, groans and mortifications, 'he makes satisfaction to God,'[1] 'he purchases both God's pardon now, and also a crown of glory.' Thus readily do such external requirements and enforced mortifications rise into a kind of meritorious round of performances, and take to some extent the place of the one glorious object of faith and hope. For the lapsed it came practically to be salvation, *remotely* no doubt through the redeeming grace of God in Christ, but *directly* through the rigid observances of a prolonged discipline, the intercessions of a mediating priesthood, and the authoritative absolution of the Church. And we may well be content to want such awful pomp and circumstance in connection with the recovery of fallen members, in order to escape from the deadly errors out of which it in a great degree sprang, and to which it in turn most powerfully ministered.

[1] *De Lapsis.*

Still it is possible here, as in other things, while shunning excess in one direction, to be guilty of it in another. And one can readily apprehend, when no marked difference of outward treatment appears between those who have fallen into scandalous sin and such as have maintained a consistent Christian behaviour, when, even though some pains may be taken privately to bring them to a better mind, the path of admission to the more distinctive privileges of the Church is left equally open to them as to others, the inevitable result must be a lowering, in the general sense of the community, of the estimate formed of their misdemeanour. So far as overt acts are concerned, no account seems to be made of it by those who have the charge of God's house ; how natural, then, for others to treat similar transgressions lightly, or, if more seriously inclined, to take offence at the seeming indifference of their spiritual guides ! Yet, as matters now stand, it is not quite easy to adopt a procedure that shall present very broad and cognizable distinctions ; it is only within narrow limits that they can be found. In post-Reformation times the practice of public confessions and rebukes, closed with a formal absolution and a charge to go and sin no more, was set up as a regular part of the discipline of the Kirk in this country, and continued to prevail for several generations.[1] In most churches there was even what bore the name of the ' repentance-stool,' placed nearly in front of the pulpit, on which the offending person was obliged to sit for two or three successive Sundays, and to rise up a little before the close of the service and receive solemn admonition and rebuke in the presence of

[1] ' The extremitie of sackclothe was also prescrivt be the acts of the generall discipline,' and was not to be dispensed with for any 'pecunial sum' (*Book of Universal Kirk*). Nor was any exemption allowed to persons in high life. Among those who made public satisfaction we find the Lord Treasurer in 1563 ; the Countess of Argyll in 1567 ; in 1568 the Bishop of Orkney (M'Crie's *Life of Knox*, p. 454).

the congregation ; on the last, a formal absolution was pronounced.   But as times changed, the practice first became
irregular in its administration, and then fell into desuetude.
Fines in many places were taken as a substitute, the money
so obtained being forfeited to the poor, which could only
be characterized as a species of simony ; and as it would, of
course, be chiefly taken advantage of by the richer portion
of the congregation, it was attended with the additional evil
of forming one kind of discipline for the wealthier and
another for the poorer classes of the Church.   This was to
do the work of God with respect of persons, therefore doing
it so as certainly to defeat the ends which it should have
been mainly directed to promote.   Such a halting procedure
could not last ; and as the spirit of the times changed, the
repentance-stool for the one class and the money fines for
the other were disused ; public rebukes, also, in great
measure disappeared; while acts of formal excommunication
and acts of absolution ceased to be delivered from the pulpit
in presence of the assembled congregation.

Is this change to be regretted ? It is not quite easy to
say ; indeed, it turns very much upon the further question,
whether the general state and tone of society now be upon
the whole more favourable, or the reverse, to vital godliness,
than they were in earlier and ruder times ?   Without debat-
ing the point as to the absolute merits of the two, there can
be no doubt that in the conventionalisms and proprieties of
life there is a decided change for the better in that part of the
population which constitutes the life and stay of Christian
society ; so that, as in familiar discourse and in current
literature, in the formal proceedings also of a Church, things
would appear unseemly and indelicate in present times,
would grate upon people's feelings, and tend rather to annoy
than to edify, which at an earlier period would have been
heard or witnessed without emotion.   It is impossible to
deny, and hopeless to fight with success against, this altered

style of things ; it is an essential part of the civilisation and refinement of modern times ; and it is the policy of the Church to accommodate her procedure to it, retaining as far as possible the substance, while she lets go the form of the older discipline. The form is, for the most part, gone anyhow ; public professions of repentance and rebukes are no longer practicable as in the olden time ; and in the few cases where I have known a return to them attempted, under a zealous pastorate, the attempt has always failed, and it was found necessary, for the interests of righteousness themselves, to have them abandoned. But if matters be otherwise rightly ordered, especially if those who have the spiritual oversight of a particular Church be men of principle, discretion, and probity, and enjoy the respect and confidence of the members, the real objects in view may be substantially served through their instrumentality. As representing the spiritual community, let them, in their more private inter- course with the parties interested, do what was wont to be done in public, so far as reproof, admonition, confession of sin, promise of amendment, suspension from Church fellow- ship, restoration or final excision are concerned. What is done thus is really done by the Church, and, one may say, in its presence ; just as what is done by the representative body of a commonwealth is done by the commonwealth itself, and is so regarded by its constituent elements. And if it is done conscientiously, prayerfully, judiciously, it will also be done to edification, more so a great deal than by a rigid adherence to the letter and form of proceedings which may be no longer adapted to the state and temper of society, and which, for the sake of an *apparent* conformity to Scripture precedent, would sacrifice the *reality*.

CHAPTER IX.

SUBSIDIARY MEANS AND AGENCIES.

BY subsidiary means and agencies, I mean things not directly and strictly belonging to the pastoral office, but still so closely connected with it, that in most cases it will be both the interest and the duty of the pastor to encourage and promote their employment. For, aiming as they do at the reformation of existing abuses, or the bringing about of a more healthful state of society, they so far tend to subserve the objects which a minister of the gospel should have in view, and become handmaids to him in his work. They will, however, necessarily differ to some extent according to the nature of the locality in which his sphere of labour is cast, and the classes of society with which it brings him more especially into contact. Experience here, as in various other things which have come under our consideration, must be the great teacher and guide; and nothing more is needed, or would be proper in this outline, than to indicate quite briefly some of the leading points to which attention should be given. They fall into two divisions, those which have an incidental bearing on religion, and those which relate to social economics.

1. Under the first class may be mentioned efforts to promote a taste for religious and instructive reading. When such a taste is diffused, both itself and the habits associated with it prove among the best auxiliaries of the pulpit. For, if those who frequent the house of God are in any measure

accustomed to the quiet and thoughtful occupation of the kind referred to, they will grow in intelligence, in their capacity for appreciating the discourses of the Sabbath, and also in their ability to profit by them. A certain dulness of apprehension, sluggishness of spirit, and consequent indisposition or incapacity to follow the train of thought in a well-digested discourse, are the usual characteristics of audiences which are utter or comparative strangers to reading of a cognate description during the week. And with such audiences the danger is, that when serious impressions are made upon them by what is addressed to them on the Lord's day, these are apt to disappear again by the total withdrawal of the mind from similar lines of meditation during the week.

To some small extent the object in view may be attained by the circulation of tracts, but not very materially. These are more suited, as a whole, for originating right thought, and leading people's minds into the way of truth, than for imparting much knowledge, or forming habits of thoughtfulness and attention. When judiciously selected, however, they have their use, and even in the way of directing and sustaining thought will sometimes profitably fill up a little spare time which would otherwise run to waste. But better adapted for the purpose more immediately contemplated are the monthly or weekly periodicals which are now issued in considerable variety, with special reference to private and family use on the Lord's day. Though not to be indiscriminately recommended, as if all were equally adapted to promote their professed object, some of them are worthy of all praise. The stated circulation of such productions, and missionary records, containing accounts of evangelistic operations at home and abroad, is well deserving of attention. Associations might, at various localities, be with advantage formed for carrying it the more easily into effect; and for the more remote and isolated rural districts much may be

done to promote the end in view by a judicious encouragement of the colportage system.

Sabbath-school, and, where possible, congregational libraries, belong also to this line of things, and should receive
the considerate attention, and, when formed, the watchful
superintendence of the pastor. It is one of the special
advantages of present times, that books for the young exist
in such numbers and variety. There is now a pretty extensive literature conducted expressly for them, and a literature
predominantly religious in its tone, as also in the subjects
of which it formally treats. Every pastor should use his
influence with the young of his flock to induce them to form
some acquaintance with this juvenile literature, which will
also react on the older members of the family. In rural
situations it may sometimes be needful, or at least expedient,
for him to take the charge of such libraries, as otherwise
there may be a danger of the books being badly kept, and
the youthful applicants also may be apt to light upon
books of a somewhat unsuitable kind. When the young
grow up and join themselves to the communion of the
Church, it may be well, if their numbers are not very great,
to present each with a good practical treatise suited to their
respective capacities, a treatise or manual of the kind of
which Doddridge's *Rise and Progress* may be cited as a favourable example ; such a gift being fitted at once to form a
pleasing memorial of that important period in their religious
history, and also to exercise an influence for good on their
further advancement.

I am quite disposed to reckon among the subsidiary
means under consideration the practice which has of late
become common in towns, and has been extending to
villages, of lectures on week-day evenings, lectures perhaps
sometimes having a directly religious interest, but more
commonly on subjects of a historical, literary, or scientific
nature, treated in a manner fitted to improve and elevate

the minds of the people, as well as strengthen indirectly their religious convictions. Such lectures must be delivered chiefly by ministers of the gospel, though with occasional help from others; and the time and study necessary to take their part occasionally in such employment will be far from being misspent. But more directly bearing on their proper function is the promotion of prayer meetings among their people, and some perhaps would add, of fellowship meetings. But in regard to the latter, there is need for much caution on the part of a pastor. Fellowship meetings are formed with a view, not merely to engage in exercises of worship, but also to interchange thoughts among the members on matters pertaining to divine truth or religious experience; safe enough, probably, and improving if the membership is small, and composed of such as have much confidence and fellow-feeling one with another, so that they can really speak heart to heart; but when it is otherwise, they are extremely apt to become loquacious, disputative, and even to gender strifes. A prudent pastor will therefore rarely intermeddle with meetings of this description, and neither directly encourage nor discountenance them. But in respect to the establishment of prayer meetings he need have no scruple, if he can only find persons who have the requisite zeal and gifts for conducting them. Here for the most part lies the main difficulty, and it is of such a kind that no undue pressure should be made upon individuals with the view of overcoming it; for if there be a defect in the requisite intelligence, piety, or power of utterance, the meetings in question cannot be instituted with much prospect of continuance or success. The spirit of prayer, it should ever be remembered, is of more importance than any particular mode of exercising it.

2. Passing now to the other branch of subsidiary means, that relating to social economics, a pretty large field till lately lay open here for parish ministers in connection with

the management of the poor, calling for the exercise of discretion, sagacity, and good feeling. It was in this field that Dr. Chalmers won for himself his first claim to distinction as a philanthropist ; and to the discussion of topics connected with it one of his most elaborate works is devoted, his *Parish Economics.* The work may still be read with interest and profit, as it is pregnant with views and principles which admit of a certain application in every age ; but as a guide-book for pastors in a specific department of official duty it may justly be said to be antiquated. This whole branch of social economics is now directed by an agency of its own, in which ministers of the gospel, whether of the Established Church or not, have but a subordinate part to perform. But, of course, it will never cease to be their duty to interest themselves in the state of the poor, and to be forward in devising liberal things in those more peculiar cases of want and distress which from time to time occur, and for which a legal machinery affords no adequate source of relief.

In the present circumstances of our country, it belongs more to the province of a minister of the gospel to concert, or lend his countenance and support to those who may be concerting, measures which have for their object the reduction of pauperism and other social evils ; in particular, the repression of prostitution, and the diminution of that intemperance which is a fountain of innumerable disorders. For this purpose he will readily co-operate in the efforts made to curtail, in particular localities, the number of public-houses, to establish coffee-rooms and places of healthful refreshment and innocent resort, and to form where they are obviously needed temperance societies. For things of this description, lying outside, in a manner, the pastoral sphere, yet pressing closely on its border, no general rule can be prescribed, or any uniform practice recommended. If there be but high Christian principle first, then an enlightened Christian expediency, wisely considering the circumstances of the place and time with a view to the rectification of any flagrant social evils existing, there will be no need for special instructions and stereotyped modes of working. Here also the love of benefiting one's generation by the removal of what tends to minister to disease, slovenliness, and vice, will be a law to itself, and not only a law, but a well-spring of beneficent action, fruitful in resources, striving in every way possible to lessen the inducements to evil, and raise up bulwarks for the protection of the weaker elements in human nature against the stronger, the tempted against the tempting, the young and simple against the wiles of the profligate and the wicked. Thus will Christian love earn the blessing promised to those 'who sow beside all waters.'

THE END.

MURRAY AND GIBB, EDINBURGH,
PRINTERS TO HER MAJESTY'S STATIONERY OFFICE.